ESSENCE OF INDECISION

Essence of Indecision

Diefenbaker's Nuclear Policy, 1957–1963

PATRICIA I. McMAHON

McGill-Queen's University Press
Montreal & Kingston • London • Ithaca

ISBN 978–0–7735–3498–8

Legal deposit first quarter 2009
Bibliothèque nationale du Québec

Printed in Canada on acid-free paper that is 100% ancient forest free
(100% post-consumer recycled), processed chlorine free

McGill-Queen's University Press acknowledges the support of the
Canada Council for the Arts for our publishing program. We also
acknowledge the financial support of the Government of Canada
through the Book Publishing Industry Development Program (BPIDP)
for our publishing activities.

Library and Archives Canada Cataloguing in Publication

McMahon, Patricia I., 1972–
    Essence of indecision : Diefenbaker's nuclear policy, 1957–1963 /
Patricia I. McMahon.

Includes bibliographical references and index.
ISBN 978-0-7735-3498-8

1. Nuclear weapons – Government policy – Canada – History.
2. Canada – Politics and government – 1957–1963. I. Title.

FC615.M39 2009   971.0642   C2009-900252-3

Typeset by Jay Tee Graphics Ltd. in 10.5/13 Sabon

Contents

Abbreviations

CCF	Co-operative Commonwealth Federation
CCCRH	Canadian Committee for the Control of Radiation Hazards
CDC	Cabinet Defence Committee
CCND	Canadian Campaign for Nuclear Disarmament
CND	(British) Campaign for Nuclear Disarmament
CUCND	Combined Universities Campaign for Nuclear Disarmament
DEW	Distant Early Warning
ICBM	Intercontinental Ballistic Missile
IRBM	Intermediate-Range Ballistic Missile
LAC	Library and Archives Canada
NATO	North Atlantic Treaty Organization
NLF	National Liberal Federation
NORAD	North American Air Defence
OAS	Organization of American States
PCP	Progressive Conservative Party
RCAF	Royal Canadian Air Force
SACEUR	Strategic Air Command Europe
SAGE	Semi-Automatic Ground Environment System
SUPA	Students United for Peace Action
UNEF	United Nations Emergency Force
USAF	United States Air Force
VOW	Voice of Women

Introduction

Diefenbaker in full oratorical flight is a sight not soon to be forgotten ... The India-rubber features twist and contort in grotesque and gargoyle-like grimaces; beneath the electric gray V of the hairline, the eyebrows beat up and down like bats' wings; the agate-blue eyes blaze forth cold fire. Elderly female Tory supporters find Diefenbaker's face rugged, kind, pleasant, and even soothing; his enemies insist that it is sufficient grounds for barring Tory rallies to children under 16.[1]

Such was the description of Prime Minister John G. Diefenbaker offered by *Newsweek* magazine in February 1963. By that time, Diefenbaker had every reason to fear for his political future. Long gone was the support that had helped him lead the Progressive Conservative Party to power in 1958 with the greatest parliamentary majority in Canadian history to that time. His apparently indecisive handling of Canada's nuclear policy did much to contribute to his dwindling popularity. The political turmoil that surrounded the debate about Canadian nuclear policy in the late 1950s and early 1960s, and the interplay between the development of Diefenbaker's nuclear policy and the anti-nuclear movement, are the subjects of this book.

The stock portrait of Canada's thirteenth prime minister is one of an indecisive populist who naively discounted the growing use of public opinion polling data in favour of letters from ordinary Canadians. According to this view, Diefenbaker made indiscriminate use of his mailbag's contents to determine substantive government policy, including matters of national security. Anti-nuclear activists, with their organized letter-writing campaigns, are said to have been particularly influential in this regard. This portrait is compelling, but as this book demonstrates, it is incomplete.

Diefenbaker's indecision was more apparent than real. This book makes it clear that he wanted Canada to join the nuclear club; any dithering surrounding the negotiations was the result of political considerations, not genuine indecision. Simply put, Diefenbaker feared the potential political fallout that could accompany the acquisition of nuclear weapons. This preoccupation with political consequences is what lent an air of indecision to his behaviour. Moreover, the concern was a reasonable one for a figure beholden to the electorate for his success. It was also a rational worry for someone who had faced more defeat than success at the hands of the electorate.

This book shows how Diefenbaker took a two-pronged approach to nuclear policy. On the one hand, he promoted the possibility of nuclear disarmament; on the other, he actively supported the acquisition of nuclear weapons from the United States. Although this approach appears to be contradictory, it was not. Nor was it the result of uncertainty. Diefenbaker believed that Canadians would be more willing to accept nuclear weapons (and the leader who made the decision to acquire them) if they knew that their prime minister had done so only as a last resort.

When the world entered the nuclear age in 1945, C.D. Howe, Canada's wartime minister of munitions and supply and postwar minister of reconstruction, announced in Parliament that Canada would not develop a nuclear arsenal. The wartime government had played a significant role in the development of the first American atomic bomb by supplying uranium to the Manhattan Project, but a home-grown nuclear weapons program was too expensive for the Canadian government to contemplate developing. Nor did there seem to be a need for Canada to acquire its own weapons of mass destruction; the Americans had a nuclear monopoly, and Canadians – firmly ensconced under the US nuclear umbrella – were content to leave nuclear hardware to them. There the matter seemed to rest for the foreseeable future.

By the late 1950s, the postwar world did not resemble what Canadian officials had envisioned in 1945. Not only had the wartime alliance between the Soviet Union, Great Britain, and the United States dissolved, but the American nuclear monopoly also had been short-lived; in 1949 the Soviet Union exploded its first atomic device. A nuclear arms race followed as the British joined the nuclear club in 1952. That same year, tensions increased again when the Americans detonated the first thermonuclear (or hydrogen) bomb. Not to be outdone, the Soviets kept pace, exploding their own thermonuclear device a year later, with the British following suit in 1957.

The arrival of the Republican general Dwight D. Eisenhower in the White House in 1953 transformed American nuclear strategy. He was the first president to have a solid understanding of nuclear weapons, having served as the first strategic allied commander in Europe under NATO. Together with his secretary of state, John Foster Dulles, Eisenhower introduced the "New Look" and a policy of "massive retaliation" at the end of 1953 and beginning of 1954. Both anticipated that nuclear weapons would play the dominant role in defending the West from Soviet attack. The New Look required that nuclear weapons be treated as weapons like any other. As Dulles explained, massive retaliation, at its most basic, "was to depend primarily upon a great capacity to retaliate, instantly, by means and at places of our choosing."[2] As the manned bomber of the early Cold War years was widely expected to give way to remote delivery systems comprising intercontinental and intermediate-range ballistic missiles, a transition period for weapons systems accompanied this shift toward the doctrine of massive retaliation. All this combined to make the late 1950s a period of reassessment in which nations around the world reevaluated their strategic priorities. And thus the Canadian government turned its attention again to the subject of nuclear weapons.

The first glimmers of the nuclear debate in Canada predate the election of the Progressive Conservative Party in 1957. However, it was not until the arrival of John Diefenbaker that the debate reached full force. As prime minister from 1957 to 1963, he was at the centre of the ensuing controversy, and his attitudes and actions are a large part of the story. This book examines the development of Canada's nuclear policy during this period.

First, a word about what this book is not. *Essence of Indecision* is not a global history of nuclear policy; it deals with global context only where that is directly relevant to Canadian considerations. Nor does it deal with nuclear theory or the strategic considerations of defence policymakers.[3] Instead, it focuses on the political considerations that influenced Diefenbaker's nuclear deliberations. As a result, it relies extensively on material from the manuscript collections of those involved in the political development of nuclear policy rather than on departmental records related to national security and defence.

Contemporaries and historians alike have been harsh in their criticism of Diefenbaker's handling of the nuclear issue. Words such as "inept" and "indecisive" are routinely employed to describe his behaviour, and "Why Diefenbaker dithered" could easily have been the title of this book. Nevertheless, the standard explanation that Diefenbaker was indecisive is insufficient. It does not explain why he took so long to decide whether to acquire nuclear weapons. *Essence of Indecision* addresses these questions and seeks to explain why Diefenbaker behaved as he did in moving Canada first toward and then away from a nuclear role in the world. In sum, it outlines how an appreciation of Diefenbaker's political aspirations, not Canada's national security, is fundamental to an understanding of his nuclear policy.

There are several possible explanations for Diefenbaker's apparent indecision. This book argues that although he believed that Canada ought to acquire nuclear weapons from the Americans, he hesitated because he feared that it could jeopardize his political standing and electoral support. The position of Diefenbaker's political opponents and the growing mobilization of the anti-nuclear movement only served to heighten this fear. Alternative explanations that have been suggested include the influence of Howard Green, Diefenbaker's second minister of external affairs and a disarmament enthusiast, and the prime minister's personal antipathy toward US President John F. Kennedy. As *Essence of Indecision* demonstrates, neither of these explanations is satisfying.

There is little mystery in determining the general history of the deliberations between Canada and the United States. In 1957 Eisenhower asked Diefenbaker to consider allowing the Americans to store nuclear weapons on US bases in Canada, bases that had been leased during the Second World War. The following year, American officials asked that Canada's armed forces accept nuclear warheads from the Americans for Canadian use. Although Diefenbaker was privately willing to acquire nuclear weapons, publicly he appeared uncertain. The explanation of this anomaly is the essence of Diefenbaker's apparent indecision. His political insecurities, both real and imagined, made it impossible for him to conclude a final agreement with American officials on nuclear weapons. While he understood that a majority of Canadians supported the acquisition of nuclear weapons, he worried that this support was malleable.

Why was Diefenbaker persuaded to believe that the nuclear issue was so volatile politically? The answer lies in the development of a Canadian anti-nuclear movement. When Diefenbaker commenced nuclear negotiations with the Americans, the anti-nuclear movement in Canada was in its infancy, little more than a ragtag collection of peace groups. Yet these groups managed to convince Diefenbaker that there would be a political price to pay if he acquired nuclear warheads for Canada's armed forces, even if they did not persuade him that their more basic proposition – that the acquisition of nuclear weapons was morally repugnant – was a valid one. Over the course of several years, Diefenbaker received letters, briefings, and personal pleas from anti-nuclear activists. Only when they offered a potential show of force did he begin to retreat from his willingness to acquire nuclear weapons.

Preoccupied with maintaining his political support, Diefenbaker was reluctant to do anything that might threaten his position as prime minister. This concern meant that his deliberations centred on the more nuanced issue of how to make nuclear policy palatable politically. They did not focus on the more basic consideration of whether his government ought to acquire nuclear weapons. Because of these concerns about electoral viability, Diefenbaker kept two things in mind when he formulated his government's nuclear policy: the state of public support and, by extension, the policies put forth by his political opponents.

Critics have argued that Diefenbaker was unduly swayed by his correspondence on this subject. In my view, this criticism is exaggerated. It was clear that Diefenbaker was conscious of the concerns raised by ordinary Canadians – and as a self-styled populist, this was to be expected. But most who wrote to Diefenbaker did so as part of an organized campaign to ban the bomb. And while the prime minister catalogued the letters sent to him from ordinary Canadians, he recognized that much of the correspondence he received from anti-nuclear activists did not represent the general state of public opinion. He knew and understood that most Canadians wanted the government to accept nuclear weapons. What his correspondence indicated was that nuclear policy required delicate political handling. With a high percentage of the public undecided about, though not opposed to, acquisition (at least in the early years of the debate), correspondence from the anti-nuclear movement represented the potential volatility of public support.

In order to understand how anti-nuclear activists set out to influence policy, this book examines how Canada's three most prominent anti-nuclear organizations tried to persuade Diefenbaker that Canadians wanted his government to forgo nuclear weapons. Each group – the Canadian Committee for the Control of Radiation Hazards, the Combined Universities Campaign for Nuclear Disarmament, and the Voice of Women – had its own approach, strengths, and weaknesses. Ultimately, each failed. This book explains why.

The anti-nuclear movement was not Diefenbaker's only concern. He was also plagued by fears that Liberal leader Lester Pearson would rally the anti-nuclear forces and take their support to victory in the next federal election. A Nobel Peace Prize, won for efforts to settle the Suez Canal crisis, and extensive experience in international affairs gave the former secretary of state for external affairs great credibility when it came to matters of peace and the conduct of foreign relations. The prize also added to Diefenbaker's fears that Pearson would make use of the government's acceptance of nuclear weapons for the Liberal Party's political gain.

Essence of Indecision begins by examining the atmosphere surrounding the Progressive Conservative Party's victory in June 1957 and the government's first defence-related dilemma: whether to accept the outgoing Liberal government's plans for an integrated North American air defence scheme. Next, the book details how Diefenbaker dealt with defence policy in the first year of his majority government, examining how his government handled the conclusion of NORAD, the acceptance of the Bomarc missile, and the cancellation of the Avro Arrow. With an enormous majority, Diefenbaker could rest easy in the knowledge that his political position was secure. During this period, 1958 and 1959, it was clear that the government was willing to accept nuclear weapons from the Americans.

Defence policy changed very little in 1959 and 1960, despite some major changes in the Diefenbaker government. Chapter 3 examines the context within which Canada's ambassador in Washington began nuclear negotiations with the Americans in the spring of 1959. Nuclear policy continued to move forward even after Howard Green became secretary of state for external affairs in June 1959. Although Green questioned some decisions related to nuclear policy in late 1959, there was little doubt on either side of the border that an agreement between the two countries was simply a matter of time. This was so, even when the Americans suspended talks in the spring of 1960 as they prepared for presidential elections. At the same time, the Liberal Party's position remained a source of concern to Diefenbaker. Pearson was outspoken in his opposition to the acquisition of nuclear weapons, and Diefenbaker was beset by anxiety that the Liberal leader would make nuclear policy into a political issue. During the same period, Canada's anti-nuclear movement was beginning to take shape.

Chapter 4 deals with a period of great change in Diefenbaker's nuclear deliberations. In late 1960, Canada's nuclear policy began to come into sharper focus. In October, Diefenbaker appointed Douglas Harkness to succeed George Pearkes as his minister of national defence. Within the month, John F. Kennedy defeated Richard Nixon to become the next American president. Together, Kennedy and Harkness had a major impact on Canada's nuclear policy as both sought to push Diefenbaker to move beyond a general willingness to accept nuclear warheads for Canada's armed forces toward the specifics of an agreement. In this regard, Diefenbaker's encounters with the new American president had a profound impact on the formulation of Canada's nuclear policy. After meeting with their Canadian counterparts in February and May 1961, American officials believed that Diefenbaker was on side when it came to arming Canada with nuclear weapons. By all accounts, he promised American officials that Canada's acquisition of nuclear warheads was only a matter of time. Although he raised concerns about the level of public support for nuclear stockpiles in Canada, he seemed ready and willing to move forward, and nuclear negotiations were resumed in August 1961.

By mid-1961, Diefenbaker was already thinking about the next federal election and the possible political consequences of acquiring nuclear weapons. Yet despite his growing dislike for Kennedy, he was nonetheless willing to proceed apace with the nuclear negotiations, and in preparing for the upcoming campaign, there was little to indicate that nuclear policy might be a political liability. But, just as the two countries were on the verge of reaching a pact in late September, Diefenbaker backed away. Suddenly, his hesitation was more than mere rhetoric. Now, he truly believed there was the potential for political harm if he concluded an agreement with the

Americans. As a result, by the end of October the negotiations that had once seemed so promising were once again on hold. Diefenbaker's return to power with a minority government in June 1962 ensured that the backburner was where those negotiations would stay for the foreseeable future. The disarmament groups were responsible for the prime minister's change of heart in the autumn of 1961, and chapter 5 deals with the events surrounding these changes.

While anti-nuclear activists had made an impression on the prime minister insofar as they demonstrated the potential volatility of public opinion, they did not have the same impact on the average Canadian. Nor did they influence the substance of Canada's nuclear policy. That task fell to international circumstances. Chapter 6 examines how the Cuban Missile Crisis of October 1962 broke the stalemate and resulted in significant changes to Canada's nuclear policy. The crisis led Diefenbaker to resume nuclear negotiations with the Americans. It also inspired Pearson to begin considering whether to reverse his party's stand on nuclear weapons. There were also political considerations that influenced both leaders to pursue an agreement with the Americans. Indeed, Pearson's announcement in January 1963 that he would accept nuclear warheads from the Americans if Canadians elected him prime minister finished what the Cuban Missile Crisis had started. That announcement also set off a series of political crises that led to the demise of Diefenbaker's minority government in Parliament and its subsequent defeat at the polls in April. With the Liberal Party's electoral victory, Pearson – dubbed the "unfrocked priest of peace" by Pierre Trudeau[4] – concluded an agreement with the Americans to provide nuclear warheads for Canada's armed forces, at long last.

Before turning to the story of Diefenbaker's nuclear policy, I offer a note about my sources. There is an excellent collection of papers pertaining to the peace movement at the William Ready Archives at McMaster University in Hamilton, Ontario. This collection includes the papers of the Canadian Committee for the Control of Radiation Hazards/Canadian Campaign for Nuclear Disarmament and the Combined Universities Campaign for Nuclear Disarmament/ Students United for Peace Action. These archives also house the Canadian Peace Congress papers which, though outside the scope of this book, are a wonderful resource for those interested in the Canadian peace movement, particularly during the Vietnam era.

This manuscript was completed without access to most documents on nuclear policy from either the Department of National Defence or the Department of External Affairs. I was actively discouraged from continuing my pursuit of material from these record groups when I applied for permission to see them. I was told that the documents I had requested were closed for the foreseeable future and that most of the information I would find there was available in published form elsewhere. In addition, I was told that these restricted documents would add nothing new to what was already known about Canada's nuclear policy during this period.

Although an examination of these departmental papers might have added some detail about the intricacies of the negotiations, their absence does not detract from this study. This is a book about the politics of nuclear policy, and it argues that Diefenbaker's personal political considerations governed his decision on whether to accept or reject nuclear warheads. For this reason, material outlining the political process of Diefenbaker's policy formulation was integral to my research. I was fortunate to find rich resources in collections of the personal papers of those involved in the formulation of Canada's nuclear policy; the papers of H.B. Robinson in Ottawa and John G. Diefenbaker in Saskatoon contain detailed files and reference material on this subject and were especially helpful. Similarly, the papers of both of the major Canadian political parties contain valuable material about the formulation of policy. Without these collections, the reinterpretation of one of the most written-about periods in Canadian history would not have been possible.

Finally, a number of people provided invaluable assistance with the research and preparation of this book. Many archival staff were exceptionally helpful, most notably Kathy Garay at McMaster University, Joan Champ and R. Bruce Shepard at the Diefenbaker Canada Centre in Saskatoon, and Tim Cook, Paul Marsden, and Loretta Barber at Library and Archives Canada. All provided great guidance.

I owe thanks to those who read and commented on various drafts of this manuscript: Robert Bothwell, R. Craig Brown, Ronald Deibert, John English, Francine McKenzie, and Beth Fischer.

Thanks, too, to the staff at McGill-Queen's University Press, particularly Philip Cercone and Joan McGilvray, for their assistance in the preparation of this book. Carlotta Lemieux's helpful comments and copyediting greatly improved the book.

ESSENCE OF INDECISION

1

The Conservatives Return to Power, 1957–1958

The irony of political longevity is electoral alienation, and never was this truer than in the 1957 election. On the morning of 11 June, Americans were greeted with the news that President Eisenhower had been hospitalized, the result of blueberry pie-induced nausea; and Canadians awoke to find newspaper headlines detailing the possibility of a new political party in Ottawa for the first time in more than a generation. "Liberals Lose Control," proclaimed the *Globe and Mail*, "Stalemate in Ottawa." Few had anticipated the results, marking as they did the end of an era. The Progressive Conservative Party had defeated a government that had been in power for twenty-two years. Certainly, the Liberal Party had not expected to suffer defeat at the hands of John Diefenbaker, the new Conservative leader, a Prairie populist known for his fire-and-brimstone style of delivery.

Notwithstanding their new leader, the Conservatives had not appeared to pose much of a threat to the Liberals. A Gallup poll in February 1957 had shown that a plurality of Canadians still supported the government. At the national level, the Liberals led with 44 percent support, with the Conservatives trailing nearly twenty points behind at 25 percent. The Co-operative Commonwealth Federation (CCF) and Social Credit Party barely registered, with 8 and 7 percent, respectively. A similar pattern was evident with respect to regional support; in the Maritimes, Quebec, Ontario, and the West, the Liberals outpaced the Conservatives every time.[1] When the election was called in mid-April, the Liberals were stronger still, at 49 percent, with the Conservatives trailing at 32 percent,[2] and even in mid-May members of the Liberal Party campaign staff were certain that Prime Minister Louis St Laurent was going to be returned to office with a majority.[3] Cabinet ministers such J.W. Pickersgill[4] and Senator C.G. ("Chubby") Power, a Quebec Liberal from the Mackenzie King era, agreed, the latter estimating that the party would win 142 seats in Parliament.[5] Many Liberals sympathized with Pickersgill's view that Diefenbaker's lofty but empty rhetoric was no match for the solid record of the St Laurent government.[6] Even Diefenbaker's own aides did not expect victory, anticipating at best a showing of between 75 and 111 seats in the House of Commons.[7]

Yet not all was as predictable as it seemed. Despite the encouraging figures and polling data, the Liberals were vulnerable to attack. With more than two decades in office, the party appeared to be tired and arrogant, and the twelve months prior to the 1957 election had been difficult ones for the Liberal government. Two foreign policy controversies, the Trans-Canada Pipeline debate and the Suez Canal crisis, caused the government particular trouble and were major factors in its electoral defeat.

The fiasco surrounding the Trans-Canada Pipeline in 1956 is aptly described as a black moment in parliamentary history.[8] In 1951, Parliament granted a charter to the American-owned Trans-Canada Pipelines Limited to build an all-Canadian gas pipeline from Alberta to Montreal. By 1956, the project had come to a standstill. It could not proceed until Parliament created a crown corporation in order to pay for the portion of the pipeline that ran, at great expense, through northern Ontario.[9] In order to begin construction in 1956, Parliament had to pass the bill by 7 June. Having introduced the motion in May, the Liberals left themselves little time.

With opposition filibusters threatening the bill's very survival, the St Laurent government introduced closure, which required the completion of discussion on the bill within the day, thus prohibiting adjournment. The government's predicament was that closure had not been used since 1932, when the Conservatives had used it to pass the Unemployment and Farm Relief Continuance Bill. The leader of the opposition, William Lyon Mackenzie King, had called the procedure "autocratic power to the nth degree."[10] What the Liberals now contemplated was unprecedented – and, arguably, worse than what Prime Minister R.B. Bennett had done some two dozen years earlier – for they proposed to use closure to pass the bill through each stage: resolution, second reading, committee, and third reading. Compounding the reliance on closure was the growing fear of American economic influence in Canadian industry, which the pipeline seemed to illustrate so fittingly. Opposition parties called the government arrogant for stifling parliamentary debate, and many Canadians were hard pressed to disagree. Although the Liberals passed their pipeline bill, they did so at the expense of their credibility with the electorate.[11]

The credibility of the Liberal Party was undermined further when it responded to the Suez Crisis later in the year. Prime Minister St Laurent faced a dilemma. Although he agreed with the Americans, who had condemned the invasion, he wanted to find a settlement that would preserve the unity of both the Commonwealth and NATO. Lester Pearson, the secretary of state for external affairs, helped to resolve the crisis by creating the United Nations Emergency Force, which was sent to Egypt to keep the peace.

Ironically, while Pearson's actions won accolades abroad, he received a mixed response at home. Today, the tendency is to recall the handling of the crisis as a high point in the conduct of Canadian diplomacy. After all, Pearson's solution earned him the Nobel Peace Prize. However, there may be more than a hint of nostalgia to this celebration. At the time, a Gallup poll based on a sampling from Toronto indicated that Canadians were divided over the government's handling of the crisis, with slightly more Canadians rejecting the government's position than supporting it.[12] The Progressive Conservative Party reflected the views of Gallup's narrow plurality and criticized the government for refusing to support the British effort, arguing that Canada had betrayed both Britain and the Empire.[13] That a plurality of Canadians (at least, according to one poll) opposed the Liberal response to the crisis and feared severing ties with Great Britain illustrated that Canadians were still loyal to Britain, and the Tories seemed to be more in touch with these attitudes.

It seems clear, then, that the Liberal Party did as much to lose the 1957 federal election as the Conservatives did to emerge victorious. However, victory in 1957 did not belong to the Progressive Conservative Party but to John Diefenbaker. The campaign strategy had focused attention on the new leader, distinguishing him from the Liberals and their arrogance, with Allister Grosart and Dalton Camp (both of whom had experience in advertising and public relations) leading the charge.[14] A Liberal in his student days, Camp had organized Robert Stanfield's campaign for premier in Nova Scotia

in 1956, and he was now responsible for making Diefenbaker the
Conservative Party's showpiece, as the Tory campaign focused on
personality, not policy.[15] It was a wise decision.

The Conservative leader's splendid performance on the campaign
trail was a decisive factor in the party's electoral success. With eyes
flashing and voice booming, Diefenbaker could deliver a stump
speech like few others; what mattered on the hustings was style, not
content. He loved "mainstreeting," talking to average Canadians in
order to get a feel for the locals and their thoughts on the issues of
the day. It also provided Diefenbaker with the opportunity to see
whether the people supported his policies.[16]

Campaign literature tried to create a folksy image, painting the
Conservative leader as a different kind of politician, a man of the
people, with the common touch: "Everywhere he goes ordinary
men and women seek him out to shake his hand."[17] However,
Diefenbaker's fondness for campaigning masked one of his great
insecurities. Despite campaign literature to the contrary, he was not
a "natural winner."[18] He always worried about the level of his support, whether national or local,[19] and with good reason. Diefenbaker's road to victory was one that had been paved with repeated
defeat. Having failed to secure elected office five times – federally in
1925 and 1926, provincially in 1929 and 1939, and municipally in
1933 – he finally secured elected office in 1940.

Election to Parliament did not end Diefenbaker's string of electoral defeats. He ran unsuccessfully for the party leadership twice,
once in 1942 and again 1948, before finally winning the leadership
in 1956. At the age of fifty-nine, Diefenbaker had sixteen years of
experience on the opposition benches. And though he became Canada's thirteenth prime minister – a job he had coveted since child-
hood – within two years of becoming party leader, he had a
resoluteness borne of successive failures. Within this context,
Diefenbaker had an understandable awareness of public opinion.
Yet more than political preservation fuelled his preoccupation with
popular sentiment, for he viewed himself as a grassroots politician
and defender of the downtrodden.

International relations provided Conservative organizers with the
ideal opportunity to blend a focus on Diefenbaker with an emphasis
on Liberal arrogance. The Liberals, one pamphlet noted, "have been
inept, arrogant and injudicious in dealing with our traditional friends
and allies abroad. In so doing they have lost valuable markets for

Canadian farm products, disrupted traditional Commonwealth ties, and raised unfavourable trade balances to the highest levels in history."[20] The literature stressed Diefenbaker's personal interest in external relations, describing him as "an expert on foreign affairs through his work at the United Nations, NATO and elsewhere."[21]

The pamphlets also signalled a shift in attitude. In discussing foreign affairs, the literature mentioned only in passing Canada's relations with the United States and membership in NATO and the United Nations. Instead, it emphasized the importance of Canada's ties to Britain and the Commonwealth. One brochure reminded Canadians that the Conservatives "resent the British people being derisively condemned as 'supermen,'"[22] a reference to St Laurent's comments in Parliament during the Suez Crisis that "the era when the supermen of Europe could govern the whole world is coming pretty close to an end."[23] Intended to remind Canadians that the Liberals governed in a heavy-handed fashion, from parliamentary debate to relations with Great Britain, Conservative Party literature sought to use the Liberal record to Diefenbaker's advantage.

Just as the Conservative's campaign focused on the merits of Diefenbaker, the Liberal Party built its platform on St Laurent and the achievements of his government. But St Laurent was not up to the task of carrying a campaign in 1957. At seventy-five years of age, he was tired and ready for retirement. And after years in office, the Liberal Party had alienated various segments of the electorate. Whether it was C.D. Howe's handling of the pipeline debate, Pearson's and St Laurent's dealings at the United Nations during the Suez Crisis, or Finance Minister Walter Harris's somewhat stingy offerings in the area of old age pensions in his pre-election budget, the Liberals had done plenty of things to make Canadians think twice about returning the "Government Party" to office for the sixth time since 1935.[24]

Canadians may have thought twice about re-electing the Liberal Party, but the election results illustrate that the choice was not clear for everyone. In the Canadian first-past-the-post parliamentary system, the party with the greatest number of votes does not always have the greatest number of seats in the House of Commons. Such was the case in 1957. The Liberals won 43 percent of the popular vote, which translated into 106 seats in the House of Commons. By contrast, the Conservatives won only 39 percent of the popular vote but gained 112 seats in Parliament. The remaining seats in the House

were won by the CCF with 25, Social Credit with 19, and Independ-
ents with 4.[25]

The Conservative Party's minority government shocked some
Liberals, who urged St Laurent to fight for his position as prime
minister, a response that more than a few Conservatives feared.[26] St
Laurent was of a different view. He had already stayed in politics far
longer than anyone had expected. Arriving in Ottawa in 1941 to
become Mackenzie King's minister of justice, he had joined the cabinet
on condition that he would return to private life after the war. But
when the war ended in 1945 he was persuaded to remain in Ottawa,
becoming the secretary of state for external affairs a year later. When
King retired in 1948, St Laurent was the natural successor as Liberal
leader and prime minister of Canada. Having considered retirement at
various times since the early 1950s, St Laurent had no interest in cling-
ing to power in 1957, and after reconciling his concerns about his
obligations as party leader, he announced his retirement from politics
in September.[27]

While the Liberals were planning their leadership convention for
January 1958, the Conservatives busied themselves with running the
country. There was a great deal for the government to do during its
first weeks in power. What was to be done with government offices?
Cabinet committees? What about government secrets? There was
much to learn, and little time. After years out of power, the transition
from opposition to government was a difficult one, and Diefenbaker's
personality made a complicated process even more so.

The new prime minister was a deeply suspicious man, conscious
of personal slights, both real and imagined. Since he had failed so
often to secure elected office, power, when finally achieved, was a
prized possession. At the same time, his many past failures meant
that he had plenty of political opponents, which made forming a
cabinet a particularly difficult task. He resigned himself to the fact
that he would have to include many of his opponents in the group
of MPs who were to be his closest advisers. Included among this
body were Davie Fulton, Donald Fleming, George Nowlan, J.M.
Macdonnell, and Léon Balcer, all of whom had opposed him at the
most recent leadership convention. As Diefenbaker commented melo-
dramatically to Ellen Fairclough (also in cabinet and another who had
not supported his leadership bid in 1956), "I have to form a cabinet,
and it begins to look as though I shall have to form it largely of
my enemies."[28]

Not everyone was pleased about the change of government. Many civil servants worried about the new regime. The civil service was not sympathetic to the Liberal Party per se but, like many bureaucracies, disliked change. Things had been done a certain way for a very long time. After years of one party in power, there was a certain level of comfort and ease of communication between the Liberals and the civil service. A new government would do things differently, might even question the manner in which things were done.[29] Officials in the Department of External Affairs were especially concerned about the incoming government. One diplomat, passing through New York on his way to a posting just after the election, captured this sentiment nicely. "The Canadian people just can't do this to us," he was heard complaining to a travel companion.[30] The suspicions were mutual, and Diefenbaker dubbed members of the department "Pearsonalities."[31]

Both Diefenbaker and the Department of External Affairs had legitimate concerns about one another. It was natural for Diefenbaker to be leery of an institution whose undersecretary had gone on to become its minister. Worse still, that minister, Lester Pearson, was poised to become the next leader of the Liberal Party. In the House of Commons, when Pearson's participation in debate revealed that he knew more about a foreign policy issue than Diefenbaker thought he should have known, the prime minister tended to believe the worst. It was easy to think that the "Pearsonalities," friends such as Norman Robertson, had divulged confidential information. But Pearson had been a member of the department, in his various capacities, longer than the Liberals had been in power under King and St Laurent. He certainly did not need broken confidences to know about matters of foreign affairs, having been in the thick of external policy until his party's defeat. Yet Diefenbaker's concerns were not manifestations of paranoia; they were due to his inexperience and insecurity in office.

Members of the Department of External Affairs also had understandable concerns. There was an ease of communication between the department and its former minister. Aside from his experience as a diplomat, Pearson had been minister for almost nine years. Now the department had to adapt to a new minister and a new style of politician. Jules Léger, the undersecretary of external affairs, complained that he did not yet know how Diefenbaker functioned, what his interests were, how he absorbed information, and how much information he needed from the department.[32] Department officials needed to know this kind of seemingly trivial information in order to prepare the most appropriate briefing material for their new political boss.

Despite these concerns, not everyone was worried about the havoc Diefenbaker could wreak. For instance, John Holmes, a member of the department, regarded the prime minister as "considerate, attentive, and quick to absorb the broad lines of an issue."[33] R.B. Bryce, the clerk of the privy council, was enormously helpful to Diefenbaker and aided the transition to power with his forthright opinions and advice.[34] An engineer by early training, Bryce had also studied economics at Cambridge and Harvard. He joined the Department of Finance in 1938 and remained there until 1954, when he replaced J.W. Pickersgill (who left the civil service to represent Newfoundland in Parliament for the governing Liberals) as secretary to cabinet and clerk of the privy council. Bryce was more than an intelligent adviser to the prime minister; he also served as a bridge between Diefenbaker and the civil service, trying to reassure each about the intentions and concerns of the other. It was a contribution that Diefenbaker appreciated, acknowledging on at least one occasion, "I couldn't have carried on without him."[35]

Diefenbaker had little time to prepare for his first experience in the conduct of foreign relations, since he departed for his first Commonwealth Conference in London within days of coming to power. Upon his return to Canada on 7 July he committed his first foreign policy gaffe. Ending his trip on a high note, Diefenbaker pledged to a group of reporters gathered at the airport to await his return that he would divert 15 per cent of Canada's trade with the United States to Great Britain. The remark was off the cuff, and the civil service was taken aback; the bureaucrats had not been consulted about the viability of the proposal or the proposed figure,[36] nor was it feasible to funnel 15 per cent of Canada's trade away from the United States and toward Britain. Diefenbaker's enthusiasm betrayed his inexperience, and this inexperience quickly got him into more trouble.

Diefenbaker admired Britain and the Commonwealth, and was less enthusiastic about relations with the United States. Nevertheless, the relationship he developed with President Dwight D. Eisenhower was a warm and genuine one, and this helped to draw attention away from the fact that the two countries had to deal with difficult issues in a tense international atmosphere. Diefenbaker was more cautious and uncertain about Eisenhower's secretary of state, John Foster Dulles, whom he regarded with suspicion. Diefenbaker, like others, found Dulles to be cold.[37] But while many people disliked Dulles personally, the prime minister's feelings had more to do with what the secretary of state stood for than his personality.

Dulles embodied all the elements of the American establishment that Diefenbaker loathed and even feared, and though many have argued that he had a penchant for anti-Americanism, his attitude was far more complicated. It is perhaps best described by H.B. Robinson, who acted as the liaison between the Prime Minister's Office and the Department of External Affairs, and viewed Diefenbaker's attitude as anti-establishmentism. "There was a certain 'caste' of American," Robinson recalled, "highly educated, professionally secure, and socially well-connected, whose attitude and style he thought betrayed an insensitivity or indifference to the interests of others, including ... Canadians."[38]

Educated at Princeton, Dulles has been called the most accomplished individual to be secretary of state since John Quincy Adams.[39] He was almost bred for his position: his maternal grandfather was John W. Foster, Benjamin Harrison's secretary of state, and his uncle was Robert Lansing, Woodrow Wilson's secretary of state during the First World War. Dulles's own experience in foreign affairs was formidable prior to his appointment, and in this regard he had far more in common with Pearson than with Diefenbaker. Acting as his grandfather's assistant, Dulles had attended the Second Peace Conference, held at The Hague in 1907 to deal with issues in international humanitarian law and disarmament. He also participated in the Versailles talks following the First World War. Although he became a lawyer, he continued to be involved in foreign affairs, advising government officials through the 1940s. He was part of the American delegation at the founding conference of the United Nations at San Francisco, and he attended meetings of the UN General Assembly in the years that followed. He also participated in council of foreign ministers meetings after 1945 and helped to negotiate a peace settlement with Japan in 1950. It was these experiences and Dulles's pedigree, placing him firmly within the establishment, that made Diefenbaker so uncomfortable.

The perception that Diefenbaker was anti-American was of immediate importance in the summer of 1957 as the new prime minister turned his attentions to Canada's military relations with the United States. NORAD – the North American Air Defence Agreement – was the primary reason for this attention, an issue inherited from the Liberals. An agreement between Canada and the United States, NORAD was designed to integrate continental air defence under an American commander and Canadian deputy commander.[40] In many respects, it was the logical culmination of the defence cooperation between Canada and the United States that had started in 1940 with the Ogdensburg Agreement. St Laurent's Liberals had promised to respond to the American proposals by 15 June, presuming that their electoral success was assured. Diefenbaker's election on 10 June, however, made the deadline impossible to meet.[41] The new government did not even know what kind of representation would be required on External Affairs and Defence committees until two days after the deadline had passed, let alone the intricacies of continental air defence.[42]

Procedurally, the agreement should have been approved first by the Cabinet Defence Committee (CDC) and cabinet before it was announced to Canadians. But the Conservatives had not yet reconstituted the CDC, and Diefenbaker believed that time was of the essence.[43] The chairman of the Chiefs of Staff, General Charles Foulkes, in conjunction with Jules Léger and R.B. Bryce, tried to persuade Diefenbaker to accept the Liberal-negotiated agreement. All three agreed that NORAD should move forward, and the defence minister, George Pearkes, presented the proposal to Diefenbaker on 24 July, securing his approval.[44] The new cabinet did not discuss NORAD and its implications until the end of July, and only then to deal briefly with the appointment of Air Marshal C. Roy Slemon as deputy commander.[45]

That Diefenbaker failed to follow the consultative procedures established by the Liberals earned him, then as now, a stern rebuke in many quarters.[46] Critics highlighted what they saw as procedural bungling and argued that the prime minister's rapid decision to accept NORAD was a sure sign of both the government's ineptitude and the prime minister's inexperience – he was, after all, his own minister of external affairs at this time – in matters of foreign affairs.

This assessment is not altogether fair for a number of reasons. The major criticism implies that there could be no responsible assessment of NORAD and its implications without the CDC in place.

Yet the composition of the CDC calls this criticism into question. The committee included the prime minister, the minister and associate minister of national defence, the secretary of state for external affairs, and the ministers of finance, defence production, justice, and health and welfare. Members of the civil service also advised the committee, including the secretary to the cabinet, the undersecretary of external affairs, the deputy minister of national defence, the chairs of the Chiefs of Staff and the Defence Research Board, and the chiefs of the naval staff, general staff, and air staff.[47]

In fact, many of the CDC's most prominent members discussed the matter with Diefenbaker. Foulkes continued to support the NORAD negotiations and the agreement after the Liberals were defeated, and he dealt with Léger and Bryce. Together, they agreed to discuss the matter with Pearkes, who then spoke to the prime minister.[48] It seems, then, to be an exaggeration to claim the prime minister accepted NORAD by himself, without benefit of outside information or consultation. The CDC may not have been formally constituted, but Diefenbaker consulted many of the people who would become its key members before approving NORAD in principle.

The role of the Department of External Affairs is also a matter of some debate in that part of the critique is that Diefenbaker failed to consult with its professionals.[49] For example, Hilliker and Barry have noted that External Affairs was left in the dark until the US ambassador called the acting undersecretary, John Holmes, about the press release that was to be released jointly by the two governments on 1 August.[50] There are, however, some problems with this assessment.

Foulkes consulted with Léger about NORAD in the early days of the Diefenbaker government, and if department officials were not apprised of the pending agreement, perhaps Léger is to blame, not Diefenbaker. Furthermore, members of the department had been involved in the previous government's negotiations with the Americans. An agreement had been close at hand in the spring of 1957, and the subject had been on the agenda of the 15 March meeting of the CDC. It was removed from the agenda before the meeting, and formal approval of the agreement was postponed pending the outcome of the federal election, which the Liberals called on 6 April.[51] However, the proposal was submitted once again to the CDC at the final meeting of the committee under the Liberals on 13 June (just three days after the general election), but the freshly defeated government wisely decided to defer consideration of the proposal for the new government.[52] Thus, when the Liberals later responded that the agreement had not been formally introduced to the CDC or cabinet, it was true, but the implication was disingenuous. They had intended to approve the agreement after the election, expecting to win another majority mandate.[53]

Diefenbaker's insistence that the agreement include a written guarantee that Canada would be consulted before any order placing NORAD troops on alert delayed final approval of the diplomatic notes constituting the North American Air Defence Agreement. In Canada, consultation was a perennial concern, whether dealing with the British or the Americans, and Diefenbaker's fears were genuine and legitimate. Who would not want guaranteed consultation before committing troops to military action? Not surprisingly, the language associated with this insistence was the source of much debate between officials from the two countries.

Another element of Diefenbaker's concern was political. He knew that American economic influence could inflame public opinion, and he feared the same was true of defence issues.[54] He remembered the outcry after the pipeline debate, only part of which resulted from the manner in which the debate was handled. It was not anti-American to promote Canada first; and in this case, it did not fit Diefenbaker's brand of political nationalism to ignore it. For these reasons NORAD was not formally approved in Canada until after Diefenbaker secured a majority government in 1958.

There seems to be some confusion over what Diefenbaker accepted in late July 1957. It was an "informal understanding" between the two countries, in which the military was originally allowed to work out the arrangements.[55] With time and criticism, however, Diefenbaker was persuaded to undertake further formal negotiations with the Americans to allow an exchange of diplomatic notes. These talks took place though the fall of 1957 and the spring of 1958. Essentially, in July 1957 Diefenbaker had agreed to the principles underpinning the integration of North American air defence; he did not agree to the formal terms on which that integration would occur.

Problems with the language in the official notes plagued the negotiations between the Canadians and Americans through the spring of 1958. Diefenbaker was especially worried about the implications of the language used to describe the link between

NORAD and NATO. He wanted the link between the two alliances to be explicit, but the Americans feared that such a connection could inspire unwelcome interference on the part of other NATO countries, presumably France. Diefenbaker also stressed the importance of consultation within the NORAD alliance, so much so that the subject – which had been omitted in the original terms – was included in the final version of 12 May 1958.[56] This change was not an insignificant one, and Diefenbaker's willingness to pursue negotiations did not mean that an air defence agreement was a foregone conclusion. With Diefenbaker, there was no such thing as a final agreement until it had been signed.

NORAD marked the culmination of Canadian-American defence cooperation that dated back to the early days of the Second World War. And while the agreement may have been the natural extension of that relationship, it also made it more difficult for the Canadian government to pursue an independent defence policy. Diefenbaker had demanded that the Americans consult with Canada before commanding NORAD forces on alert. This guarantee of consultation entailed a certain level of reciprocity and cooperation on the part of the Canadians. In this regard, the NORAD agreement may have made Canada's acquisition of nuclear weapons more likely than not. The issue, then, is the price at which Diefenbaker secured the promise of consultation from the Americans. More to the point, to what extent would consultation require cooperation with the United States? There is no evidence to suggest that Diefenbaker considered this potential consequence of NORAD, and the criticism that he failed to recognize that NORAD might restrict Canadian sovereignty may have some merit.[57] However, it is equally plausible that in the depths of the Cold War, security mattered more than sovereignty. What is clear is that the creation of an integrated system of air defence in North America served to limit the Progressive Conservative government's ability to maintain Canada's position as a member of the non-nuclear world. At the same time, there is nothing to suggest that Canada's prime minister or anyone else in his cabinet regarded this reduced flexibility as problematic.

Parliament, now with Diefenbaker at its helm, did not resume sitting until mid-October 1957. In the interim, St Laurent announced his retirement, and the Liberals planned their leadership convention for January. The Progressive Conservative government continued to work on its legislative agenda and efforts to shape Canada's foreign and defence policies. On 14 September, Diefenbaker finally appointed a secretary of state for external affairs, announcing that Sidney Smith, president of the University of Toronto, would join Parliament after a by-election in October. Smith had little political experience, though he had considered running for the party's leadership in 1942. He was a university administrator, not an expert in foreign relations, and the appointment came as a genuine surprise to the media and the Department of External Affairs alike. Most, however, welcomed Smith's appointment.[58]

As Smith campaigned for his election to Parliament, the government decided to reassess Canada's defence expenditures. By 1957 the defence budget was more than what the Tories thought Canada could afford. Cost was a priority for the new government, and this was apparent at a CDC meeting in mid-September 1957. Nuclear weapons were discussed as a cost-saving measure, a point on which the Departments of External Affairs and Defence could agree. Where they differed was on the issue of control. Officials from External Affairs insisted that any interdepartmental discussions must emphasize civilian rather than military control of the warheads.[59] Nevertheless, the defence budget had to be reduced, and a number of proposals were considered, including reductions in the number of reserve and auxiliary forces, as well as some university-based officer-training programs. Other options included the transfer of various activities from National Defence to other ministries. The most obvious target, however, was the Avro Arrow, the CF-105 supersonic jet aircraft being developed by A.V. Roe of Canada.[60]

On Pearkes's recommendation, the CDC agreed to reduce the number of university-based officer-training programs and cancel the CF-100 jet fighter and related Sparrow engine program. But cancelling the Sparrow increased costs for the Avro Arrow, the growing expense of which was the subject of heated discussion in cabinet, particularly since it was clear that there was no foreign market for it to help offset costs.[61] The Arrow had the feel of a white elephant: costs spiralling out of control, efficacy in doubt, and future relevance uncertain. Relevance was a particular concern when the Soviets launched the missile age with *Sputnik* on 4 October 1957. The success of the Soviet satellite, which heralded the coming of the intercontinental ballistic missile, seemed to call into question the pertinence of an aircraft such as the Arrow, which had been designed to intercept manned bombers that were now expected to be obsolete in the not too distant future.

Despite this uncertainty, the Arrow won a stay from cabinet at the end of October for reasons of pure politics. Diefenbaker refused to terminate the Arrow program because the project's manufacturing base was in Ontario, a province that had been crucial to the Conservative Party's success in the 1957 election[62] and one where strong support was needed if the Tories were to secure a majority government in the next election. Cancelling the Arrow would cost 14,000 jobs in the Toronto area, which Diefenbaker believed would harm the party politically.[63] The result was cabinet's determination to proceed with the project for another twelve months, ordering twenty-nine pre-production aircraft and further development of the Iroquois engine.[64] At best, this was a stopgap measure, designed to keep the Conservatives out of trouble in Ontario until after the next election; at worst, it justified a strategy of procrastination that emboldened Diefenbaker to delay rather than decide in the face of a controversial or contentious issue.

While cabinet members debated the future of the Arrow in October 1957, Canada's nuclear status at home and abroad was also a matter of some consideration. The Americans were in the midst of discussing whether to upgrade the aircraft and weapons system used by the US Air Force at Goose Bay in Labrador. In particular, the question was whether the USAF should acquire nuclear warheads for the MB-1 rocket stored at the American base at Goose Bay. As a result, Diefenbaker was forced to contemplate that President Eisenhower might ask the Canadian government for permission to store nuclear weapons at the base. Anticipating this possibility, he wanted to discuss the subject with cabinet.

R.B. Bryce, however, persuaded Diefenbaker to forget about the subject for the time being, reassuring him that the storage of nuclear material at Goose Bay was neither pressing nor complicated. In his view, it was certainly not something that required immediate attention, since there would be no changes in US policy before 1958 or 1959. Regardless, Bryce felt confident that the American proposal would be straightforward, one that the Canadian people would accept without hesitation. After all, the Liberal government had previously authorized the Americans to carry the MB-1, armed with nuclear warheads, in Canadian air space. For

Bryce, there was not really any difference between carrying nuclear weapons over Canadian territory and storing them at an American base on Canadian soil.[65]

Nuclear issues also preoccupied officials at External Affairs. In the months preceding the December 1957 meeting of the NATO alliance in Paris, Canadian officials noted that nuclear stockpiles presented only one potential problem. Smaller powers had been pressuring the Americans for access to nuclear weapons, and US officials were increasingly concerned about the implications of such a measure. In particular, they feared nuclear proliferation, and it took time for them to see the merits of such a proposal. On this subject, Canadian officials sided with the smaller members of NATO, and as the December meeting approached, Canadian experts argued that nuclear stockpiles in the alliance would serve to increase European security. So confident were officials that this was the right policy to pursue that they believed negotiations between the European allies and the Americans would be concluded without a hitch.[66]

Officials noted only one potential difficulty: precedent. It was a pitfall that should have caused more concern than it did. If, through NATO, American forces in Europe were permitted to have nuclear weapons on foreign soil, would US forces expect the same treatment on their bases in Canada? In truth, the potential for conflict in this area was minimal. Agreements between the Americans and their European allies included provisions that contemplated the possibility of nuclear stockpiles at those NATO bases; but there was no similar reference to nuclear weapons in arrangements governing US bases in Canada.[67] Too much should not be made of this omission; the leases covering the Canadian bases were concluded during the Second World War when nuclear weapons did not yet exist.

Officials at External Affairs also thought the prospect of European nuclear stockpiles might benefit both disarmament talks and fiscal responsibility. By the middle of 1957, disarmament talks were underway in London, but without any real end in sight. Officials thought that the mere threat of national nuclear stockpiles might serve to make complete disarmament more palatable. As well, a collective cache of nuclear weapons (as would be the case in NATO) would be more secure and would constitute "less" proliferation than individual national holdings.[68] In terms of budgetary constraints, the timing of these NATO talks could not have been better.

There were signs of an economic downturn worldwide and in Canada particularly, and the Conservatives had promised that Canadians would get more for their defence dollar than they had under the Liberals.[69] When it came to nuclear weapons, a single NATO stockpile would be more cost effective than individual nuclear arsenals throughout the alliance.[70] Any proposal that encouraged greater security and fiscal responsibility in a single stroke was welcome indeed.

The Canadian position was confusing in one way. Officials commented that the Canadians would be willing participants in a NATO scheme, but they also noted that the RCAF did not want tactical nuclear weapons for its own use in Europe at this time. Despite some hesitation on the part of the RCAF, officials at External Affairs fully expected that Canadian forces would eventually play a nuclear role in NATO.[71]

There were also some practical shortcomings to consider. Foremost was a concern about control: Which country or entity would control the use of the stockpiled weapons and in what situation would they be used within the North Atlantic alliance? Canadian officials were firmly opposed to the idea that a single member of NATO should be allowed to have unilateral authority to use the weapons, and they believed the United States had to be treated like any other ally for this purpose. They proposed a system of checks and balances for Europe that was similar to the two-key system that lay at the heart of an existing Anglo-American nuclear agreement. The debate, then, was not whether NATO should have nuclear weapons or whether Canadian forces should play a nuclear role in the North Atlantic alliance; rather, it was a matter of control.[72]

Canadian officials were in the midst of discussing the intricacies of controlling nuclear stockpiles in NATO when General Lauris Norstad, the supreme allied commander of NATO, came to Ottawa in mid-November 1957 to brief members of the CDC about the state of affairs in the alliance. In 1956 Norstad had proposed adding nuclear weapons to NATO's arsenal, and the Paris summit in December 1957 offered an opportunity to deal with developments since that time. Having called late 1957 "one of the most critical periods since the end of World War II,"[73] Norstad told members of the CDC that he was worried that the reductions in defence spending, though a legitimate means of coping with fiscal pressures at home, were undermining the strength of the alliance abroad.[74]

Norstad also spoke of the apprehensions of the European members of the alliance. The Europeans continued to have reservations about nuclear stockpiles within NATO, but whereas Canadian officials were worried about control, the Europeans feared that the United States, as the atomic guarantor of the alliance, would refuse to intervene should a crisis occur in Europe. There were serious concerns that the Americans would not risk war with the Soviet Union in order to intervene on behalf of a European ally, regardless of the obligations set out in NATO. As a result, the smaller members of NATO increasingly believed that they would be vulnerable to Soviet attack if they did not have their own stockpiles. Cost, however, was a prohibiting factor. If most European nations could not afford to expand their conventional armaments and forces, they certainly could not afford to pursue their own individual nuclear weapons programs. Thus, nuclear stockpiles within NATO, in which the European allies borrowed American nuclear weapons in some kind of shared arrangement, seemed to be the best solution.[75]

The December summit in Paris would have been an ideal opportunity to clarify Canada's position on nuclear stockpiles in NATO, but the new minister of external affairs, Sidney Smith, quickly caused a political storm. In early December, he had commented that the meeting in Paris was about "increasing our deterrent forces against aggression."[76] The opposition in Parliament reacted swiftly and negatively. Rather than stand his ground, Smith back-peddled, stating that he had not meant to imply that Canadian forces would acquire nuclear weapons either at home or abroad. In an address before the External Affairs committee, the minister took great pains to distinguish between Canada's policy and NATO's policy. The Conservatives, Smith intoned as he clarified the government's policy, supported nuclear weapons only for the European members of NATO. Canada, he maintained, did not need them.[77]

Diefenbaker echoed Smith's caution when he spoke at the summit about the expense of nuclear weapons and the possible political consequences of their acquisition.[78] Despite these sentiments, the Americans approached Diefenbaker's government as anticipated about the possibility of stockpiling nuclear warheads in Canada for the benefit of both countries. This proposition led to a discussion in cabinet on 10 January 1958 about the merits of nuclear stockpiles in Canada.

The proposed bilateral talks were to take the form of "exploratory discussions at the military level" that Washington claimed "would in no way whatsoever bind the government when it came to making future decisions of substance on these matters."[79] Given these assurances, Diefenbaker was willing to enter negotiations with the Americans at the beginning of 1958, and within days, cabinet accepted the US proposal as a logical extension of existing bilateral agreements.[80] Although Diefenbaker was always worried about his level of public support, which was especially relevant given his minority government in Parliament, he did not think the nuclear issue was particularly contentious at this time. It appears never to have occurred to him that the nuclear issue might undermine his prospects for a majority in the next election.

The January 1958 meeting would have been the perfect opportunity for any member of cabinet to express concern or to question the basic merits of these talks with the Americans. Yet no one raised any objections. Neither Douglas Harkness (the future minister of national defence) nor Howard Green (the future minister of external affairs) – nor any other member of cabinet – contributed to the discussion on nuclear weapons. That Harkness said nothing is not surprising; he was, after all, still the minister of agriculture in early 1958, and he had no reason to be involved in nuclear issues or to have concerns beyond a personal nature that he was unlikely to share at a formal cabinet meeting. Green, on the other hand, was not merely the minister of public works but was the former acting minister for defence production, which put him in the midst of the nuclear debate because of the potential implications for defence production. Cabinet's support for preliminary discussions was not necessarily an endorsement of nuclear weapons for Canada's armed forces, but it does suggest that there was no obvious opposition or division within cabinet on the subject at that time.[81]

While the Progressive Conservatives set about governing, the Liberals were trying to rebuild their party. Many had reconciled themselves to the 1957 defeat because they believed that their time on the opposition benches would be short. They blamed defeat on their tenure in office: the party had been in power too long, and defeat by way of minority government was a reasonably painless remedy.[82] Implicit in this assessment was the thought that the election results were an aberration, and Canadians would return the Liberals to power with another majority when they saw the error of their ways. Some Liberals remarked that the election results reflected a certain well being in Canada; for the electorate to hand over the reigns of power to the Conservatives meant that Canadians felt confident about their future. Proponents of this explanation regarded the Liberals' downfall as change for its own sake. Times were good, governing was easy, and anyone, even Diefenbaker, would do.[83]

Concern about the state of the Liberal Party was a less common view but a more realistic one. The Liberal defeat was a sign that something was wrong with the party and its organization, and the party's electoral fortunes would not change until the Liberals reassessed their policies and structure. Proponents of this view looked for similarities between the 1957 election and others. The more optimistic compared the results with those of 1926, while the more pragmatic likened the election to that of 1930, when R.B. Bennett had soundly defeated Mackenzie King. The latter comparison was far more apt. Although the 1957 election resulted in a minority government whereas the 1930 campaign had produced a majority, there were similar reasons for the outcome. In both cases, Canadians were tired of a Liberal government that seemed out of touch with issues that concerned ordinary citizens, and the results reflected the electorate's desire for change.[84]

Liberals contemplated how best to reinvigorate the party as they mobilized for the Leadership Convention in January 1958. Lester B. Pearson was the clear favourite to replace St Laurent, especially in view of his Nobel Peace Prize for his efforts to resolve the Suez Crisis. Paul Martin and Walter Harris also entered the race, but Pearson was the obvious choice for most delegates. He had the profile and the prestige many believed would help to rejuvenate the party and return it to power.

Leadership was going to be an important factor in the next election; it was a strength for Diefenbaker and the Conservatives, and had been a weakness for the Liberals under St Laurent. On the surface, Pearson seemed to be the ideal candidate to lead the Liberals to victory. He was a Protestant from Ontario (two of the key criteria according to the National Liberal Federation)[85] and was both well known and well respected by Canadians – precisely the sort of person the party hoped would deflect public attention away from Diefenbaker and his recent round of achievements and would draw attention to the Liberal Party, Liberalism, and the new leader. As for issues, foreign policy was a weakness for Diefenbaker and the Tories, and it was something that the Liberals, under Pearson's leadership, seemed well positioned to exploit.[86]

If the Liberals had hoped that Pearson would be the man to lead the party to power, those hopes were soon dashed. Four days after becoming leader, on 20 January 1958, Pearson introduced a motion in the House of Commons that undermined both his political credibility and his party's electoral fortunes in one fell swoop. The government had introduced a motion for supply – which presented the opposition with an ideal opportunity to include an amendment that criticized the government's conduct – and it quickly became a non-confidence motion. J.W. Pickersgill, clerk of the privy council under Mackenzie King and St Laurent and now a Liberal politician representing Newfoundland, was responsible for telling Pearson about the opportunity presented by the supply motion, and together they wrote an amendment and a speech moving non-confidence in the government.[87]

On 20 January 1958, Pearson rose in the House of Commons and urged the Conservative government to resign, blaming Diefenbaker and his ministers for Canada's economic woes and for a lack of vision. Ordinarily, resignations of this magnitude would lead to a general election, but Pearson assured the Commons that this was not his intent. Instead, he proposed that the Liberal Party be allowed to form the government, one that would govern according to the policies adopted at the recent leadership convention, "ending the Tory pause and getting this country back on the Liberal highway of progress from which we have been temporarily diverted."[88]

In essence, the motion called the Conservatives incompetent and concluded that the business of governing should be returned to the Liberals. It was an arrogant thing to do; more importantly, it gave Diefenbaker the opportunity to demolish Pearson in response. Diefenbaker attacked the Liberal leader and the motion for almost two hours – or, as he liked to describe it, "I operated on him without anaesthetic."[89] The core of Diefenbaker's attack was based on a confidential economic report entitled "The Canadian Economic Outlook for 1957," which the prime minister revealed in the heat of debate. Produced by the Finance Department for St Laurent's government the previous March, the report predicted a downturn in the Canadian economy. The implications of the report were clear: it was now impossible for the Liberals to blame Canada's economic woes on the Conservatives, and Diefenbaker took the wind out of Pearson's sails. And instead of turning over the government to the Liberals, Diefenbaker called a snap election.

Nuclear matters were not high on the government's agenda as it prepared for its second election campaign in less than twelve months. Cabinet discussed defence production and the construction of refuelling sites for the United States Air Force at Canadian bases, but it focused on the importance of production as the economy declined. As long as Canadians would receive the jobs that were related to the construction of these sites, Diefenbaker was willing to allow the plan – another Liberal project – to proceed.[90] Behind the scenes at National Defence, the minister, George Pearkes, was working on his own proposal to deal with the talks Diefenbaker agreed to have with the Americans on the subject of stockpiles at Goose Bay.

In early February 1958, Pearkes prepared a memorandum for the CDC urging the government to allow the storage of nuclear weapons at the existing facilities in Goose Bay. Emphasizing that these stockpiles would strengthen the defensive position of the Strategic Air Command by providing a greater second-strike capability, the minister stressed that the weapons stored at Goose Bay were for defensive purposes only. Retaliatory capabilities were consistent with the strategic doctrine of deterrence as well as with Canada's commitment to both regional security and NATO. Pearkes also pointed out that Canada was not being asked to fill a unique role, since there were similar stockpiles in Great Britain, Spain, North Africa, and the Pacific. Finally, and perhaps most importantly, he offered reassurances that nuclear weapons at Goose Bay would not require a major increase in the number of American personnel at the base or involve additional risk to Canadian security. These final points were perhaps the most important aspects of the proposal for nationalists in Diefenbaker's cabinet.[91]

This was the state of Canada's nuclear policy as the 1958 election campaign began. As the Conservative Party's election material makes clear, the nuclear issue was a low priority for the government. Although the Conservatives had not yet accepted stockpiles for Goose Bay, it seemed only a matter of time before nuclear weapons would arrive in Canada (even if they were restricted to US bases).

More prepared and better organized for the 1958 campaign than they had been for the 1957 contest,[92] the Conservatives praised the accomplishments of Diefenbaker's minority government and attacked the Liberals for their arrogance. At Diefenbaker's opening rally in Winnipeg, he focused on the Liberals' non-confidence motion, mocking the leader of the opposition. "Pearson must have had help drafting that motion," he railed, "Could one person, without assistance, have produced anything so stupid?"[93] Over the next six weeks, the prime minister never missed an opportunity to remind Canadians of the Liberal leader's blunder.[94]

Throughout Diefenbaker's "whistle-stop" tour in 1958, he focused overwhelmingly on local issues. Old age pensions, building grants, housing loans, labour legislation, and the like were top priorities.[95] External affairs and national defence ranked well down the list of concerns – number six on a list of eight major policy areas – though party literature stressed the prime minister's "knowledge" and "credibility" in these areas.[96] As in the 1957 campaign, pamphlets made a special point of stressing Diefenbaker's experience in international affairs, and they gave particular attention to his decision to serve (briefly) as his own minister of external affairs. The campaign literature reminded Canadians that the Conservatives viewed Canada as a North Atlantic nation, highlighting Diefenbaker's involvement in the Commonwealth and the Commonwealth Trade and Economic Conference, as well as the nation's role in the United Nations and the United Nations Emergency Force, in Egypt (despite the party's earlier opposition). The only reference to nuclear weapons was the government's support for disarmament and vague references to the general abolition of nuclear weapons. Nothing in its campaign literature reflected the government's contemplation of nuclear stockpiles.

The Conservatives realized that excessive attention to foreign affairs worked to Pearson's advantage, and organizers initially advised candidates to avoid attacks on the Liberal leader's experience "and particularly any reference to any prizes that he may have won."[97] This strategy changed in mid-March after the *Globe and Mail* applauded Diefenbaker's efforts to make foreign policy a bipartisan matter.[98] The praise was particularly important because the newspaper also criticized the Liberals for taking a partisan approach to external relations by using the slogan "Pearson for Peace."[99] Conservative organizers seized on the *Globe*'s criticism and now encouraged candidates to attack the Liberals openly on this subject. Candidates were similarly urged to take aim at Paul

Martin's suggestion that the Canadian automobile industry start making missiles as a means of job creation.[100] Rather than address these criticisms, Pearson added fuel to the fire when he pledged to fill to capacity various military bases in the Maritimes.[101]

Despite these attacks, Liberal strategists knew that foreign affairs was Pearson's bailiwick and emphasized his experience in "The Pearson Story." "This is the man," the story read, "whose sure, skilled hand is needed now to guide Canada out of this period of difficulty and doubt. He is the man of peace, the man of action who in times of emergency comes through with positive workable solutions." With repeated references to the peace prize – despite Pearson's claims not to use the prize to appeal for votes – the pamphlet concluded with a photograph taken at a Liberal rally, the leader centre stage in front of a sea of "Peace Prosperity Pearson" signs.

The Liberals had called for "less politics more statesmanship,"[102] but their behaviour during the campaign set a tone that was anything but statesmanlike. Efforts to portray Pearson as apolitical were equally at odds with the opposition leader's role in a parliamentary system, namely, to criticize government policy. At the same time, the portrayal created an unrealistic impression of Pearson, suggesting that he would be different from other politicians; he would not sling mud at the government, he would not "play politics."[103]

More problematic than this contradictory image on the campaign trail was the Liberal leader's actual performance. Pearson was no match for Diefenbaker's oratorical style. He could mingle on the world stage, in the back corridors of the United Nations, but with ordinary Canadians he seemed to hold little appeal. He simply could not reach out to them, nor could he rally support on the hustings, making only a modest impression on those who witnessed his efforts at political gatherings. Commenting on these rallies, a Conservative aide – admittedly, a biased observer – remarked, "I didn't blame the farmer who sat next to me popping Crackerjack clusters into his mouth and slowly, with eyes closed, mechanically chewing and chewing. There wasn't much else to do."[104]

The 1958 election resulted in a massive majority for the Progressive Conservatives. Diefenbaker had asked Canadians to "Follow John." They did. In droves. Out of a possible 265 seats in the House of Commons, the Conservatives won a staggering 208. After travelling some 23,800 kilometres in six weeks, delivering more than a hundred speeches along the way, Diefenbaker felt entitled to take credit for the victory.[105] The CCF won 8 seats, while Social Credit lost every riding in which it ran a candidate. Major figures from all opposition parties were defeated. The CCF lost M.J. Coldwell and Stanley Knowles, and Social Credit lost its party leader, Solon Low. The Liberals were hit even harder. Only five ministers from the St Laurent years survived the storm: Pearson, Martin, Pickersgill, Lionel Chevrier, and Jean Lesage. At worst, the Liberals had expected to win between 80 and 100 seats.[106] No one had anticipated the Canadian electorate would return a meagre 49 Liberals to Parliament. If Canadians were uncertain about which path to choose in 1957, their intentions were abundantly clear eight months later. In 1958, Canadians gave Diefenbaker the greatest parliamentary majority in Canadian history to that time.

The majority proved to be a mixed blessing for Diefenbaker and his party. On the one hand, it was a reward for a job well done with a minority government. But the reward raised expectations that the Conservatives would continue to perform vigorously. The majority was also a curse of sorts for Diefenbaker. Given his previous electoral and political struggles, he must have known that his party's standing (and his own) had nowhere to go but down. He knew that potentially contentious issues such as NORAD and the Avro Arrow had been shelved only temporarily for the sake of electoral expediency. Now, with those issues pressing and a huge majority, he had to act. But the majority also gave Diefenbaker time to delay, which he did with great frequency, particularly in matters of foreign and defence policy. Like Canada's longest serving prime minister, William Lyon Mackenzie King, Diefenbaker believed that there was little reason to act when a decision could be made another day. However, he lacked King's political skill and luck, and "another day" was often just around the corner. It is within this context that Diefenbaker and his government conducted foreign and defence policy in the early days of their majority government.

2

Diefenbaker and Defence Policy, 1958–1959

Governing with a majority did not come easily to John Diefenbaker. As in 1957, his cabinet consisted of his challengers, if not his enemies, but the prime minister himself had begun to change. After his landslide victory in the spring of 1958, Diefenbaker began to turn away from the kind of consultation that had made him popular with his caucus after the 1957 election. As one Conservative MP commented, "Caucuses became John Diefenbaker telling of his readings from Mackenzie King. At every caucus, we were regaled with something from Mackenzie King, who had become for some reason or other that nobody could quite understand, John's great hero."[1] Diefenbaker came to believe that Canadians had elected him and him alone, not the Conservative Party, and he was not far off in his assessment.

Nevertheless, he was unable to enjoy his newfound political security and record majority. Instead, he spent more time worrying about public opinion and public perceptions of his government than consulting with either cabinet or caucus. This preoccupation with maintaining his electoral support led Diefenbaker to launch what Donald Fleming later called a "perpetual campaign."[2] He came to worry so much about electoral support that he began to dwell on the importance of unsolicited letters on any number of subjects. As journalist Peter C. Newman observed, Diefenbaker treasured the letters sent to him by ordinary Canadians: "Dief regarded his mail as an extremely important political listening-post. It was filed away by subject-matter, with a geographical cross-index, so that the PM could quickly obtain a sampling of public opinion on any important issue."[3] Such a characterization of the prime minister's rather elaborate filing system is an exaggeration – the material was filed alphabetically by surname, not subject matter – but the sentiment is correct.[4] Diefenbaker's belief that he could quickly take the pulse of the country by turning to his correspondence was particularly important when it came to potentially controversial issues, including those involving national defence. The key is what Diefenbaker understood these letters to mean.

Notwithstanding this attention to his correspondence, Diefenbaker did not have an unsophisticated understanding of public opinion. He appreciated, for example, the distinction between scientific polling and unsolicited letters of support or opposition. What correspondence from ordinary Canadians helped to point out were contentious issues and possible political vulnerabilities. It was this sense that the anti-nuclear movement sought to exploit.

Diefenbaker understood that the nuclear movement was not large, but noise mattered more than numbers when political considerations were at stake. During the first year of his majority government, Diefenbaker made three major decisions regarding defence policy, and the manner in which he made them set the backdrop for his conduct in foreign relations and defence policy more generally. On all three issues, Diefenbaker and his cabinet tried to balance defence priorities, on the one hand, with political popularity and fiscal prudence, on the other. Over time, the latter came to take priority over the former.

Within weeks of his landslide victory, Diefenbaker laid the foundation of his nuclear policy at a meeting of the Cabinet Defence Committee (CDC) in late April 1958. While the committee discussed a variety of issues that day, including Canada's role in NATO, progress in the NORAD negotiations, and a proposed ballistic missile early warning system, the bulk of the meeting centred on the merits of nuclear stockpiles. Cost was a factor with some of the other proposals, but not with nuclear weapons. For example, the Americans agreed to assume responsibility for the expense and logistics of laying the required cable underneath Canadian territorial waters for the proposed early warning system. There had been some talk about whether the Canadian government should purchase the cable from the Americans in order to make the warning system a true joint venture, but there was simply no way the government could afford the financial expenditure in 1958, or anytime in the foreseeable future. There were also secondary benefits to consider; an important advantage of the arrangement was the fact that Canadian contractors and companies would be used wherever possible to construct the Canadian portion of the system.

As talks turned to storing nuclear weapons at Goose Bay, Charles Foulkes, chairman of the Chiefs of Staff, George Pearkes, minister of defence, and Sidney Smith, minister of external affairs, each made presentations. Foulkes and Pearkes spoke in favour of acquiring nuclear weapons, while Smith was more cautious though not entirely opposed to the proposition. Military representatives at the meeting stressed that the weapons proposed for Goose Bay were defensive; the base would be on a par with US bases in Britain, Spain, North Africa, and the Pacific, which already had nuclear weapons intended to aid the second strike capability of the United States. Nuclear stockpiles would not transform Goose Bay into a base from which an initial attack could or would be launched.

By all accounts, Goose Bay was a unique situation within Canada as an American base on Canadian soil,[5] where American forces – not Canadian forces – would be responsible for nuclear weapons; there was no reason to believe that the Americans would ask for permission to store nuclear weapons at any other base in Canada. The proposed arrangement seemed to be so straightforward that the Americans would not even need to amend their Atomic Energy Act, which severely limited the exchange or transfer of nuclear information and material.

The plan that defence officials presented for Goose Bay was actually part of a much larger proposal involving talks between Canadian and American officials in late 1957 and early 1958. A range of nuclear possibilities had been discussed – from the Bomarc missile in Canada and MB-1 rockets for the Royal Canadian Air Force in Europe (both of which would be used by Canadian forces) to nuclear weapons at leased bases such as Goose Bay and Argentia. During this meeting of the CDC in late April 1958, Foulkes reminded the participants that the St Laurent government had already authorized the creation of nuclear storage facilities at Goose Bay in 1951. Clearly, he argued, storage facilities indicated that the Liberals would have agreed to allow nuclear stockpiles if the Americans had asked.[6]

Sidney Smith and John Diefenbaker were not as certain as their Defence Department colleagues that Canada ought to jump into nuclear negotiations with the Americans. Their concerns, however, were not philosophical. Both men worried about the possible precedent that would be set by the military's proposal as well as the political consequences that might flow from Canada's acquisition of nuclear weapons. Smith was more practical and less political than Diefenbaker, wondering about issues of control. His solution was to pursue an agreement with the Americans on the same terms as the British, who had secured a veto over the use of the nuclear weapons stored in Britain.[7] Diefenbaker's concerns were more overtly political than those of his minister of external affairs. He feared that the acceptance of nuclear weapons might undermine his political support, and he ruminated that "public opinion in the UK was divided on the issue and it would be unfortunate if conditions were created which would lead to a similar division in this country."[8] But Diefenbaker had no moral or principled objection to the acquisition of nuclear weapons.

His musings about whether to consult Pearson about the possibility of nuclear stockpiles in Canada reflected similar concerns. With 208 seats in the House of Commons, Diefenbaker did not need Pearson's support to acquire nuclear weapons. Even if Pearson criticized him as a warmonger or accused him of slavishly following American nuclear policy – a distinct possibility – time was on Diefenbaker's side. The discussion about nuclear weapons at the CDC came only weeks into the government's new mandate, and there was still plenty of time to counter any public outcry, the possibility of which was remote. Indeed, Diefenbaker's fears outpaced public sentiment, given that Canada's anti-nuclear movement was both tiny and quiet in the spring of 1958.

The discussion within the CDC illustrates that the issue of stockpiles at Goose Bay was neither strategically nor philosophically contentious, though a certain amount of caution was expressed about the value of a Canadian veto, and with good reason. The Americans might promise Canadian officials a veto over the use of jointly held warheads, but it was unlikely to be of any use in the event of an emergency. In any case, the decision to accept or reject nuclear stockpiles at Goose Bay was not a pressing one. International tensions seemed to be waning, removing the urgency that had accompanied the first American proposal in December 1957. As a result, the CDC decided to defer a decision on the subject until the Americans asked again.[9]

The following day, cabinet turned its attention to the possibility of storing nuclear weapons at Canadian bases leased to the United States. Overnight, Diefenbaker had grown more concerned about Pearson's position on the issue, and he expressed his fear that the opposition leader would probably make it a matter of public debate. The government, he warned, needed to respond effectively.

Diefenbaker's was a reasonable concern, given that Pearson had campaigned as the "man for peace" (even if he had been a key minister in the Liberal government that had approved nuclear installations at Goose Bay). Meanwhile, Smith continued to focus on issues of control, proposing a system of joint control between the Canadians and Americans. Since the proposed agreement was based on the existing arrangement between Britain and the United States, Smith did not anticipate that Washington would oppose the formula. Pearkes was noticeably silent during these talks, contributing to the discussion only to detail the three types of missiles the Americans might ask to store in Canada: air-to-air missiles armed with atomic warheads, designed for continental defence; atomic bombs carried by the US Air Force's Strategic Air Command for defensive purposes or retaliation; and nuclear weapons for use by either the Canadian or American navy against submarines.[10]

Cabinet was decidedly unenthusiastic in response to Diefenbaker's musings on whether they should talk to the Liberals about the possibility of storing nuclear weapons in Canada. No doubt, such an approach would be a show of good faith in the pursuit of a bipartisan foreign policy (for which the media had praised the government in the recent campaign), but it could be construed as a sign of insecurity and uncertainty. Moreover, the Liberals had not formally approached the Conservatives on an issue of national defence or foreign affairs – at least, not in recent memory – and there was no reason to talk to them before the government had made a formal decision to acquire nuclear weapons from the Americans. It seemed to be asking for trouble, leaving the government vulnerable to attack in Parliament. Raised only to inform cabinet of CDC's current thinking on nuclear weapons, no decision was required for the time being. And there the matter stood.[11]

Diefenbaker's handling of the nuclear issue in April 1958 highlights his preoccupation with public opinion and political support. Only mild concern was warranted at the time. In the spring of 1958, Diefenbaker began to receive letters from members of the public who expressed their general opposition to nuclear weapons. The letters emphasized the perils of nuclear fallout, not stockpiles, and focused on the state of international affairs. In particular, the writers focused on the dangers of Soviet and American nuclear testing. Most urged the prime minister to make use of Canada's special relationship with the United States to encourage a moratorium on testing or to use Canada's "international reputation" to promote a global test ban. There were no letters expressing concern that the Government of Canada might acquire nuclear weapons.[12]

These letters show that it would be wrong to suggest that Diefenbaker had absolutely nothing to fear politically about nuclear policy. There was reason to be concerned about the volume of correspondence on the subject, and it did not take much to imagine that those who were inspired to oppose nuclear testing would quickly put pen to paper to oppose Canada's acquisition of nuclear warheads. The very existence of letters related to nuclear matters underscored to Diefenbaker the potential controversy that could accompany talks to acquire nuclear weapons from the Americans.

While cabinet began to discuss the prospect of nuclear stockpiles in Canada, Diefenbaker was also trying to work out the final details of NORAD. By the spring of 1958, the difficulties associated with concluding the NORAD agreement were ones of style not substance, and negotiations for a formal agreement reached their final stages at that time.[13] Diefenbaker and his cabinet colleagues were firm in their belief that Canada ought to join with the United States in defending North American air space, and within days of the 1958 federal election they resumed consideration of the proposed agreement.

The Canadians sent their final draft agreement to Washington in early April, and cabinet discussed the proposal several days later. In the prime minister's absence, Howard Green, Diefenbaker's minister of public works and most trusted member of cabinet, presided over the meeting as acting prime minister. George Pearkes and Sidney Smith led the discussions on NORAD, detailing a number of scenarios in which Canadian forces would be required to act under the agreement. No one considered that joining NORAD might require Canada to acquire nuclear weapons for its armed forces, nor did anyone seem to care about this possibility. Thus, by mid-April 1958 there were no questions or concerns about the implications of NORAD or the principles that underpinned the agreement.[14]

Cabinet did not discuss NORAD again for almost a month. During that time, negotiations progressed quickly. By the end of April, the two governments had reached an agreement on bilateral alert declarations. Only the issues of ministerial consultation and NORAD's role within NATO remained to be settled. When the cabinet finally returned to the subject on 8 May, its members were pleased to see the progress that had been made, particularly that the Americans had accepted annual consultations with the Canadians and seemed to understand that there was "widespread public interest" in the subject of alerts and the carriage of nuclear weapons over Canadian territory.

As he led the discussion in cabinet that day, Diefenbaker remained preoccupied with the fear that Canadians might not accept the agreement. He also worried that Pearson would "create problems in parliament" over the agreement. As noted above, Pearson had been involved in the initial NORAD negotiations, and Diefenbaker was worried that he might somehow accuse him of neglecting Canada's national interest. It is not clear how a North American security arrangement could undermine Canadian interests, especially if the Liberal government had also planned to approve it, but it was something that Diefenbaker feared.

To this end, Diefenbaker tried to protect Canada's national interest by asking for a strong link between NORAD and NATO. The Americans, however, were firmly opposed to anything that might draw Europeans into North American affairs, and they rejected the request. Diefenbaker was pragmatic in his response. He understood that the Americans feared possible foreign meddling in local matters and was willing to concede the point. As he explained to his cabinet colleagues, this was simply the price one had to pay for a much-needed defence arrangement. In any event, he confessed, the connection between NATO and NORAD would have been more symbolic than real, a multilateral counterweight to the bilateral defence agreement in appearance only. The link would have played well in Parliament and with the Canadian public, but it would not have served any utility beyond basic politics.[15]

Despite these reassurances, cabinet was not unanimous in its support for the proposed concession. While most ministers regarded it as trivial, some argued that the suggested changes were so different from what the Conservatives had already said about the nature of NORAD that the government would be open to criticism. Ultimately, cabinet's only decision on 8 May was to await a formal response from Washington.[16]

This slight rift within cabinet had no immediate consequences. Canadian officials had already drafted a new agreement in view of the new language they had received from the Americans, and they were literally preparing to transmit the new agreement to Washington as cabinet discussed the matter. Within days, everything was resolved. Midway through a cabinet meeting on 10 May, H.B. Robinson passed a note to Diefenbaker indicating that the Americans had finally consented on the outstanding consultation provision. All that remained to be negotiated was the actual mechanism for ministerial consultation between the two countries.[17] Believing they had their guarantee of civilian control over NORAD and joint ministerial consultation – in some form – the members of Diefenbaker's cabinet quickly approved the agreement.[18]

The NORAD notes were exchanged on 12 May, and were introduced in the House of Commons a week later. The opposition responded quickly, calling for a formal debate and parliamentary approval. In truth, the opposition parties were not interested in a debate on the substance or merit of the agreement. They simply sought instead to embarrass the government, just as Diefenbaker had feared.[19] Diefenbaker's decision to submit the NORAD agreement to Parliament for approval came only after he had considered the ramifications of discussing the agreement in the House of Commons. He was concerned that a debate on NORAD might set a precedent, requiring that any future military arrangement be submitted to Parliament for its approval.[20] His cabinet ministers agreed, but they believed it was worth submitting the agreement to Parliament to demonstrate the government's openness on the issue. However, formal approval was far from certain; although the Conservatives controlled the House of Commons, the Liberals still had a majority in the Senate. And while it was unlikely that the Liberal-dominated Senate would reject NORAD, the mere possibility weighed heavily on the prime minister.[21]

Canadian politicians debated the NORAD agreement in the House of Commons from 10 to 19 June. Diefenbaker may have conceded the proposed link between NATO and NORAD to the Americans during the negotiations, but in Parliament he tried to draw a connection between the two alliances. Pearson called his bluff, citing from the transcript of NATO Secretary General Paul-Henri Spaak's recent press conference in which Spaak had stressed, "NORAD is not under the command of NATO."²² But Diefenbaker would not budge.

In his reluctance to concede the point, Diefenbaker tried to evade Pearson's assertion by focusing on the symbolism of NORAD within the context of NATO. Symbolism, after all, was ultimately what Diefenbaker had in mind when he had raised the subject with the Americans during the negotiations. He explained to Parliament that NORAD extended "the principles of NATO" to North America in the sense "that it makes provision for the joining together of free nations within the context of NATO and for the purpose of NATO." Putting aside the question of formal linkages between the two alliances, he concluded that NORAD served to strengthen NATO, "which is all that matters."²³

In June 1958, as Diefenbaker and his government prepared to put the NORAD debate behind them, the subject of nuclear stockpiles returned to the fore. In May the Americans had asked again for permission to store nuclear weapons at Goose Bay. This request went further than the one from earlier in the year. It was no longer just a question of storage. Now the Americans were asking if they could "hold discussions on integrating atomic capabilities for continental air defence."²⁴ When members of the CDC met in late April, they had already decided to defer making a decision on both subjects, "pending further consideration of the various matters involved and further discussions with the US authorities as required."²⁵

On 8 May, at the same cabinet meeting at which NORAD was discussed, Diefenbaker led a discussion on the subject of nuclear stockpiles. Pearkes, minister of national defence, attended the meeting; Smith, minister of external affairs, who had previously expressed reservations about the circumstances surrounding the acquisition of nuclear weapons from the Americans, did not. The discussion was brief, and no one opposed "discussions on integrating atomic capabilities for continental air defence."²⁶

Despite this lack of opposition, cabinet postponed making a formal decision about the talks, just as the CDC had done earlier. Since the last time the nuclear issues had come before a cabinet meeting (the end of April), Diefenbaker – despite his reservations – had decided to talk to President Eisenhower and Lester Pearson before making a formal decision. Nonetheless, the cabinet meeting of 8 May was an important one in the development of Canada's nuclear policy. Although cabinet did not make a formal decision to pursue stockpiles for Canada, this was the first time it had contemplated the acquisition of nuclear weapons for Canadian forces. This was a clear step beyond allowing the Americans to stockpile warheads at US bases in Canada. More to the point, it was a decision made within the context of NORAD, and the cabinet ministers understood the implications of what they were doing.

After the conclusion of NORAD, Diefenbaker could not consider Canada's defence situation without considering Canada's relations with the United States. And although relations were very good on a personal level between Diefenbaker and Eisenhower, there was trouble brewing in the defence relationship between the two countries. By the summer of 1958, with NORAD approved, more was at stake than ministerial consultation. Before Eisenhower's visit to Ottawa that summer, Smith and Pearkes had met with John Foster Dulles on 10 July. A prominent feature of the Dulles-Smith talks was the possibility of an agreement on shared defence production.

At the meeting, Smith complained to the American secretary of state that Canada was overburdened by the ever-increasing expense of continental defence; as Canadian involvement in North American defence had increased, so had the costs. Smith pointed out that the Avro Arrow had cost the Canadian government $250 million in development by 1958 and was expected to cost another $530 million by 1961. The semi-automatic ground environment system (SAGE), designed to aid in Canadian air defence, cost $150 million. The Bomarc missile (expected to complement the manned bomber and complete the North American Bomarc defence network), while extending continental defence by some 400 kilometres to the north, cost $200 million.[27] Smith urged his American counterpart to consider Canada's involvement in the increase of radar coverage in the northern part of North America, with various monitoring systems such as the Pinetree System, DEW Line, and Mid-Canada Line.[28]

Smith suggested a possible solution to the financial dilemma facing the Canadian government. The two countries had a history of shared military production dating back to 1939, and Smith proposed a similar arrangement. He opposed mutual aid, but a plan involving the joint production of defence material in conjunction with a cost-sharing arrangement for development and production was altogether different and entirely acceptable to him.

During the meeting, Pearkes pointed out that NORAD brought with it plenty of cooperation operationally, and he urged the American officials to consider that now was the time for "co-operation in production." The Canadians proposed that US air squadrons at Harmon Field and Goose Bay agree to use the CF-105 (the Avro Arrow), thereby reducing the costs of its production. Pearkes also appealed to past cost-sharing agreements, specifically the construction of the Pinetree, DEW, and Mid-Canada lines, explaining to Dulles, "We are reaching the stage where it is not possible to develop or produce complicated weapons purely for Canadian use." There were other considerations, namely, "that we should be able to maintain and repair all weapons that are used on Canadian soil." Finally and perhaps most importantly, Pearkes stressed the necessity of maintaining Canadian "defence industrial facilities for availability in the event of an emergency." Dulles sympathized with the Canadians about the costs of postwar defence, noting that his country was also concerned about such problems. "The cost of modern weapons," he remarked, "is almost fantastic. Last week the secretary of defense indicated the mounting costs by comparing a World War II plane at $100,000 with a modern plane at approximately $5 million."[29]

The Canadian proposal for a joint defence production sharing agreement underscores the economic constraints within which the Diefenbaker government formulated its defence policy.[30] It also illustrates the pragmatism of the Canadian officials, who appreciated the economic attraction of nuclear weaponry. Again, no one expressed philosophical concerns about the possibility that Canada would acquire weapons of mass destruction.[31] In essence, the Canadian officials told the secretary of state – the architect of "massive retaliation" – that Canada could not afford the most modern (and, by extension, the most destructive) military accoutrement unless the Americans helped out. By contrast, no one ever pointed out to cabinet that modern missiles, including Bomarcs, were probably too expensive for the Canadian budget.

Thus, by the summer of 1958 it seemed to be only a matter of time before the Canadian government would acquire nuclear weapons. R.B. Bryce, the clerk of the privy council and Diefenbaker's most trusted adviser, offered advice to the prime minister on a number of defence issues that shaped the last half of 1958. In particular, he encouraged the government to maintain the Arrow program, despite its growing costs and likely obsolescence. Bryce also supported the acquisition of nuclear warheads, urging Diefenbaker to accept the MB-1 nuclear missile in place of the Sparrow and Astra components of the Arrow. This would "minimize great technical risks and possible delays," he noted, and would "save money at the critically important time." Perhaps most importantly, he said that, such an approach "should not cause serious political difficulties."[32]

Bryce was also convinced of the Bomarc's viability, and he urged Diefenbaker to accept two bases in and around Ottawa. However, the Bomarc missile was intended to supplement, not replace, the Arrow for air defence; as far as Bryce was concerned, acquiring the Bomarc did not mean cancelling the Arrow program. This was not a naive acceptance of the Bomarc, nor was it a failure to comprehend its role in defending North America, for Bryce realized full well that the bases involved were situated to defend the United States and not Canada.

In presenting nuclear weapons to Diefenbaker as a defence option that was viable both economically and politically, Bryce stressed that nuclear-tipped Bomarc missiles were the most cost-effective means of securing Canada's defence. Given this emphasis, it is difficult to accept, as some have argued, that Diefenbaker and his cabinet overlooked the nuclear component of the Bomarc missile in their haste to deal with the growing crisis surrounding the Arrow. Bryce's forthright advice makes clear this was not the case.[33]

Although Bryce and others did not worry that Diefenbaker would lose political support as a result of nuclear policy in 1958, the practical details of acquiring the warheads remained complicated. American law prohibited the selling of nuclear warheads (though, in an age of fiscal restraint, this was just as well as far as the Canadians were concerned). Leasing the warheads was an alternative, but it raised concerns about custody and control. It also presented a predicament for Canadian officials.

Since the Second World War, Canadian officials had been adamant that they contribute to allied assistance in partnership with the Americans; they did not want to be dependent on American aid. The latter was precisely what had worried Smith and other Canadian officials when they met with Dulles in July to propose a defence production sharing agreement. Nuclear weapons were no different. And while Bryce encouraged Diefenbaker to accept nuclear weapons from the Americans, he also advised a certain amount of caution. Nuclear weapons marked a "departure in Canadian policy," he warned, and "if followed by other steps could lead to a clearly dependent position for Canada and its forces."[34] The difficulty lay in determining how to balance the desire for costly nuclear weapons with concerns about national sovereignty and fiscal responsibility.

The interplay between economics and defence policy continued through the summer of 1958. At the beginning of August, cabinet approved two recommendations of the CDC that involved considerable expenditures for the government. The first was the extension of the Pinetree radar line. The other was the implementation of the SAGE program in Canada.[35] The Pinetree line included five radar stations, as well as thirty-nine intermediate gap-filler stations between the radar stations, and was expected to cost $87 million. The anticipated cost of the SAGE system was $107 million, with the Americans paying for two computers worth almost half that sum, leaving the Canadians to pay $54 million.

At the same time, Smith began to change his position on the acceptability and necessity of nuclear weapons. By the summer of 1958, he had come to believe that the Soviet threat, both current and future, outweighed budgetary constraints. His staff at External Affairs had warned him that the Soviets were a threat because of their missile holdings. Although these were not expected to outnumber American bombers any time in the near future, there was a dual threat when Soviet missile holdings were added to the assessment, and thus North America needed to defend itself "against every possible attack." Canada had an obligation to do its fair share in this defence of North America.

Smith now believed there were only two options for Canada. The government could increase the defence budget or it could accept mutual aid from the United States for the first time. Reversing his earlier position, he recommended the latter. Membership in NATO and NORAD, he argued, had already reduced Canadian sovereignty. The true test of national sovereignty was whether a country could defend itself, and therefore any defence arrangement with the Americans that increased Canadian security was "not an unreasonable diminution of sovereignty."[36] Of course, the terms of the arrangement were crucial to shoring up Canada's independence. Only if theirs was an equitable contribution to North American defence would the Canadians maintain their influence with the Americans; by extension, only if Canada paid its fair share of continental defence costs could national sovereignty be maintained.

Smith offered other strong arguments in favour of nuclear weapons. Although the Bomarc could be armed with a non-nuclear warhead, it seemed pointless to have a state-of-the-art weapons system operating at less than capacity. Furthermore, Canadian forces in NORAD would be working side by side with the Americans, who were armed with nuclear weapons. The Canadian public was unlikely to accept that their soldiers were not as well equipped to protect North America as their American counterparts.

Even the issue of control was no longer insurmountable. Smith continued to promote the idea that the Canadians pursue a veto along the lines of the arrangement that the British had with the Americans. That agreement stated:

The United States Government shall provide nuclear warheads for the missiles transferred to the United Kingdom Government pursuant to this Agreement. All nuclear warheads so provided shall remain in full United States ownership, custody and control in accordance with the United States law.

The decision to launch these missiles will be a matter for joint decision by the two Governments. Any such joint decisions will be made in the light of the circumstances at the time and having regard to the undertaking the two Governments have assumed in Article 5 of the North Atlantic Treaty.[37]

In this light, Canada's acceptance of nuclear weapons seemed to be a necessity, a foregone conclusion even, in the summer of 1958 as Smith was encouraging the government to accept nuclear stockpiles at Goose Bay.

Thus, by the fall, everything the Diefenbaker government did pointed toward the acquisition of nuclear weapons. In September cabinet approved Bomarc bases in Canada,[38] and on 23 September, Diefenbaker announced that his government would acquire the Bomarc missile as part of its air defence program. At the same time, he announced revisions to Canada's defence policy that suggested the impending demise of the Avro Arrow, despite Bryce's advice to the contrary. Although Diefenbaker worried about how best to tell Canadians that his government intended to scrap the Arrow, all evidence suggests that it was only a matter of time before the program was terminated.[39] The result was the government's announcement that it intended to continue the development (but not the production) of the Arrow and the Iroquois engine until March 1959, at which point the program would once again be subject to re-evaluation. The Astra and Sparrow programs were cancelled altogether.[40]

Diefenbaker decided to continue the development of the Arrow not because of some inner turmoil or indecision, but because he wanted to secure a cost-sharing agreement with the Americans for the purchase of the Bomarc and the F-106 American-made interceptor before finalizing plans to cancel the Canadian-made interceptor. While the F-106 was inferior to the Arrow in terms of its capabilities, it was far more affordable and thus easily justified as a better choice for the Canadian government.[41]

By the beginning of October the government had approved the procurement of a battery of Lacrosse surface-to-surface guided missile systems for Canadian forces in Europe. In cabinet, Diefenbaker supported the army's efforts to modernize its forces, explaining, "The Lacrosse ... appeared to be the most suitable system available. Since it was essential to provide this type of support for the brigade group in Europe, the minimum quantity necessary was one battery of four launchers and twelve missiles."[42] Cabinet agreed. Far from failing to grasp the implications of the Bomarc missile or other nuclear warheads, Diefenbaker's conduct during discussions about the Lacrosse indicates that he knew exactly what he was doing.

Meanwhile, officials at the Department of External Affairs realized that the government was starting to make major changes to Canada's defence policy, and they had reservations about Canadian forces acquiring nuclear weapons. This had been apparent when members of NATO began talks on the possibility of stockpiles in Europe in the spring of 1958.[43] Jules Léger, the undersecretary of external affairs, wrote to Norman Robertson, Canada's ambassador to the United States, expressing his apprehension about the growing clamour for nuclear weapons among members of the North Atlantic alliance. He was particularly distressed about the possibility of tactical nuclear weapons and urged that Canadian officials try to promote disarmament over nuclear negotiations. Political considerations, Léger argued, had to be used to rein in the military's enthusiasm for nuclear warheads. Robertson agreed.[44]

By October, officials at External Affairs were even more distressed by the government's move toward the acquisition of nuclear weapons. In a letter to General Charles Foulkes, the chief of staff, Léger echoed his earlier emphasis on the importance of political control, urging that military and civilian authorities work together on the negotiations. Léger – like Smith – was most concerned about who would control nuclear weapons in Canada; he could accept collective NATO control in Europe but did not support NORAD control in North America. The NORAD commander was an American, and Léger opposed subordinating Canadian forces to American control. Yet he was nothing if not pragmatic and was willing to concede NORAD control if there was no other way to secure an agreement with the Americans for nuclear warheads. But he insisted that if NORAD were given control, joint control must govern the actual use of the weapons.⁴⁵

Joint control, then, was the fundamental concern and the minimum requirement for an agreement as far as Léger was concerned. This point was made time and again over the course of the negotiations between the two countries. Similarly, Léger's encouragement that civilian and military authorities work together on the negotiations was a clear reminder that military representatives were only too willing to rush ahead of the civilians in their pursuit of nuclear weapons.

On 15 October the government's deliberations culminated in cabinet's formal decision to undertake negotiations with the Americans to acquire nuclear weapons for Canada's armed forces, provided that three conditions were met. First and foremost, the talks had to be kept secret. Just as important was cabinet's determination that the Canadian government obtain as much freedom as possible to determine how the warheads would be used in an emergency. And finally, cabinet insisted that Canadian authorization be required before any nuclear warheads could be released in Canada, regardless of whether they were released by Canadian or American forces.⁴⁶

Echoing the concerns of the officials at External Affairs, the ministers focused exclusively on issues of control at this cabinet meeting. No one questioned the merits of nuclear stockpiles in Canada. As Donald Fleming, the finance minister, recalled, "No final conclusion was reached on the storage of defensive nuclear weapons in Canada, but only details remained to be discussed."⁴⁷ Yet even this assertion ignores the nuance of the cabinet's decision.

The cabinet record is more tentative than Fleming's recollection suggests, stating simply: "The minister recommended that agreement in principle be given to investigate with the US authorities, SACEUR, and Commander-in-Chief NORAD, the possibilities of nego-

tiating agreements for the disposition of nuclear warheads as he
had outlined. If agreements were ultimately negotiated, they would
be submitted to cabinet for final approval."[48] The words "investigate" and "possibilities" suggest that the cabinet was committed to
the *idea* that nuclear weapons could be acquired for Canadian
forces, not that the acquisition was a foregone conclusion. This
said, in late 1958 it still seemed more likely than not that the
Diefenbaker government would accept nuclear warheads if the
appropriate arrangements regarding control and custody could be
negotiated. And given the recent experience negotiating the terms
of NORAD, these conditions did not seem to pose an insurmountable
obstacle to a nuclear arrangement between the two countries.

The three cabinet conditions guided the debate within the civil
service and the government. External Affairs responded to the decision by outlining where its opinions differed from those of National
Defence, again emphasizing the importance of civilian control; it
hoped that joint control would allow Canadian officials to dampen
American enthusiasm should there come a time when US officials
considered using nuclear weapons. These concerns about civilian
control dovetailed nicely with Diefenbaker's worries about public
opinion and Canadians' support for the measure, because the consultation requirement would make the issue more acceptable to the
electorate.[49] It is noteworthy, however, that the primary concern
was consultation before use, not consent.

While External Affairs considered the political acceptability
of nuclear weapons, National Defence questioned the military viability of Canadian custody and control. Defence officials argued
that time did not permit the luxury of sovereignty; any situation
that required the use of nuclear weapons was sufficiently serious
that political officials would have to subordinate their control to
the military. The military representatives thus thought that NORAD
should use the proposed NATO formula, which was based on a
policy of delegated control for the use of nuclear warheads within
the alliance.

The problem with this position was that the NATO negotiations
had stalled by the end of 1958, in large part because the French had
demanded greater national control over the nuclear warheads that
would be stationed in France. In many respects, French officials had
similar concerns to their counterparts at External Affairs. And as
negotiations with the Americans moved forward, the differences

between External Affairs and National Defence continued to grow. This difference of opinion represented "the classic dilemma" of nuclear weapons, one that Diefenbaker noted carefully: national security versus national sovereignty.[50]

External Affairs responded to the Defence proposals with a strategy of delay. Its officials realized they needed their own proposal to deal with the issue of control, one that could counter the criticisms raised by National Defence – primarily that there would not be enough time in an emergency to worry about national sovereignty. For the time being, External Affairs officials encouraged the military representatives to begin preliminary discussions with their American counterparts. However, they were equally adamant that arrangements could not be finalized until after the talks within NATO were complete. They also considered the implications of SAC nuclear weapons at Goose Bay. While the military urged separate discussions and agreements to govern different situations, External Affairs officials suggested a general agreement that had sufficient breadth to encompass both strategic and tactical weapons.[51]

As officials at External Affairs began to work on their own proposal to address issues of control in the autumn of 1958, the department had a change of management. Norman Robertson replaced Jules Léger as undersecretary of external affairs, and Robertson was not as certain as his predecessor – if Léger had been truly certain – that Canada ought to acquire nuclear weapons.[52] Nonetheless, the officials continued to work on how best to counter the concerns about control expressed by the military. They did not question the basic premise that Canada should acquire nuclear weapons, and NATO was particularly germane to the department's proposal, for they examined the British, French, and Italian positions within the alliance.

In Britain, the Americans provided nuclear warheads, but a joint decision by the two governments was required before the missiles could be launched. This was political control, not necessarily "practical control." The arrangement with France was entirely different. The French demanded control of both the launching mechanisms and the warheads stored on their territory. The French proposals to deal with this situation were elaborate, and Canadian officials did not expect they would lead to an agreement any time soon. The Italian situation was akin to that of Great Britain and the other NATO nations (aside from France) in that a joint decision was

required before nuclear weapons could be launched from their territory. There was, however, at least one significant difference between
Britain and Italy: whereas the British were on the verge of building
their own bombs, the Italians had no such prospect.[53]

By the first week in November, External Affairs finally had its
own proposal to govern control. The department now agreed with
National Defence that a veto would be pointless, despite Smith's
suggestion to the contrary. An attack on North America would acti-
vate NORAD, and an emergency situation would render a veto moot.
Given this scenario, fighting for a veto hardly seemed worth the
effort. But while forgoing a veto made practical sense, it posed
potential problems with respect to public opinion. External Affairs
therefore urged Diefenbaker to be forthright with the Canadian
people about the situation. There seemed to be no way around the
fact that ultimate control would rest with the president, not with
the prime minister or Parliament. Yet not even this possible difficulty was expected to harm the government politically. Canadians
had accepted continental air defence with NORAD, and the department's nuclear proposal seemed to be a logical extension of this
pact. As far as External Affairs officials were concerned, nuclear
weapons would be like any other weapon controlled by NORAD and
its command.[54]

As Christmas 1958 approached, Diefenbaker faced difficult decisions about Canada's defence policy. Despite the efforts of External
Affairs, there was no formal Canadian proposal for the custody and
control of nuclear weapons on Canadian territory. This was problematic. At a cabinet meeting in December, the defence minister
argued that the real issue was quite simple, revolving around
whether Canadian forces would be properly equipped to fulfill their
obligations. He accepted that under US law the president was the
final arbiter of use when it came to nuclear weapons, and he
believed that a request for joint control and custody would be as
pointless as asking for a veto over actual use.[55]

Pearkes's comments revealed a growing sense of frustration over
the subject of nuclear negotiations and the amount of time it was
taking to secure an agreement, as did the brief cabinet discussion
that followed. One minister commented on the apparent futility of
the debate: "Whatever the government decided would be criticized.
A good many Canadians would not want the weapons stored here
for use by Canadian or US forces under any circumstances." Ignor-

ing the possibility of political consequences, but with more resignation than enthusiasm, cabinet approved Pearkes's proposal to undertake discussions with the Americans at the Canada–United States ministerial committee in Paris.[56]

The Paris meeting proved to be a success. Pearkes secured US approval to begin drafting a nuclear agreement based on the conditions approved by cabinet.[57] And as 1958 came to an end, cabinet contemplated whether Diefenbaker should make a formal announcement that negotiations were underway with the Americans. There was also a discussion about how the talks might influence the government's support for disarmament. On the surface, the two seemed to present a contradiction in policy. In fact, the two different positions were the beginnings of a two-pronged approach to nuclear policy.

In an ideal world, Diefenbaker would have preferred a global disarmament agreement. There was, however, little hope for such a result; the Soviets would never support a Western disarmament proposal, just as the West was not likely to support a proposal that originated from the Eastern Bloc. As a result, the government's decision to enter negotiations with the Americans was a means of maintaining Canadian security when the disarmament talks broke down, as they inevitably would. The Americans seemed to understand this Canadian strategy and accepted it. They appeared not to be in any hurry to secure an agreement, and it was sufficient that talks were underway. On the Canadian side, American willingness to enter into a defence production sharing agreement to offset the exorbitant cost of these modern weapons was crucial. With that, cabinet agreed that the government would make a statement early in the New Year outlining the talks on acquisition and nuclear stockpiling in Canada.[58]

That statement came on 20 February 1959, when Diefenbaker announced his government's intention to pursue an agreement with the United States for the acquisition of nuclear weapons for Canada's armed forces. The nuclear component of the statement was overshadowed by the concurrent announcement that the Arrow had been cancelled. The statement was the culmination of six months of deliberation on the fate of the CF-105. As estimated costs climbed to $2 billion, the Arrow's expense was a primary factor behind the decision. There was no hope of selling the interceptor abroad and thus no possible way of offsetting the rising costs. There were also concerns about the interceptor's relevance as militaries moved away from bombers toward intercontinental ballistic missiles, though some questioned the wisdom of abandoning the Arrow when it was unlikely that the Soviets would move to a defence strategy that involved only missiles.[59]

Diefenbaker knew, as did the rest of the cabinet, that the Arrow made little financial sense. He also believed that it would soon be obsolete, most likely by the time it was produced. There was simply no reason to continue the project. But the prospect of enormous job losses in the Toronto area, the Tories' political heartland, was a concern. Yet the longer the government waited, the more likely it was that a federal election would be looming around the corner. By then – 1962 or 1963 – hundreds of millions of dollars would have been wasted. Although the Arrow's economic feasibility was the government's primary concern, political liability was a close second. Ultimately, the government hoped, "the Canadian public would give credit to the government in the long run for good housekeeping and it appeared that on defence and on sound economic grounds it was good housekeeping to discontinue the programme now."[60]

Bryce had encouraged Diefenbaker to contextualize the cancellation of the Arrow by pointing out that Canada was going to acquire nuclear weapons to protect itself against the Soviet threat.[61] He did not expect the announcement about nuclear weapons to be controversial, so it is unlikely that he encouraged Diefenbaker to link it to the cancellation of the Arrow in order to bury it as unpleasant news. The fact that Diefenbaker followed his advice calls into question the suggestion that the Bomarc's nuclear capacity was lost in the Arrow debate. Bryce was aware of it, made sure that Diefenbaker was equally apprised, and even viewed it as an asset when it came to announcing the cancellation of the Arrow.[62]

Diefenbaker's statement on 20 February satisfied the pledge he made to cabinet to announce the government's nuclear talks with the Eisenhower administration, and it is worth noting at length because of his subsequent references to it:

> The full potential of these defensive weapons is achieved only when they are armed with nuclear warheads. The government is, therefore, examining with the United States government questions connected with the acquisition of nuclear warheads for Bomarc and other defensive weapons for use by the Cana-

dian forces in Canada, and the storage of warheads in Canada. Problems connected with the arming of the Canadian brigade in Europe with short-range nuclear weapons for NATO's defence tasks are also being studied.

We are confident that we shall be able to reach formal agreement with the United States on appropriate means to serve the common objective. It will of course be some time before these weapons will be available for use by Canadian forces. The government, as soon as it is in a position to do so, will inform the House, within the limits of security, of the general terms of understanding which are reached between the two governments on this subject.

Diefenbaker softened his stance by emphasizing that Canada would not produce nuclear weapons, but pointed out that "we must reluctantly admit the need in present circumstances for nuclear weapons of a defensive character."[63]

The reaction that followed Diefenbaker's two announcements focused more on the Arrow than on the prospect of nuclear weapons coming to Canada. The headline in the *Globe and Mail* read "Drop Arrow; 13,800 idle"; only a secondary headline noted the real importance of Diefenbaker's statement to Parliament on 20 February: "Canadians to Get Nuclear Weapons."[64] In March the *New York Times* picked up the story, noting Canada's willingness to accept nuclear weapons.[65]

The prime minister received bags of mail as a result of his statement before the House of Commons. Most expressed concern about the economic consequences of the Arrow's termination, not the possibility of nuclear weapons coming to Canada.[66] Only a handful of letters expressed some concern about the story that had appeared in the *New York Times*. There was also a small proportion of correspondence that took issue not with the article but with the substance of Diefenbaker's statement to Parliament, opposing Canada's acquisition of nuclear weapons. If Diefenbaker had worried about the political consequences of permitting nuclear stockpiles in Canada in April 1958, after his government had so recently won a landslide majority, a letter from David Gauthier in March 1959 now heightened these concerns. In February, immediately following the prime minister's statement, Gauthier, a lecturer in the Philosophy Department at the University of Toronto and a burgeoning anti-nuclear activist, wrote to the student newspaper, the *Varsity*, protesting the government's decision to cancel the Avro Arrow and to accept the Bomarc missile.[67] The following month he organized a petition to condemn Diefenbaker's contemplation of nuclear stockpiles and to urge him to cancel the Bomarc. The petition was a modest success, garnering approximately seventy faculty signatures.[68]

Diefenbaker responded in Parliament. Based on the advice of External Affairs officials, he concentrated on the *New York Times* article, calling its conclusions "inaccurate." He stressed that his 20 February statement did not mean that the government intended to acquire nuclear warheads in the immediate future, only that negotiations would be complicated and the government would provide information to the public when it could.[69] The approach was neither a ringing endorsement nor an outright rejection of nuclear weapons, and it left the government with room to manoeuvre.

It is clear that only a very small percentage of the prime minister's mail revealed that Canadians were opposed to the acquisition of nuclear weapons. This correspondence, however, had an importance that exceeded its numbers. Organized efforts to promote the maintenance of Canada as a nuclear-free country did not yet exist, but anti-Bomarc letters like those from Gauthier confirmed to the prime minister that anti-nuclear groups could exist in Canada just as they already existed in Great Britain. What Diefenbaker could not know then was that his 20 February statement served as the catalyst for a home-grown anti-nuclear movement in Canada, and this limited response to the Bomarc announcement was the beginning of efforts to organize Canadians to oppose nuclear weapons. Although the announcement indicated that talks with the Americans were only exploratory, many would-be anti-nuclear activists believed the government had already made its decision to proceed. And they were not far off the mark.

Just as Diefenbaker and his cabinet were on the verge of a significant decision, one of the most important posts in the government unexpectedly fell vacant. On St Patrick's Day, a mere week after Diefenbaker's clarification of nuclear policy in the House of Commons, Sidney Smith died. Diefenbaker filled the void himself temporarily, but although he was clearly intrigued by foreign affairs, there was simply too much to learn in too short a time.[70] In the months between Smith's death in March and the appointment of his replacement in June, Canada's nuclear policy crystallized.

3

Canada's Nuclear Policy Takes Shape, 1959–1960

Sidney Smith's sudden death in March 1959 left a void in Diefenbaker's government. Smith's successor at External Affairs, Howard Green, was appointed in June, shortly after the government agreed to begin formal negotiations with the United States to acquire nuclear weapons. More dove than hawk, Green was an unlikely candidate to facilitate Canada's entry into the nuclear club. Why, then, did Diefenbaker appoint him to such an important portfolio at such a crucial moment? What was his influence on nuclear policy? These questions are important when examining the critical period from the spring of 1959 to the autumn of 1960. Throughout, Diefenbaker continued to worry about public opposition to nuclear weapons as well as the Liberal Party's nuclear policy. Criticized for cancelling the Arrow, he was reluctant to incur the wrath of voters on another defence issue. As well, Pearson was opposed to Canada's acquisition of nuclear weapons, and Diefenbaker feared that the Liberal leader's perceived moral authority on the subject would persuade Canadians to reject nuclear weapons and, by extension, the Tories.

The international situation and the rate of technological change influenced the pace at which Diefenbaker made decisions about Canada's defence policy. No pressing international crisis demanded an immediate decision on nuclear weapons, and thus there was no need to make a decision that was bound to upset at least some Canadians.[1] And although Soviet premier Khrushchev continued to threaten Western interests in Berlin, Soviet threats in West Germany were not new, and nothing indicated that outright conflict was imminent. Moreover, in the midst of the shift from manned bomb-

ers to ICBMs no one could be certain how long it would take for the
Soviets to change their weapons systems. It seemed unlikely that
they would abandon manned bombers altogether, and consequently
the nuclear threat to North America was a mixed one for the foreseeable future.

Critics have argued that Diefenbaker's greatest weakness as a
leader was his indecisiveness, and they point to the nuclear debate
to illustrate this flaw.[2] But to label Diefenbaker as indecisive does
not explain why he behaved as he did. He was not indecisive so
much as a poor political strategist. He knew that public procrastination had served William Lyon Mackenzie King well during the
Second World War, and he hoped to use a similar strategy of delay
to his own advantage.[3]

Although King may have been a sound political role model, the
situation with nuclear weapons was entirely different from the conscription issue. There was no evidence to suggest that nuclear weapons threatened national unity as conscription had done in both
world wars. There was, however, some evidence that the issue, like
conscription, might undermine the prime minister's political support. Diefenbaker thought, to paraphrase Mackenzie King, that a
strategy of "not necessarily nuclear weapons, but nuclear weapons
if necessary" might persuade opponents that he had no other option
to safeguard national security but to accept nuclear warheads for
Canada's armed forced at home and abroad. Disarmament was
Diefenbaker's preference in an ideal world, but that was not the
world of the late 1950s. Promoting disarmament as the first option
with the acquisition of nuclear warheads as a fallback seemed to be
a sensible alternative. Seen in this light, Diefenbaker's public procrastination was a conscious political calculation, not the result
of indecision.

In the spring of 1959, cabinet decided that the initial talks with the
Americans for the acquisition of nuclear weapons would use the
existing Anglo-American arrangement as a template. That agreement could form only the basis for the talks because there were two
important differences between the circumstances in Canada and
those in Great Britain. The Canadians were not entitled to "classified information concerning atomic weapons" because, unlike the
British, they did not actually intend to produce or develop their
own nuclear weapons; and unlike the British agreement, there was

no provision for Canada to acquire "a complete submarine nuclear propulsion plant, together with spare parts and the fuel elements required to operate this plant."[4] Aside from these two points, the projected Canadian-American agreement would be identical to the one between Britain and the United States, whether it involved "classification policies," "responsibility for the use of information, material, equipment and devices, conditions and guarantees," "patents," or "definitions."[5]

On 22 April 1959 the Cabinet Defence Committee authorized negotiations with Washington.[6] Cabinet granted its approval a few weeks later, with Diefenbaker at the helm. No discussion accompanied approval of the talks, and the only record was brief: "Cabinet agreed that the Canadian ambassador in Washington be authorized to sign the agreement negotiated with the United States for co-operation on the uses of atomic energy for mutual defence purposes."[7] Words to this effect were telegraphed to the Canadian Embassy in Washington, and Diefenbaker signed the ambassador's official note formally authorizing the talks on 22 May.[8] This official note concluded more than six months of deliberations and indicated that Diefenbaker and his government were ready to move toward the acquisition of nuclear weapons, at least for joint use with the Americans. As Robinson noted, "The questions for discussion with the Americans and the NATO authorities in 1958 and 1959 had mostly to do with the how and the when rather than with the whether or the why."[9]

The Canadian government was well on the way toward acquiring nuclear weapons when Green became secretary of state for external affairs at the beginning of June 1959. Sidney Smith had been a disappointment in the position. Although he was just getting accustomed to his portfolio when he died,[10] he never really understood the prime minister. Whereas Diefenbaker failed to comprehend that Smith was not a partisan Tory in the leader's mould, Smith did not appreciate Diefenbaker's devotion to the politics of parliamentary life.[11] Because the two men never developed close ties, their working relationship was awkward at times.[12]

There were a number of ways in which Smith and Green differed. Unlike his predecessor, Green had experience in both Parliament and cabinet when he came to the foreign affairs portfolio. First elected to the House of Commons in 1935 representing Vancouver South (later Vancouver Quadra), Green had spent even longer on the opposition benches than Diefenbaker. And although he had not supported Diefenbaker in his various attempts to win the party's leadership, he was nonetheless the prime minister's close and trusted colleague. Indeed, Green was one of the few ministers about whom Diefenbaker wrote fondly in his memoirs.[13] The two shared a desk in the House of Commons, and in Diefenbaker's absence Green often served as acting prime minister. Within cabinet, Green had been minister of public works in 1957 as well as acting minister of defence production until the majority in 1958, when Raymond O'Hurley took over the job. As a result, not only did Green have cabinet experience, but he had been a member of cabinet when major decisions were made about nuclear policy, having attended most of the meetings in which these decisions were made.

Green's greatest attribute was not his ministerial expertise but his political experience and close relationship with the prime minister. Diefenbaker's confidence in Green was apparent to the Department of External Affairs, and it improved relations between the department and the prime minister. Unlike Smith, Green had immediate access to Diefenbaker, which led to frequent meetings to discuss matters – a privilege reserved for only a few cabinet members. "Green's appointment," H.B. Robinson has rightly noted, "opened up opportunities of influence which had simply not existed since Pearson's departure two years before."[14]

There were, however, some major problems with Green's appointment. First, he seemed somewhat overwhelmed by his new position in cabinet and more than a little star struck.[15] More importantly, although he had greater access to the prime minister than the previous minister, he had little knowledge of international relations. Born in 1895, Green had served in England and France during the First World War, but he did not leave North America again until he became the minister of external affairs some forty years later. Nor did he have a broad view of the world or Canada's role therein. One official recalls meetings at which Green read various UN disarmament resolutions aloud and asked, "What's wrong with that?" External Affairs officials had to explain to their new minister that Canadian membership in NATO and NORAD made it impossible for Canada to promote a policy of neutrality for Western defence.[16]

Green arrived at the department at a time when many foreign service officers were beginning to have doubts about Canada taking on a nuclear role, whether in Europe or North America. Norman Robertson, the department's undersecretary, was particularly uncomfortable with this prospect. He worried that Canada's acquisition of nuclear weapons would add to the perils of nuclear proliferation, a sentiment he made known to Diefenbaker before Green's appointment as minister – he had sent Diefenbaker a copy of an article that argued the futility of nuclear weapons and the merits of unilateral nuclear disarmament in conjunction with increased conventional preparedness on the part of the Western alliance.[17] Although Diefenbaker read and made note of the article, he disagreed with it.[18]

In mid-June, cabinet was primarily concerned about possible changes in American defence policy and the consequences that would follow for Canadian policy. On 12 June US Secretary of Defense Neil McElroy appeared before the US Senate Armed Services Committee with a new "master plan" for air defence. Pearkes and others feared that the Americans were going to withdraw funding for the Bomarc system, thereby reducing its prominence in North American defence and leaving Canada with another obsolete (and possibly ineffective) system. However, McElroy was quick to reassure Canadian officials. The "new American position regarding air defence would in no way affect the defence of the North American continent so far as Canada is concerned," he told them. "The defense department's plans embraced the deployment of Bomarc weapons systems on both coasts and across the northern perimeter of the United States and included the Canadian Bomarc sites as integral parts of the entire system."[19]

What Diefenbaker and his cabinet worried about was the public's perception of these possible changes. In particular, he feared that Canadians would think his government had allowed the Eisenhower administration to dictate Canada's defence policy. Even the mere hint that US officials had consulted with their Canadian counterparts about the possible change might make the situation more palatable politically.[20] Such consultation tied nicely into the Canadian demands for joint care and control. Diefenbaker was afraid that Canadians would believe the nation's sovereignty was in jeopardy if Canadian officials did not participate – in at least some capacity – in the decision to release weapons in Canada. He himself had raised this fear in his attacks on the previous Liberal government when he was in opposition; his government could not now appear to have the same kind of relationship with the Americans as the one he had criticized.

Green had a lot to learn about external affairs generally, let alone the intricacies of nuclear policy, so it is not surprising that he said very little about Canada's acquisition of nuclear weapons during his early days as minister. Over the course of the summer, he was briefed on a variety of subjects, including nuclear weapons within NATO and NORAD. Jules Léger, the former undersecretary who was now Canada's ambassador to NATO, penned an eighteen-page review of NATO-related issues to help provide the basics to the new minister. He stressed the growing debate on nuclear stockpiles within the alliance, reiterating information that Green already had, but focused on the custodial issues related to the American offer of IRBMs to members of NATO. He explained that in the event of an emergency, the weapons would be released to the appropriate NATO commander, not to the local (i.e., national) government or national forces directly. The same provisions applied to tactical nuclear weapons. Given the oft-repeated emphasis by Canadian officials on the importance of care and control, there can be little doubt that the provision was problematic for the government and departmental officials alike.

Aside from these challenges, Léger reminded the minister that Canada still had an important role to play in NATO. For example, there remained the possibility that the Canadians might be able to help devise a means of control for nuclear weapons within the alliance.[21] Canadian officials preferred the multilateral approach of NATO to the simple bilateral framework with the Americans, believing that the North Atlantic alliance offered at least the potential for other allies against the Americans if US demands were ever too great. The same security would not exist in a bilateral arrangement between Canada and the United States. Yet NORAD was not completely without benefit, and Canadian officials began to realize there might be greater flexibility within NORAD than within NATO, for it was probably easier to reach an agreement with the Americans when the other Atlantic allies did not have to be taken into consideration.

This greater flexibility was apparent in the summer of 1959 as Canadian officials continued to negotiate with their American counterparts. The negotiations progressed to the point where the defence minister, George Pearkes, recommended to the Cabinet Defence Committee that it approve the American request to stockpile nuclear weapons at Goose Bay and Harmon Field for use of the US Air Force squadrons under NORAD command. It was an approval in principle only, since the details were yet to be determined,[22] but the CDC agreed and accepted the recommendations on 4 August, with a concluding note of caution: "United States authorities should be informed of the need for avoiding publicity on the matter at the present time."[23] Although Diefenbaker had promised to keep Parliament informed of the nuclear negotiations as they progressed, he now wanted them to be concealed.

The negotiations quickly ran into trouble, and consultation – or a lack thereof – was at the heart of the problem. At the end of August, cabinet learned about an American air defence exercise code-named Sky Hawk, scheduled for 4 October. The exercise was to test NORAD's ability to respond to a Soviet attack, and the Canadian cabinet had to approve the exercise before it could proceed. However, cabinet members had some misgivings. First, there were questions about the timing of the test, coming as it would on the heels of Khrushchev's visit to the United States in September. Second, the ministers worried about the need to ground Canadian civilian air traffic for six hours. Above all, they were annoyed that the Americans had not bothered to consult the Canadians in any meaningful way before scheduling the exercise. In view of these drawbacks, cabinet concluded that it was not an "appropriate time" for such a display of force.[24]

Diefenbaker had every reason to be annoyed. Once again, his concern was about consultation. While military authorities had been planning and discussing the operation since May, cabinet had not learned of the operation until the end of August.[25] Even Pearkes, who thought the test and amount of notice were reasonable, had found out about the operation from the Americans only at the beginning of August. Livid, Diefenbaker demanded to know how a "major air defence exercise involving the grounding of civil aircraft had been approved without a cabinet decision."[26] One minister said that officials at External Affairs had found out about the operation through the Canadian Embassy staff in Washington, while another pointed out that Eisenhower himself had only recently learned of the operation. True though these points may have been, they were cold comfort to Diefenbaker when he had stressed so many times to American officials the premium he placed on consultation.[27]

After much discussion, Pearkes failed to provide Diefenbaker with a satisfactory explanation of why cabinet had been left in the dark about the operation. The overriding impression was that the military, both Canadian and American, had planned the exercise without giving so much as a thought to whether their civilian masters would give their approval.[28] It was an ill-conceived assumption, and cabinet decided to send a memorandum to the Eisenhower administration rejecting the proposed exercise.[29]

The Americans were undeterred, and US Ambassador Richard Wigglesworth met with Diefenbaker to discuss the matter. Cabinet discussions about the exercise continued through early September, while Diefenbaker adamantly refused to reconsider cabinet's rejection of the exercise. Undaunted, Eisenhower sent a personal note to Diefenbaker asking for approval of the operation. Again, Diefenbaker refused, explaining only his concern about the need to ground civilian flights during the exercise. Frustrated, the Americans finally gave up, formally cancelling Sky Hawk on 15 September.

The debacle surrounding Sky Hawk undermined Diefenbaker's confidence in the Eisenhower administration. If the Americans could not be counted on to consult with the Canadians about a joint military exercise involving the armed forces of both countries, there was no reason to expect them to consult in the event of a crisis that called for the use of nuclear weapons. This failure to consult rekindled Diefenbaker's fears that the Americans would take Canadian support for granted.

By coincidence, the subject of nuclear negotiations had followed the debate about Sky Hawk on the agenda of the 26 August cabinet meeting. Pearkes made his case in favour of allowing the Americans to store nuclear weapons at Goose Bay and Harmon Field, echoing the recommendations of the CDC from earlier in the month. As if to answer Diefenbaker's concerns about Sky Hawk, he stressed the importance of joint control. While the Americans would be responsible for the storage facilities and security, the Canadians would have to give permission before the weapons could be removed from storage. The same would be true for their use. In fact, the Americans were hesitant to commit to consulting the Canadians about removing the warheads from storage, though Pearkes did not believe this was an insurmountable obstacle to an agreement. Reminding his cabinet colleagues that US officials were already willing to seek Canadian permission for USAF flights over Canada involving nuclear cargo, he said he was confident that they would eventually consent to the consultation requirement in order to secure an agreement. Cabinet agreed and accepted his submission, concluding that he and Green should prepare a draft agreement that took joint responsibility into account.[30]

Nuclear weapons remained uncontroversial at these meetings in mid-1959, and no one objected to their acquisition. Even Howard Green did not questioned the idea of nuclear stockpiles. The sole point of contention during the discussions around the cabinet table, and a mild one at that, involved which nation would be responsible for the security around the stockpiles (i.e., issues of custody and control). Here, Green's only concern, as Smith's had been before, was that Canadian forces be jointly responsible for the nuclear weapons stored on Canadian bases. He was content to let the Americans take full responsibility for security on the bases they leased from Canada. Diefenbaker agreed that the security issue might be worth pursuing, but that was the extent of his comment on the subject. Ultimately, cabinet decided to give Diefenbaker and Pearkes more time to discuss the matter in greater detail before reaching a final decision.[31]

On 22 September, cabinet approved the text of a Canadian proposal to allow nuclear weapons at Goose Bay and Harmon Field. Although Green did not attend the meeting, he had helped Pearkes and Diefenbaker prepare the note that cabinet approved.[32] Furthermore, Green had become an active participant in the meetings of the cabinet and the CDC, and his concerns – restricted to issues of care and control – were well known in the autumn of 1959. Never once did he question the basic proposition that Canada should acquire nuclear warheads.[33]

Although it is possible that Green promoted a policy of joint control knowing it would impede negotiations, it is unlikely. Green had been minister of external affairs for only a few months, and he was still trying to grasp the details of his portfolio. Furthermore, his personal papers indicate that he was willing to accept a nuclear arrangement with the United States as long as Canadian officials were involved in deciding whether and when the weapons were released from Canadian territory.[34] Two things helped to refine Green's views on disarmament during this period. One was his experience at the United Nations General Assembly, where he introduced a disarmament proposal. The other was his wife, a scientist, who taught him about the hazards of nuclear fallout.[35] It is within this context that Canadian and American officials met at Camp

David in November 1959 as part of the Canada–United States Cabinet Committee on Joint Defence.

The complexities of storing nuclear weapons in Canada were apparent during the preparation for the Camp David meeting as Canadian officials came to appreciate that the nation's obligations to various military alliances complicated nuclear policy. Within NORAD, Canada might be able to acquire nuclear weapons under a straightforward bilateral agreement with the United States, one that guaranteed joint control and custody of the warheads. Certainly, such an arrangement would suffice for Goose Bay and Harmon Field. The North Atlantic alliance, however, was different. The Americans had also asked the Canadians to station weapons at Argentia, a US naval base under the control of the Supreme Allied Commander Atlantic. Because Argentia was a base used in NATO operations, there were multilateral implications to consider. More importantly, the nuclear warheads destined for NATO could be classified as offensive, unlike the purely defensive weapons to be stored at Goose Bay and Harmon Field.

The desire for consistency was problematic; the Canadians did not want to accept one arrangement within NORAD and another within NATO, fearing that this would set a dangerous precedent. Instead, they wanted the Americans to treat Canada the same way in both cases, regardless of the alliance. The last thing Canadian officials wanted was to complicate the debate by having two separate nuclear arrangements with the Americans. The Americans found the situation difficult to manoeuvre for similar reasons. After all, they had other allies to consider; if the Canadians received "special treatment," the Europeans were bound to demand the same.[36] For these reasons, those within the Canadian government who had believed it would be straightforward to negotiate an agreement with the Americans for the storage of nuclear weapons in Canada were forced to reconsider their position as the meeting at Camp David approached.

Briefing papers prepared for the November meeting with US officials highlighted the potential problems with Canada's nuclear policy. Successive drafts stressed the importance of the relationship between the two countries, joint cooperation and consultation in matters of defence, and, most importantly, civilian control. They underscored Canada's opposition to nuclear proliferation, a position it shared with the United States. Both countries, for example, opposed the efforts of individual nations such as France to produce their own nuclear weapons. The Canadian proposal would not constitute proliferation because there was no need to divulge nuclear secrets in order to establish joint control.[37]

Although the Canadian plan did not constitute proliferation, officials were worried about the potential for controversy. In particular, there was growing concern that Canada's acquisition of nuclear weapons would contradict the government's policy on disarmament. Notes of caution were struck to this effect (though there was no direct discussion of this problem in the Camp David briefing material), warning that the acquisition of nuclear weapons would undermine Canada's efforts to promote international disarmament.[38] However, External Affairs officials were mixed in their views on the likelihood of a disarmament agreement. On the one hand, an unlimited military program was expensive and potentially damaging politically, and a general disarmament agreement could serve as an incentive to resolve these problems. On the other, there was a big obstacle to such an agreement: the Soviet Union. The Soviets had been next to impossible to deal with in disarmament matters, and there could be no agreement without their participation.[39]

There is an interesting omission in the briefing material. Notwithstanding the attention paid to other nuclear issues in preparation for the meeting at Camp David, there was no discussion of the significance of the nuclear-tipped Bomarc missile. Nuclear negotiations in 1958 and 1959 had centred on whether Canada would allow SAC squadrons at Goose Bay and Harmon Field to have nuclear weapons (the MB-1), and the weapons proposed for SAC had little to do with nuclear warheads for the Bomarc anti-aircraft missile accepted in September 1958. Although there was a presumption that nuclear tips would be ordered to accompany the missiles, it was never stated formally, and the briefing papers for Camp David revealed the first hint that acquiring nuclear tips for the Bomarc might be more complicated than initially anticipated.

Final notes referred to the new possibility of intercontinental ballistic missiles, though the officials concluded that the Americans had not yet asked about stationing these missiles in Canada.[40] The reference to ICBMs came as a surprise to Diefenbaker, who made a special note of it in the margin of his briefing papers.[41] There was a difference between an anti-aircraft nuclear missile like the Bomarc and an ICBM, and this new mention of intercontinental missiles must have made Diefenbaker wonder what else was being left to the last minute.

During the same period (November 1959), the Department of External Affairs was finally willing to endorse the storage of nuclear weapons at Goose Bay and Harmon Field. No one objected in cabinet.[42] Yet Diefenbaker continued to worry that the Americans would not consult with Canadian officials in an emergency. The source of this fear was not the Eisenhower administration per se but the military, both Canadian and American. There remained now but one source of disagreement within cabinet: the likelihood that the current round of disarmament talks would reach a positive conclusion.

Here, Diefenbaker and Green were at complete odds; the prime minister doubted that much progress could be made, but the minister was more confident about the prospects for a disarmament agreement because everyone was "frightened over the future." Green tried to persuade his colleagues that NATO and General Norstad supported disarmament, as did Khrushchev and the Soviet Union. He even went so far as to argue that Canada "was in a good position to use [its] influence, which was what the U.K. hoped we would do, and make an important contribution. The only people who were being really intransigent were certain elements in the Pentagon." Green's urgings seemed to hold little promise for most cabinet ministers, though the disarmament issue remained unresolved. Instead, cabinet decided to revisit the likelihood of a disarmament agreement after the meeting at Camp David.[43] What is so significant about this particular cabinet meeting is the disagreement between Diefenbaker and Green. It marks 6 November 1959 as the first open difference in cabinet over the merits of disarmament talks and the likelihood of a disarmament agreement.

The Camp David meeting of the Canada–United States Cabinet Committee on Joint Defence in November 1959 turned out to be an informative one. It gave the Canadians an opportunity to air some grievances and determine the American position on a number of issues. Like Diefenbaker, the American officials were not overly optimistic that a disarmament agreement could be reached. More positively, though, there was general agreement that Khrushchev's recent visit to the United States suggested to the Americans that international tensions were on the decline. The officials also discussed the cancelled Sky Hawk exercise, agreeing to keep civilian authorities abreast of plans for future air defence exercises. The Canadians were mollified by these promises, and another exercise was tentatively scheduled for sometime in 1960.

A great deal of time was spent discussing the logistics of nuclear stockpiles in Canada. In early October, the Canadians had sent a draft note to the Americans outlining their position on Goose Bay and Harmon Field. That draft had been returned just before the meeting at Camp David, and there had not been sufficient time to prepare a detailed response for presentation at the meeting. In fact, the Canadians had some objections to the American counter-proposal. In particular, they took issue with the substitution of the word "custody" for "ownership." Also problematic were proposed modifications to the provisions governing joint responsibility for security and use of the warheads. The Canadian officials rejected even the most modest delegation of authority for use. As the Canadian chair remarked, use of nuclear weapons was clearly a matter of "high policy" that could not occur until there was genuine consultation with the highest civilian authorities in both governments.[44]

The Americans understood some of the Canadian concerns, but they still had to find language that met the requirements of US law while allowing NORAD to act quickly in an emergency. Other concerns were more confusing. The use of the word "custody" was especially puzzling. They reminded the Canadians that the prime minister had said almost the same thing in his 20 February statement to Parliament, where he had stated, "We consider that it is expedient that ownership and custody of the nuclear warheads should remain with the United States."[45]

Minor disagreements aside, both governments left Camp David satisfied that language could be found to facilitate the deployment of American nuclear weapons to Canada. The Diefenbaker government agreed in principle to store defensive nuclear weapons in Canada, though the details of such an arrangement remained to be determined. There thus seemed to be little reason to doubt that the Canadian government was set to acquire nuclear warheads.

Following the success of the Camp David meeting, the Canadians believed they were in a strong position to negotiate the terms of the agreement, though it was surely a hyperbolic moment when Pearkes assured his cabinet colleagues that the Americans were so eager to store nuclear weapons at Goose Bay that the Canadian government could virtually dictate its own conditions.[46] Cabinet's discussion of the Camp David meeting was brief, centring on nuclear weapons and future air defence exercises. One minister (unnamed, but not Green, who was absent) asserted that the public was strongly opposed to the storage of nuclear weapons of any sort in Canada – though there is no evidence that this was so in late 1959.[47] Even External Affairs officials who had attended the Camp David meeting and had been lukewarm about the idea of nuclear weapons had resigned themselves to the likelihood of stockpiles at Goose Bay and Harmon Field, and they were now willing to support Canada's acquisition of nuclear warheads "under appropriate conditions."[48] Although it is difficult to ascertain whether it was Diefenbaker who made the comment about the public's reaction, the discussions in late autumn 1959 resurrected many of his old fears that Canadians would oppose the acquisition of nuclear weapons and that Pearson would use this opposition to his political advantage. It was clear that the public's willingness to support his nuclear policy remained a preoccupation for Diefenbaker.

Public opposition to nuclear warheads was growing on university campuses in the autumn of 1959, as some members of the university community began to consider how they could influence Diefenbaker's nuclear policy. At that time, a handful of faculty and students at the University of Toronto co-sponsored a petition to the prime minister that led to a meeting in mid-December between faculty members and Diefenbaker.[49] Inspired by the response, some faculty members encouraged students to form anti-nuclear groups of their own.[50]

Norman Johnson, one of the Toronto participants in the faculty-student petition, organized a meeting at University College that led to the creation of the Toronto student anti-nuclear group. Although the student anti-nuclear movement was influenced more by the British campaign than the American effort, the students named their group the Student Peace Union after a like-minded organization at the University of Chicago. The group's initial membership – seven students – represented various elements of the student left, from communists to socialists. As the membership base broadened, the Student Peace Union became the Students for Peace and eventually the Toronto Branch of the Combined Universities Campaign for Nuclear Disarmament (CUCND). The transition took a matter of months, and over time a moderate pacifist core came to dominate the organization.[51]

Students in Montreal also began to organize themselves to oppose "the bomb." While students in Toronto had begun to express their worries about the government's nuclear policy earlier than their counterparts in Montreal, it was students from the three Montreal-area universities – McGill, Sir George Williams, and the Université of Montréal – who founded CUCND, the first formal Canadian student anti-nuclear group. Inspired by the British ban-the-bombers and the Aldermaston march in 1958, the Montreal student groups formed CUCND in November 1959.[52]

CUCND's first formal activity was to gather approximately 80 members to deliver an anti-nuclear petition containing 1,100 signatures to the Prime Minister's Office on Christmas Day.[53] The result of this activity was not especially impressive. Diefenbaker was told about the petition, but he demonstrated no obvious interest in what the students had to say. The petition may have contained 1,100 signatures, but they were from people who lacked political power and credibility; these students lacked influence not because they were students but because well-known communists and radicals ran their organization. For this reason, it was easy for Diefenbaker to dismiss their views. The same was not true of the anti-nuclear movement that was taking shape beyond the university campus.

In February 1960 a group of anti-nuclear activists launched the National Committee of the Canadian Committee for the Control of Radiation Hazards (CCCRH). It was a small elite group – just forty-five people – and based on the premise that the quality of the supporters was more important than their quantity.[54] The result of months of hard work and planning, the National Committee was the brainchild of Mary Van Stolk, a "sparkplug," according to one *Maclean's* columnist, and the powerhouse behind the early growth and organization of the CCCRH.[55] In late 1958, Van Stolk had created the Edmonton Committee for the Control of Radiation Hazards, the first Canadian organization founded specifically to deal with nuclear issues. Born and raised in Milwaukee, Wisconsin, she was then a housewife in her late twenties and had been introduced to the movement by her husband, a Dutch doctor who had worked with Albert Schweitzer at his clinic in Lambaréné, Africa. Schweitzer, who won the Nobel Peace Prize in 1952, had always opposed nuclear weapons, though he had only recently been enlisted to support the anti-nuclear movement by Norman Cousins, editor of *Saturday Review* and a leading activist with the American National Committee for a Sane Nuclear Policy (SANE).[56]

The Van Stolks had moved to Edmonton, Alberta, when Dr Van Stolk took a job in the Department of Psychiatry at the city's University Hospital. Mary Van Stolk had lofty ambitions and did not settle for dealing with nuclear matters locally. The Edmonton Committee, a group of thirty-five men and women whom she gathered together, first met on 15 April 1959. Their task at that first meeting was to develop a list of prominent Canadians whom they would invite to join a National Committee, whose purpose would be to raise Canadians' awareness of the perils posed by fallout.[57] Worries about radioactive fallout were common in the late 1950s, and anti-nuclear groups around the world were urging governments to conduct more scientific research into its consequences.[58] The Edmonton group reflected this preoccupation, and the members focused on the hazards associated with radioactive fallout from nuclear testing; they did not concern themselves with whether Canada would or should acquire nuclear weapons.[59]

In the months that followed the initial meeting of the CCCRH, Van Stolk travelled across Canada, as well as to Los Angeles and New York City, to meet with members of SANE, where Cousins provided a great deal of assistance. SANE also helped Van Stolk collect educational and promotional literature to influence and educate both the general public and politicians.[60] At the end of May, she met with Hugh L. Keenleyside in New York City. It was a pivotal meeting for the CCCRH. Van Stolk convinced Keenleyside that the timing was perfect to raise public awareness about the consequences of nuclear fallout; Eisenhower and Khrushchev were planning to meet, and late 1959 seemed the ideal time to address the subject.[61]

An historian by training, Keenleyside had joined the Department of External Affairs in 1928 and then served in Japan and on the Permanent Joint Board on Defence for Canada and the United States, among other postings. Having left the department in 1947 to become the deputy minister of mines and resources, he was appointed director general of the United Nations Technical Assistance Administration in 1950. There he remained until 1958, when he left New York to become chairman of the B.C. Power Commission. It was during this period that Van Stolk met Keenleyside and persuaded him to become the provisional chairman of the National

Committee in the autumn of 1959.[62] Keenleyside played a large role in determining both the name and organizational structure of the National Committee.[63] By all accounts, he seemed to be the ideal candidate to serve as the public face of the CCCRH. He had extensive experience in international affairs, and he understood the formulation of government policy.

The CCCRH distributed hundreds of letters and circulars that spring and summer, all designed to raise awareness among Canadians about nuclear fallout. At the same time, local committees were established in Montreal and Saskatoon. These organizations were not true "branches" of the National Committee (they did not take instruction from the national office after its creation in early 1960), but they did participate in national activities, expanding the organization's reach across the country.[64] Van Stolk was serious about her nationwide mission and governed her committee accordingly, with formal operating procedures, by-laws and a formal board of directors.[65] However, an invitation-only membership policy complicated national expansion.[66]

When Van Stolk announced the creation of the National Committee in February 1960, it reflected her view that just as a group of activists could be tainted by the merest hint of communist affinity, so could it be blessed by the credibility of its most prominent and highly regarded members. Here she followed the lead of SANE and the British Campaign for Nuclear Disarmament (CND), which included such high-profile supporters as Harry Belafonte and Steve Allen (in the former) and Bertrand Russell (in the latter). SANE, which hoped to attract a broad base of support, quickly expanded its activities to include a call for general disarmament.[67] It was the more moderate of the two organisations, and Van Stolk was more comfortable with its tactics than those of the CND. For example, she copied SANE's mid-1957 debut in the *New York Times*, which featured a list of forty-eight prominent Americans who urged the government to end nuclear testing; Van Stolk used the advertisement as her model for the introduction of the National Committee.

The CND was much more vocal and more inclined toward public protest than SANE. Founded in January 1958, it included a large number of students and radicals. Although it did not formally support civil disobedience, it did advocate unilateral disarmament, and unilateral disarmament was seen as a radical proposition. As well, many members of the British CND were active in demonstrations and public protests against the bomb.[68] It was the organization that Diefenbaker had referred to with such concern in April 1958.

Such public protests held no appeal for Van Stolk. She wanted to build a credible, well-regarded organization. She understood that many Canadians were suspicious of peace activists. She also knew that the CCCRH would not be able to influence politicians and the formulation of policy unless it had a certain public authority and legitimacy; Canadians would never heed their warnings if they believed that anti-nuclear pamphlets and campaigns were little more than communist propaganda.[69] And if the electorate could not be won over to the cause, there would be no impetus for the government to listen to the movement's message, let alone adopt its views in the formulation of nuclear policy.

When Van Stolk introduced the National Committee to the world in early 1960, she did so with an impressive list of supporters from all walks of Canadian life. There was nationwide support from various university disciplines, with the sciences particularly well represented. From the University of Alberta were D.B. Scott from the Department of Physics and Dr J. Weijer, a research professor in Genetics and Plant Breeding. There was Gordin Kaplan from the Department of Physiology at Dalhousie. Perhaps the university with the greatest faculty representation was the University of Toronto, with Drs C.H. Best and D.G. Baker, both of the Banting and Best Department of Medical Research. On the humanities side was Frank Scott from the Faculty of Law at McGill, B.S. Keirstead from Political Economy at the University of Toronto, and Milton Gregg – a former minister of veterans affairs – from the University of Western Ontario.

The list of university administrators who endorsed the National Committee was even more impressive, for a number of university presidents and deans offered their support: Dr Claude Bissell, president of the University of Toronto, Dr N.A.M. MacKenzie, president of the University of British Columbia, and Dr Hugh H. Saunderson, president of the University of Manitoba. Support at the departmental level, again with particular attention from the sciences, was evidenced by the signatures of Dr John F. McCreary, dean of medicine at the University of British Columbia, Dr Pierre Dansereau, dean of science at Université de Montréal, and Dr H.G. Dion, dean of agriculture at McGill.[70]

Select members of the judiciary also supported Van Stolk's efforts.[71] Justice Ivan C. Rand, a retired justice of the Supreme Court of Canada and the founding dean of law at the University of Western Ontario, endorsed the National Committee, as did the Honourable Mr Justice Ralph Maybank from the Court of Queen's Bench (Manitoba) and the Honourable J.T. Thorson, president of the Exchequer Court of Canada in Ottawa, who later became an outspoken member of the National Committee. Both Maybank and Thorson were former Liberal politicians.

Given the traditional support of religious groups for the peace movement in Canada, it is not surprising that Protestant clerics were also well represented. They included the archbishop of Edmonton, the Most Reverend J.H. MacDonald, the Reverend W.C. Smalley, general secretary of the Baptist Union of Western Canada, and the Very Reverend Professor James S. Thomson, of McGill, a former moderator of the United Church of Canada. There was also the Reverend Leonard F. Hatfield, general secretary of the Council for Social Service in the Anglican Church, Toronto.[77] Moreover, the support cut across religions as much as it spanned the country. The Canadian Jewish Congress, for example, was well represented by Saul Hayes, the executive vice-president of the organization.[73]

The committee also included a number of prominent Canadians who were definitely not from sectors traditionally associated with the peace movement. For instance, Henry Borden, president of Brazilian Traction, Light and Power Co., Ltd, and nephew of Conservative prime minister Robert Borden, supported the CCCRH, as did A.E. Grauer, chairman and president of British Columbia Electric Co. Ltd., in Vancouver. More typical was the support offered by the labour movement, particularly Dr Eugene Forsey, director of research at the Canadian Labour Congress, whom Prime Minister Diefenbaker greatly admired, and Claude Jodoin, president of the Canadian Labour Congress.[74]

Similarly, many members of the Canadian press sympathized with the ideals represented by Van Stolk's committee. The associate editor of the *Toronto Daily Star*, Robert Nielsen, agreed to endorse the National Committee, as did John Bassett, a well-known member of the Progressive Conservative Party who was also chairman and publisher of the Toronto *Telegram*. Oakley Dalgleish, editor and publisher of the *Globe and Mail*, rounded out the representation of the Toronto print media. There was also editorial support in

Quebec, where Jean-Louis Gagnon, chief editor of *La Presse*, and André Laurendeau, editor-in-chief of *Le Devoir*, endorsed the committee.[75] Many members of the editorial staff of *Maclean's* also agreed with Van Stolk's objectives, while others wrote a series of well-placed articles featuring the newly minted organization.[76] Despite this sympathy, when Van Stolk asked *Maclean's* editor Blair Fraser if he would allow the magazine to promote the CCCRH and its concerns, he was forthright in his refusal on the grounds that the magazine covered news, it did not endorse particular causes.[77]

Van Stolk's list of high-profile supporters was designed to make political leaders in Ottawa take notice of the Canadian Committee for the Control of Radiation Hazards.[78] But a membership list alone was not enough to persuade Diefenbaker to take the views of the organization seriously. The members needed to use their influence to convince the prime minister that their support of the anti-nuclear movement was reason enough for the government to take a more cautious approach to nuclear policy. This was a more difficult task.

In late January 1960 Keenleyside, as chair of the CCCRH, had approached Diefenbaker personally in order to bring the committee to his attention and stress that it represented a broad segment of public opinion. "Our statement praises your government for steps already taken and expresses the hope that Canada will do even more to pursue its announced objectives in connection with nuclear testing and related matters," he began. "I believe that you will find our views acceptable and that the evidence our Committee provides of deep and strong Canadian feeling on this subject may sustain the hands of our representatives in their negotiations with other powers." Keenleyside went on more obsequiously to say, "May I take this opportunity to tell you how gratified I have been – and I am sure that this view is shared by a vast majority of informed Canadians – by the international policies pursued by your government? I believe that by concentrating on essentials and refusing to be diverted from adherence to principle by influence from Washington – or elsewhere – you are doing what is best for Canada and for the future of all peoples."[79]

Keenleyside received only the barest acknowledgment from the Prime Minister's Office. Diefenbaker neither wrote nor signed the reply. That job fell to one of his assistants, Gowan Guest. The response itself was a standard letter of acknowledgment: "Mr.

Diefenbaker appreciated your courtesy in giving him this information and wanted me to assure you that he had noted carefully the contents of your letter and the statement."[80] Diefenbaker's response to Keenleyside's efforts illustrates the shortcomings of Van Stolk's approach, namely that there was not necessarily a correlation between the list of high-profile Canadians and their ability to persuade the prime minister to forgo nuclear weapons; just because they were a credible group of prominent Canadians did not mean that Diefenbaker was willing to listen to their views on radioactive fallout and nuclear weapons.

Even more disturbing to Van Stolk would have been the knowledge that Keenleyside did not warrant a special reference file for his correspondence.[81] Indeed, there is little to indicate that his letter of January 1960 or the formal creation of the National Committee the following month influenced Diefenbaker's nuclear policy at that time, for the government continued its nuclear negotiations with the Americans.[82] However, while the expansion of and attention generated by the anti-nuclear movement did not lead to any public shift in Diefenbaker's nuclear policy, he was aware of its growing presence and was worried about its potential to influence Canadian public opinion.

Diefenbaker had similar concerns about Pearson's ability to persuade Canadians to oppose nuclear weapons in late 1959 and early 1960. Pearson had a great deal of experience with disarmament and nuclear weapons. He was still in Washington when Igor Gouzenko broke the news to Mackenzie King's government that there was a Soviet espionage ring in Canada, bent on learning the secrets of the atomic bomb. As the Gouzenko matter progressed, coming to public attention in February 1946, Pearson had remained involved. By the time he became undersecretary of external affairs in September 1946, Canada had joined the first international effort to control nuclear weapons at the United Nations as a member of the United Nations Atomic Energy Commission (with the unfortunate acronym UNAEC). In 1948 Pearson had moved from the diplomatic world to the political to become the minister of his old department. With this professional experience, he was more aware than most of the intricacies associated with international negotiation, nuclear proliferation, and disarmament. And while he supported efforts to control nuclear weapons, he agreed with Diefenbaker that the West could not negotiate with the Soviets.[83]

As Liberal leader, Pearson was best known for his experience abroad and his statesmanlike demeanour. Yet external affairs and defence policy played only a minor role in the initial efforts to reinvigorate the Liberal Party following its 1958 electoral defeat. These two policy areas, however, grew in importance to the Liberals as the government's position on nuclear weapons grew more publicly convoluted. Although Pearson had frequently supported the American position in matters of defence and deterrence when he had been minister of external affairs, this did not necessarily translate into a ready acceptance of nuclear warheads for Canada's armed forces. By late 1959, he was firm in his opposition to the government's nuclear policy regarding NORAD, NATO, and the Bomarc missile, even though he had gone along with the adoption of the strike/reconnaissance role for the Canadian air force in Europe in 1954.

Just as the Department of External Affairs was concerned about custody and control, so was Pearson, who argued that nuclear warheads should be under full Canadian custody and control. Yet his view was not a narrow interpretation of national sovereignty, for he proposed that nuclear stockpiles within NATO should be subject to collective rather than national control. There were two separate issues as far as Pearson was concerned: whether Canada should acquire nuclear weapons (and he believed it should not), and, matters of custody and control within NATO.[84]

Here the similarities between Pearson's position and that of External Affairs ended. External Affairs officials opposed each of the Liberal leader's proposals, noting that warheads under NORAD would remain in American custody only until the president released them for use, at which time control was subject to joint cooperation, according to the North American agreement. The logical extension of Pearson's proposal, the officials warned, was full Canadian custody and control, which would "set a dangerous precedent" if not in North America then in NATO, because NATO members would want the same arrangement. The Americans (and the Canadians) were opposed to such an arrangement within the Atlantic alliance. The officials also thought that Pearson's proposal undermined Canada's national sovereignty. According to the government's plan, Canadian military personnel would fire nuclear weapons according to NORAD procedure. Pearson's plan, at least according to officials at External Affairs, would require the stationing of Americans troops on Canadian bases. Consequently, the government's proposal – not Pearson's plan – was the best guarantee of Canada's sovereignty.

Department officials were equally unhappy about Pearson's proposal for NATO, which they regarded as impractical. Since the Americans had insisted on controlling their nuclear stockpiles in Europe, they were unlikely to allow the NATO Council to make decisions on whether and when to use their warheads. Furthermore, a Council decision required unanimous consent, thereby limiting NATO's ability to respond immediately to an emergency. While Pearson had argued that there should be no limits imposed on NATO's ability to respond to an unprovoked attack, the cumbersome procedure he proposed seemed to entail precisely the kind of constraint he sought to avoid.

Finally, department officials took issue with Pearson's assertion that the Bomarc constituted Lend-Lease aid. This reference to the Second World War military assistance agreement between the United States and Great Britain (and other allies) carried with it the connotation that Canada – like wartime Britain – was broke and was relegated to accepting a form of military charity from the Americans. Canada had not accepted Lend-Lease assistance during the war, a fact of which Canadian leaders were proud. Moreover, the Bomarc system had been accepted for the purpose of continental defence, and both countries shared the cost, with one-third paid by the Canadians and two-thirds by the Americans. Pearson's position was problematic because the Liberals had used the same formula to finance the Pinetree radar installations, and they certainly had not regarded the formula as Lend-Lease assistance when they were in power.[85]

Pearson's proposals illustrate the challenges nuclear policy posed by the late 1950s as well as the opposition's reluctance to pursue a defence policy based on consensus. By the end of 1959, the Department of External Affairs realized that nuclear policy was becoming increasingly contentious, and its officials braced themselves for an onslaught of criticism. Diefenbaker had every reason to fear that Pearson would treat the government's pursuit of nuclear weapons as a political issue, not a matter of national security.

Although cabinet's interest in disarmament increased over the course of 1959, nuclear negotiations continued with the Americans. At the beginning of 1960, Diefenbaker even prepared to make a statement to Parliament outlining the state of negotiations.[86] Thus, although he was clearly aware of and worried about Pearson's nuclear policy, it was not an obstacle to nuclear negotiations. And in the House of Commons the prime minister continued to emphasize the government's focus on consultation and control. "I want to make it abundantly clear that nuclear weapons will not be used by the Canadian forces except as the Canadian government decides and in the manner approved by the Canadian government," he told Parliament. "Canada retains its full freedom of choice and decision."[87]

Diefenbaker meant well, but his rhetoric missed the mark. A draft statement had been much more forthright, noting, "We hope that before many years have passed there will be a sufficient further relaxation of tensions, and sufficient progress made in disarmament, that it will not be necessary to keep these nuclear weapons on our bases. Until that time they will, when we complete the arrangements with the United States, strengthen our joint defences against aggression."[88] The minister of defence was forced to clarify the prime minister's statement to Parliament, commenting that any nuclear weapons in Canada belonged to the United States until released for use, at which point Canadian forces would control "sole use and direction of use of those weapons."[89]

The defence minister's statement was not entirely correct either, and it seemed to alter the government's policy. The most that Canadian officials had asked for was shared care and control; sole Canadian care and control, even after a joint agreement to release and then use nuclear weapons, was out of the question. Although officials remained optimistic about achieving an agreement, the actual negotiations were growing more complicated. It was becoming increasingly apparent that separate agreements would be required to govern each situation, whether within NATO, NORAD, or the Bomarc system.[90] Of the three, the Bomarc caused the most difficulties for Diefenbaker's government as it entered a new decade.

The Bomarc system could be designed to accept either conventional or nuclear-tipped missiles, and the government had chosen to purchase the latter. Nuclear negotiations had thus far been part of a long-range plan. In September 1958, the government had decided to build Bomarc bases, but took until July 1959 for the Canadians to reach an agreement with the Americans on who would pay for what. The Americans agreed to pay for the required "technical equipment," and the Canadians agreed to pay for the actual construction of the bases. Time had not been of the essence when dealing with the Bomarc, and there was nothing to suggest that the pace of the proceedings had changed by 1960. In early 1960 contracts for the construction of the bases at North Bay, Ontario, and La Macaza, Quebec, were just being finalized, with Bomarc missiles expected to arrive in mid-1961 to be operational the following spring.[91]

By the beginning of 1960, the opposition's demands for a defence policy review were growing louder in view of the government's apparent procrastination over nuclear policy, a fire to which the Bomarc had added fuel. Although the government refused to appoint a special committee on defence as Pearson had requested, it did strike a special committee on defence expenditures. As the name suggests, the committee restricted its examination to expenditures, not policy, and was not what the Liberals had in mind. Defence Minister George Pearkes attended most of the committee's thirty sessions, but there was no debate or detail about the future of Canadian defence policy.

Within this context, the Bomarc became the source of great controversy. By February 1960 it had failed six test flights. With each successive failure, the media and opposition criticized the government's decision to acquire what seemed to be a flop.[92] Although the Bomarc finally met with success in mid-April – which Pearkes faithfully and somewhat triumphantly announced to Parliament – Congress nonetheless wanted to cancel funding for the missile system. Then, in an instant, an international crisis changed everything.

As winter turned to spring, international tensions seemed to be on the wane as President Eisenhower and Premier Khrushchev planned to meet in Paris in mid-May. Over the course of the previous year, progress had been made toward a possible test ban agreement, which would prohibit all but underground nuclear tests.[93] Some Canadian officials had great hopes for the coming summit, particularly in conjunction with the disarmament talks recently renewed in Geneva. With the Soviets back at the negotiating table, a disarmament agreement seemed at least a possibility.[94] Diefenbaker disagreed.

Despite the growing calm in international relations, Diefenbaker did not believe that sentiment would translate into tangible progress at the disarmament talks. He grew "depressed ... when he saw the same old ideas and language being trotted out."[95] Western officials – including those from Canada's Department of External

Affairs – simply had nothing new to offer to the debate on disarmament. At the same time, Diefenbaker realized that because the Western governments had insisted on "adequate safeguards and controls," the negotiations with the Soviets were even more cumbersome. There was simply no way the West would accept the sort of sweeping statement on unilateral disarmament the Soviets would offer. As well, knowing the conditions demanded by Western governments, the Soviets were free to promote radical proposals for unilateral disarmament without fear of political repercussions at home. Unlike the democratic nations of the West, the USSR did not have to worry about public opinion. This was one of the few things about the Soviet Union that Diefenbaker envied.[96]

The already slim hopes for a disarmament agreement vanished when the Soviets shot down US Air Force Captain Gary Powers and his U-2 spy plane over Soviet territory on 1 May 1960. This incident added to the existing tensions over Berlin and was a public relations disaster for Eisenhower and the Americans. Not only did the Americans initially hesitate to explain the mission, but the Soviets had Powers – who survived the crash – in custody, along with the wrecked U-2 plane and film footage of the entire event. Although Eisenhower ultimately accepted responsibility for authorizing the flight, Khrushchev responded by threatening to cancel the upcoming summit if the American president did not apologize. Eisenhower refused, and the summit was over before it began.[97]

With the summit cancelled and Cold War tensions increasing for the foreseeable future, members of Congress felt obliged to maintain defence expenditures and developments, and reinstated funding for the Bomarc. The congressional decision was crucial to Canada's acquisition of the system because, as Pearkes had noted a year earlier, if the Americans cancelled the Bomarc, Canada would have little choice but to do the same.[98] Ultimately, the U-2 affair kept the Bomarc missile alive and well.[99]

Had members of Congress remained firm and cancelled the Bomarc, Diefenbaker would not have had to deal with the problems surrounding the missile sites in North Bay and La Macaza. Yet eliminating the Bomarc would not have solved Diefenbaker's nuclear problems altogether. The question of Harmon Field, Goose Bay, Argentia, and Canadian forces in NATO remained unsettled. At best, terminating the Bomarc would have given Diefenbaker more time but not a solution to a growing problem. More difficult than the reinstatement of the Bomarc was the outpouring of concern that followed the U-2 incident. It was an outcry that led to the creation of another anti-nuclear pressure group, which came on the heels of another protest staged by student anti-nuclear activists.

In May 1960 student activists from Toronto and Montreal decided to join forces to protest the proposed Bomarc base in North Bay.[100] While the protest helped to cement ties and boost morale among members, it did little to win support from the people of North Bay.[101] Residents of North Bay stood to benefit economically from the NORAD station and thus had few reasons to oppose the Bomarc.[102] Indeed, they seemed barely to notice the anti-nuclear activists in their midst. Without local opposition to the base, the student protest in North Bay barely registered with parliamentarians in Ottawa.

This lack of local enthusiasm for disarmament disappointed the students. They had hoped that outraged residents of North Bay would take political action, whether it was writing letters to local MPs or joining the peace movement itself. They knew the government might not bother listening to a group of university students, but thought it would pay attention to a broader segment of the electorate. If the reaction to the Bomarc protest was any indication, the movement had a long way to go before such local efforts would translate into political influence. Something more was needed to galvanize Canadians. That event was the U-2 affair, which inspired hordes of women to join the anti-nuclear movement.

The day after Khrushchev stormed out of the Paris summit, Lotta Dempsey of the *Toronto Daily Star* wrote about the crisis. "Like most women," she began, "I see the Summit in terms of my own family, my small house and garden, my quiet street and neighbors, who are now all out retraining vines, putting in plants and painting. I cannot but believe that, wherever it is spring, and wherever there is love and beauty and decency, women are trying to do the same thing. And they are greatly afraid."[103] Arguing that "the men surely have made a mess of things," she suggested that "if only the women could get together, perhaps they could do better." Dempsey struck a chord with Canadian women, and her column received great support.[104]

A few days later Dempsey wrote another column, emphasizing the common bond shared by women the world over: "I have never met a woman anywhere who did not hate fighting and killing, and the loss of husbands and the terrible tragedy of children dead, maimed or left homeless and hungry. Here lies our strength. In some way women the world over must refuse to allow this thing to happen."[105] These pleas on behalf of women and the family were not unique to the nuclear era (opposition to war was a traditional "motherhood issue" among feminists and pacifists), and they were as effective in 1960 as a rallying cry for women from all segments of Canadian society as they had been in years past.

At the end of May, Dempsey announced from her pulpit in the *Star* the creation of a new women's organization focused on disarmament and international peace.[106] Once again, the response from women was tremendous. Hundreds responded to her column, and plans were quickly underway to create what became the Voice of Women. Helen Tucker and Josephine Davis did for the Voice of Women what Mary Van Stolk did for the CCCRH. Tucker, the VOW's first president, was described by Kay Macpherson (a future president of the VOW) as "dynamic, tireless, and infuriating, a quite extraordinary woman ... Her persistence and toughness irritated many people, but she got things done, often over odds that would intimidate lesser mortals like us, and she had a remarkable list of achievements about which she would be the first to blow her own trumpet."[107] Tucker was something of a professional organizer, involved in adult education programs through the YWCA, UNESCO, and other international organizations. Like Van Stolk, she was American by birth, and she had come to Canada in the late 1930s. Perhaps most importantly, her previous experience in co-educational peace associations made her determined that women would be treated as first-class citizens in her own organization.[108]

It was Tucker who asked Davis to get involved with the VOW. After seeing Davis on a segment of the CBC's "Front Page Challenge,"[109] Tucker persuaded her to help organize a rally sponsored by the Toronto Campaign for Disarmament (the Toronto wing of the CCCRH) at Massey Hall.[110] Born in Britain, Davis had come to Canada in 1953 and was married to a prominent journalist, Fred Davis, who worked for the CBC as host of "Front Page Challenge." Although there were other founding members of the VOW, Tucker and Davis were the driving force behind the group, in conjunction with Dempsey, who helped to raise awareness through her newspaper column.[111]

The founding committee met in early June. Initially, the group called itself the Women's Committee for Peace, but it soon adopted the name Voice of Women. The goal was to promote peace through contact, based on the premise that the more contact members had with women from other cultures, the less likely was there to be international conflict.[112] This emphasis on personal contact at the grassroots level was unique within the movement.[113] Despite this broad objective, the committee focused its early efforts on Ottawa and Parliament Hill, seeking advice from the leaders they hoped to influence eventually, and trying to determine what political leaders thought about everything from the VOW's disarmament proposals to its very existence as an organization.[114] Meeting with political leaders was also an attempt to determine the attitudes of the people they would have to convert to their cause. Davis hoped that a face-to-face meeting with political leaders would be the first step in persuading them to support the VOW's position. The VOW had a marked advantage over other disarmament groups because of its size; while Van Stolk hoped that selectivity was the key to influence, Davis and Tucker realized the importance of mass appeal.

On 15 June 1960, Davis and several others met with John Diefenbaker, Howard Green, Lester Pearson, and Hazen Argue, the leader of the Co-operative Commonwealth Federation (CCF). The women received a warm welcome, and the audience seemed receptive to their views. The prime minister was pleasant enough, but there was clearly no meeting of minds. Diefenbaker's early views of the antinuclear movement were reflected in his wife's response to an invitation from the women of the VOW, who had asked Olive Diefenbaker to endorse their organization. While she agreed with its overarching objectives, the prime minister's wife worried about potential controversy. "Suppose, for example," she wrote in response to the invitation to become an honorary member, "that you want to support some stand that the governments [sic] taking – or that you want to do exactly the opposite. Inevitably my name would be associated with my husband's and in either case it would be prejudicial ... I am honoured indeed that you should think of me, but I do think that you will be better off without me."[115]

The VOW did not have any more success in its attempts to recruit other members of the Progressive Conservative Party. In addition to contacting the prime minister's wife, the women approached Diefenbaker's minister of citizenship, Ellen Fairclough, Canada's first female cabinet minister at the federal level. Like Mrs Diefenbaker, Fairclough refused to allow her name to stand as an honorary supporter of the group. Not only did she refuse the vow's invitation, but she did not take the organization very seriously. Neither the vow nor the nuclear debate more generally was even mentioned in Fairclough's memoirs.[116]

Diefenbaker was hesitant in his dealings with the anti-nuclear movement because he feared that activists in Canada would raise the same sort of fuss that the British CND had caused in Great Britain. It was a reasonable enough concern, given the anti-nuclear correspondence the prime minister had received by the end of 1959 from groups affiliated with labour, the churches, and the universities, as well as the variety of notices from the slowly growing anti-nuclear movement itself. By mid-1960, Diefenbaker's mailbag regularly contained letters from individuals and organizations opposed to Canada's acquisition of nuclear weapons. This organized opposition, even though it was in its most rudimentary form, added to his preoccupation with the state of his public support.[117]

With the vow in particular, Diefenbaker kept its material on file, though he did not sympathize with its goal of keeping nuclear warheads out of Canada. More than anything, he regarded the organization with uneasiness because of its influence. Its members were highly credible women. The very model of ladylike behaviour, wearing hats and gloves when they met with officials, they could not be dismissed out of hand as communist sympathizers. It was this credibility, combined with the movement's growing numbers, that Diefenbaker feared. A large and credible voice opposing nuclear weapons just might persuade undecided Canadians to oppose nuclear stockpiles and his government along with them.

Despite these misgivings, Diefenbaker did not allow the vow to influence policy formulation in any tangible way in the summer of 1960. He perceived the vow as a potential threat, not an immediate one, and on 22 June – the very day he received a letter from Davis thanking him for meeting with the organizers – he reaffirmed his position on nuclear weapons, announcing in Parliament the existence of nuclear negotiations with the Americans. "There have been discussions with the United States government regarding the possible conditions under which nuclear weapons for jet interceptors might be stored in United States leased bases in Canada," he told the Commons. But he also seemed to offer a glimmer of hope to the peace movement by saying that these were negotiations only and "no agreement has been arrived at."[118] The prime minister's statement in the House of Commons was a bit of a card game; while it included new references to the importance the government placed on disarmament talks, he never once endorsed the anti-nuclear movement and its objectives.

Far more sympathetic to the anti-nuclear movement generally and the Voice of Women in particular was Lester Pearson. As Diefenbaker had feared, he was a natural ally of the peace movement; he praised the movement publicly and privately, as did his wife.[119] In return, the anti-nuclear movement regarded Pearson as a reliable supporter and treated him accordingly.[120] For instance, when the VOW stated its opposition to nuclear weapons in Canada, Davis explained to the Liberal leader, "Since we are opposed to the whole concept of a nuclear war, and since we feel that the further spread of nuclear weapons increases the possibility of a nuclear war, we feel fully justified in taking a stand on this basis." Focusing on the importance of public opinion, she continued, "We hope that our action meets with your approval and the coming debate on defence appropriations will reflect some measure of public opinion on this most critical issue."[121] Other disarmament activists were congenial, even collegial, in their letters to Pearson, with an underlying sense that he was an ally who would work on their movement's behalf. Frequently cited was Pearson's Nobel Peace Prize as evidence that he had the power and influence necessary to stop nuclear testing or bring about disarmament.[122]

There was no question that Pearson sympathized with the VOW's objectives, but he had some concerns about its tactics. He was especially worried about what he viewed as Davis's tendency to proceed without consulting other members of her organization.[123] This was a minor reservation, and Pearson happily supported his wife's decision to lend her name to the VOW as an honorary sponsor. These honorary sponsors were high-profile supporters who the leaders hoped would give the organization both credibility and political influence. Of all the female politicians and politicians' wives who were approached, Maryon Pearson was one of the VOW's earliest and most ardent supporters.

In her response to the VOW's invitation to become an honorary sponsor, Mrs Pearson wrote: "I am indeed interested in Voice of Women. I think it's a most imaginative and worthwhile project and I believe that if women really set their minds and hearts on a project, they can achieve wonders." Like Lotta Dempsey, Maryon

Pearson believed that "if we women of the West could succeed in reaching the women on the other side of the 'curtain' – i.e. Russia and China – with no political overtones, but only as mothers of young children whose lives or well-being are at stake under this terrible threat of atomic fallout, not to mention bombs, I think we could start a chain reaction toward peace instead of war. Anyhow, it is certainly well worth a try." In closing her letter, she commented on the fears common to many Canadian women: "I am sure many mothers (and grandmothers) in Canada feel helpless and horrorstruck under the terrible threat that hangs over us, and would be anxious and enthusiastic to do what they could to stop it."[124] With this kind of response, vow organizers felt they could count on both Pearsons to support their crusade.

While the u-2 incident sparked the formation of the Voice of Women, it threw nuclear negotiations between Canada and the United States into a state of limbo. Pending the outcome of the summit, NATO had suspended its nuclear talks in March 1960, just as the Canadians and Americans had suspended their bilateral negotiations. Nevertheless, as the summer of 1960 approached, the Canadian government still agreed in principle to nuclear stockpiles at Goose Bay and Harmon Field for use by US interceptors under NORAD. There was also still the possibility of storing larger weapons for use by SAC forces at Goose Bay. [125]

When Diefenbaker met with Eisenhower in Washington in early June, nuclear issues were discussed only briefly and in private.[126] The prime minister stressed that his government could not accept nuclear weapons "unless we exercise joint control" like the British. Eisenhower's response was noncommittal, noting simply that a solution to the North American nuclear dilemma was unlikely to be found in the final months of his administration. Nevertheless, he was hopeful that a suitable arrangement could be found in the near future, one that did not promote nuclear proliferation yet satisfied Canadian concerns about control.[127]

These concerns occupied Diefenbaker and his cabinet over the summer. Even though formal negotiations with the Americans had been suspended, cabinet continued to deliberate the details of how best to store nuclear warheads in Canada. In June, Diefenbaker reiterated the government's position in Parliament, emphasizing that there had been negotiations but no agreement. He continued to insist on joint control as a minimum requirement before an agreement could be reached with the Americans.[128] These statements, however, did little to help clarify the government's nuclear policy. While Diefenbaker insisted that his position was entirely consistent with his statements in February 1959 and January 1960, his comments in Parliament were not as clear as he claimed. He now spoke of the difficulties imposed by US law, particularly that the Atomic Energy Act required the US government to maintain ownership of its nuclear warheads. He also spoke more frequently in favour of disarmament efforts.[129] At the beginning of July he even asked Bryce and the Department of External Affairs to prepare a response to Pearson's criticisms of the government's nuclear policy, a response that could be used as a "holding statement" by the government in the House of Commons. The end result was a statement that leaned slightly more toward disarmament (and Green's position) than before, which was not really what Bryce had in mind.[130] Soon, even the minister of defence appeared to be uncertain about the pursuit of nuclear weapons. At one point, he remarked that the government had purchased systems that required nuclear weapons, "but the decision as to the acquisition of the nuclear warheads depends on circumstances which might develop sometime in the future."[131] By mid-1960, the public could be forgiven for thinking that "when" had been replaced with "if" when it came to nuclear weapons in Canada.

During that summer, Diefenbaker's aides had begun to realize the importance their leader placed on correspondence from Canadians when it came to nuclear policy and the notice he took of the growing number of letters he had received on the subject. In late July the influx was such that he asked External Affairs to draft a form letter to send in response. As Robinson recalled, "His mood seemed genuinely puzzled as to the relative strength of the pro- and anti-nuclear arguments. His reliance on views expressed in public correspondence, even crackpot letters, to quote a member of his staff, was 'phenomenal.'"[132]

Canadian officials made the prime minister's growing concern about public opinion known to their American counterparts when the Permanent Joint Board on Defence met at Camp Gagetown, New Brunswick, at the end of August 1960. At the meeting, the American chair, Dr John Hannah, urged the Canadians to accept the US request to allow stockpiles at Goose Bay and Harmon Field, and expressed some anxiety about further delays. Dana Wilgress,

the Canadian chair, responded by singling out the political problems that the prospect of nuclear weapons created for the Diefenbaker government. "The questions of storage of nuclear weapons in
Canada for United States forces and of acquisition of nuclear weapons by Canadian forces," he emphasized, "had given rise to serious
political problems for the Canadian government."[133] Wilgress
promised to inform the government of the importance of securing
an agreement for USAF bases but refused to provide a guarantee that
an agreement would be forthcoming any time soon. Clearly, by the
summer of 1960 Diefenbaker's preoccupation with public opinion
was beginning to have an impact on Canada's nuclear policy, a
policy that just six months earlier had seemed so certain.

The growing popularity of the Liberal Party compounded Diefenbaker's uneasiness about public support for his nuclear policy. He
continued to worry about Pearson's attacks on government policy,
and with good reason. The Liberals hosted a "thinkers' conference"
at Kingston, Ontario, in early September to generate interest in the
party. Modelled after Vincent Massey's Port Hope conference 1933,
it was not an official party event, but few regarded it as anything
but a partisan affair. Notwithstanding its billing as a conference of
ideas, the organizers were more interested in attracting new members to the party (and thereby invigorating its membership) than
discussing new ideas.[134]

Domestic issues dominated the conference,[135] and only two of the
eleven papers involved foreign affairs,[136] one of these being by James
Eayrs, a political scientist at the University of Toronto, who presented
a paper that inspired much discussion about defence policy and
nuclear issues. In "Defending the Realm: A National Security Policy
for Canada in the 1960s," Eayrs proposed that Canada integrate its
defence entirely with the United States. He supported the acquisition
of nuclear weapons for Canada's armed forces, both at home and
abroad, and proposed that the Americans be allowed to decide the
kind of missiles Canada should acquire and where they should be
located. Eayrs did not stop there. He endorsed Diefenbaker's position
on control, urging the government to continue its pursuit of an agreement on this subject. Eayrs was so convinced that Canada needed
nuclear stockpiles that he was willing to allow full American control
rather than give up nuclear weapons altogether.[137]

In a clear reference to the minister of external affairs, Eayrs criticized those who believed that governments should renounce the

acquisition of nuclear weapons to make a "moral impact"; individuals could reject the acquisition of nuclear weapons, Eayrs reasoned, but it was irresponsible for a government to do so. He was emphatic in his disagreement with the proposition that Canadian officials would lack the moral authority to lead the fight against nuclear proliferation if the government acquired nuclear weapons.[138] Liberals had not supported this position in the past,[139] and Eayrs did not change many minds in Kingston. As 1960 ended, the Liberal Party and its leader remained firmly opposed to Canada's acquisition of nuclear weapons.

Through 1959, despite the appointment of Green and the efforts of Robertson, Diefenbaker had seemed firmly convinced of the merits of nuclear weapons for Canada's armed forces. Everything he said and did indicated as much. Although his public attitude began to change in 1960 as the government's disarmament policy began to take on a greater prominence, privately he remained both firm and pragmatic. He held out little hope for the current round of disarmament talks, yet he did not believe that growing international tensions required the immediate conclusion of a nuclear agreement with the Americans; the details remained to be settled, but as far as most were concerned, the decision to acquire nuclear warheads had already been made.

Eayrs's support for Canada's acquisition of nuclear weapons at the Kingston Conference highlighted the growing division in Canada. While the Liberal Party rejected Eayrs's call to arms, the majority of Canadians agreed with his suggestion. Yet Diefenbaker still worried about public opposition. Pearson exacerbated this fear in two ways: he personally opposed the acquisition of nuclear weapons and sympathised with the anti-nuclear movement; and by making his position Liberal Party policy, he offered Canadians opposed to nuclear weapons a viable alternative to the CCF (later reborn as the New Democratic Party). The Kingston Conference resulted in a higher profile for the party and its leader and was regarded as a huge success. It was reasonable for Diefenbaker to fear that this would translate into political popularity for the Liberals at the expense of his party. Moreover, on the subject of nuclear weapons, Canadians now had a clear choice between the Liberals and Conservatives.

4

A Period of Transition, 1960–1961

Diefenbaker did not welcome John F. Kennedy's victory over Richard Nixon in the presidential elections of November 1960. He was fond of Nixon, the Republican candidate and vice-president, and had hoped he would succeed Eisenhower as president.[1] Preferences aside, Diefenbaker had realised that a new leader in the White House, whether Democrat or Republican, would change relations between Canada and the United States. As Canada's ambassador in Washington remarked, the prime minister appreciated that the election meant a loss of "a number of our best informed friends in office."[2] Other changes in the autumn of 1960 also had a significant influence on Canada's nuclear policy. In October, George Pearkes left the cabinet to become lieutenant-governor of British Columbia, and Douglas Harkness succeeded him to lead the Department of National Defence. Both Kennedy and Harkness were more determined than their predecessors to conclude a nuclear arrangement.

By the time Pearkes left the cabinet, he was inextricably associated with what many regarded as the government's increasingly murky defence policy, and his departure left a void in cabinet at a crucial time. During the same period, Howard Green had become a dedicated proponent of disarmament, which only intensified the growing rift between External Affairs and National Defence over nuclear policy. Anxiety was a key reason for Green's growing interest in disarmament; he and his supporters feared that the resumption of nuclear negotiations with the Americans would undermine the potential for a disarmament agreement.[3]

This was the atmosphere in which Diefenbaker chose Harkness to succeed Pearkes as minister of defence. Harkness was fifty-seven at the time, and brought both political and military experience to the position. A former schoolteacher and farmer in Alberta, he had represented a variety of ridings in the Calgary area after he was first elected to Parliament in 1945; as a veteran of the Second World War, Colonel Harkness quickly embraced his new position. Like his predecessor, he believed Canadian forces ought to be equipped with nuclear weapons and thought it was only a matter of time before Canada would conclude an agreement with the Americans to acquire them. Cabinet had already decided to pursue negotiations with the United States, and he saw no reason for this to change.

Harkness was overly optimistic, however. Green was becoming more strident in his opposition to nuclear weapons. He now argued that a formal agreement with the Americans would be premature – unnecessary even – until the systems requiring nuclear warheads had actually arrived in Canada. The implication of Green's proposal was that the government would not need to conclude an agreement until late 1961 or even 1962. As Harkness later wrote with a certain amount of exaggeration, "To have accepted this position would really have meant that an agreement would never have been signed until a general war had broken out."[4]

Harkness realized that Green's interference might be designed to scuttle the talks, and he approached Diefenbaker to determine both the status of the negotiations and the prime minister's views on the subject. He was relieved to learn that Diefenbaker wanted Canadian representatives to continue with the deliberations. The one potential hitch was the timing. Because Canada's armed forces did not yet have the new weapons systems, Diefenbaker believed that there was not an immediate need for the warheads, and thus there was no reason to rush negotiations; agonizing over the details of a nuclear agreement at this stage seemed to be putting the cart before the horse. But there was another reason for Diefenbaker's apparent unwillingness to expedite negotiations. He was afraid that an agreement to acquire nuclear weapons would undermine Green's credibility internationally.[5] This presented a challenge for the new minister of defence.

It was clear to Harkness that something had to be done to address the government's increasingly contradictory positions of promoting disarmament while at the same time negotiating to acquire nuclear warheads. He took the initiative and developed a statement designed to reconcile these two positions. "While disarmament negotiations are going on," he wrote, "prudence and good sense dictate that preparations have to continue to be made in case no agreement is arrived at." More importantly: "These weapons will not be used except as the Canadian government decides and in the manner approved by the Canadian government."[6] The implication was that disarmament was an opportunity for Canada to forgo nuclear weapons in theory only; given the current state of the disarmament talks, an agreement was unlikely, and thus nuclear weapons were needed for Canada's national security.

There were clear advantages to this approach. As far as Diefenbaker was concerned, the possibility of a disarmament agreement, however remote, bought him time. It gave Canadians the opportunity to see that their government was doing everything possible to avoid acquiring nuclear weapons. Of course, when the talks failed, the government would accept the warheads. Only this approach, Diefenbaker believed, would secure the support of the Canadian people.

Harkness was not alone in urging Diefenbaker to continue the nuclear negotiations. R.B. Bryce also encouraged Diefenbaker to renew talks with the Americans. Bryce went even further than Harkness, suggesting that Canadian forces prepare for the inevitable breakdown in disarmament talks and formally undertake preparations to acquire the warheads. In his view, there was no reason to wait to train soldiers or prepare missile sites.[7] Bryce also supported the acquisition of SAC weapons for Harmon Field and Goose Bay, predicting that an agreement would be reached shortly within the North Atlantic alliance. While he did not dismiss disarmament outright, he did not regard it as a meaningful obstacle to Canada's acquisition of nuclear weapons. In his view, even if a disarmament agreement were reached, any weapons acquired by the Canadians would be subject to its dictates.[8]

While Bryce and Harkness worked to convince Diefenbaker to renew the negotiations with the Americans, Green and Robertson continued to promote a stand-alone policy of disarmament. Although Green was unwilling to contradict the prime minister's nuclear policy publicly, he and Robertson worked together to promote disarmament to the Cabinet Defence Committee and the cabinet. To this end, the undersecretary provided his minister with key arguments to muster support for disarmament and opposition to Canada's acquisition of nuclear armaments.

First and foremost, Green cautioned the CDC to consider the symbolism of nuclear stockpiles at Goose Bay. Allowing them at Goose Bay was a slippery slope; once government officials permitted storage of nuclear weapons anywhere on Canadian territory, they would be obliged to allow storage of nuclear warheads everywhere else for the use of Canada's armed forces. The mere existence of negotiations with the Americans was tacit approval of acquisition. The only way to resolve this problem was to end the talks immediately. Finally, there was public opinion, something sure to capture Diefenbaker's attention. Once Canadians learned of the ongoing secret nuclear negotiations with the Americans, Robertson warned, they could criticize the government for denying that Canada's nuclear policy had changed when so clearly it had.[9]

Robertson's efforts yielded few results. At a meeting of the CDC in early December 1960, Green's efforts to persuade his colleagues to suspend negotiations until all prospect of disarmament was exhausted came to naught. He was no more successful in his attempts to convince his cabinet colleagues to give up nuclear negotiations with the Americans. The United Nations had been debating the merits of an Irish disarmament proposal that committed non-nuclear nations to neither manufacture nor acquire nuclear weapons, and this was the rationale behind Green's plea to cabinet to suspend negotiations with the Americans. Although members of cabinet supported the provisions pertaining to the manufacture of nuclear weapons, they rejected the proposal's prohibition on acquisition, citing the potential conflict with Canada's nuclear policy. Green's solution was simple: change Canada's nuclear policy. The rest of the cabinet disagreed. Instead, they decided that Canada's representative to the United Nations would abstain from voting on the Irish proposal.[10]

The decision seemed to be final, but the debate was far from over. Within days, the government's position changed. Now, instead of abstaining, the Canadian representative would recommend amendments to the Irish proposal, amendments that echoed Harkness's earlier justification of Canada's nuclear policy. Now, instead of an outright ban on the spread of nuclear weapons, the ban would exist only as long as there was "no significant progress in this field in the immediate future," at which point the ban would be reassessed.[11] At the same meeting, cabinet made several major technical decisions related to Canada's nuclear policy. First, there was a consensus that Canada's policy was what Diefenbaker said it was; that is, the prime minister, and no one else, set both the tone and the direction of government policy. Other members of cabinet were certainly welcome to speak publicly on the subject, but anyone choosing to do so was expected to use the prime minister's language. Only this approach would minimize the potential for public confusion or contradictions within government policy.[12]

As 1960 drew to a close, cabinet also reached two conclusions about talks with the Americans. In late 1957 the government had agreed to provide nuclear weapons for its forces in NATO; as a result, preparations for the acquisition of all the necessary nuclear hardware continued apace. What had changed since this commitment was that acquisition was now an all-or-nothing proposition; even though there were different conditions and circumstances surrounding NORAD, NATO, and the Bomarc, only a package agreement covering all three would suffice. As a result, cabinet decided to postpone approval of the Americans' request to store warheads in Newfoundland until the more general agreement had been reached.[13]

Such a decision seemed to bode well for Green and opponents of acquisition; if a general agreement could not be concluded, the government would never be able to contemplate stockpiling nuclear warheads at Goose Bay. However, at the same time, cabinet decided to resume talks with the Americans for nuclear weapons "as soon as they can usefully be undertaken," with joint control as "a basic principle."[14] What was meant by "usefully undertaken" was not clear, but the decision in late December 1960 seemed to be a turning point in the Diefenbaker government's nuclear deliberations. Once provisions for "joint control" were secured, a nuclear agreement with the Americans seemed sure to follow. Thus, a package agreement seemed to be a matter of expediency and consistency, not of delay.

The potential difficulty with this package approach was that joint control was not an easy thing to secure from the Americans. "The only reason we haven't nuclear weapons," Diefenbaker complained to his secretary in late December, "is because the US won't let us."[15] He was referring to the restrictions imposed by the US Atomic Energy Act and the fact that the Americans had been reluctant to consider Canadian demands for joint custody and control. The implication of the statement was that Diefenbaker wanted nuclear weapons for Canada, but the Americans demanded conditions that made it impossible to conclude an agreement. Thus, by the end of 1960 the primary source of delay was neither public opinion nor Howard Green; it was the Americans, under Eisenhower's leadership, who were to blame, at least as far as Diefenbaker was concerned. Furthermore, there is nothing to suggest that Diefenbaker demanded joint control knowing that it would frustrate the talks. After all, joint control was a term of the British agreement, and there seemed to be no reason why the Canadians could not expect to negotiate the same sort of arrangement.

As Diefenbaker prepared for the new year, nuclear policy remained static, just as Green remained a devout proponent of disarmament. In January 1961, Bryce offered to speak to Robertson, whom he correctly regarded as one of the major forces behind Green's intransigence. He also offered Diefenbaker some astute political advice on the subject of nuclear weapons, urging him to deal with the matter quickly and decisively, thereby minimizing the potential for political liability. He suggested that Diefenbaker make a clear, concise statement in support of Canada's acquisition of nuclear weapons; at the same time, Diefenbaker should address the apparent contradiction in Canada's nuclear policy by stating that the various Canadian disarmament initiatives were no longer sufficient. This was imperative as far as Bryce was concerned. It would be disastrous politically, he warned, if Diefenbaker deferred the acceptance of nuclear weapons until after an election. To do so would leave the prime minister open to criticism that he had neglected national security for the sake of electoral expediency. A forthright statement in the House of Commons would have the added benefit of forcing the Liberals to clarify their own nuclear policy, which seemed to be even more ambiguous than the government's. Canadians would support nuclear stockpiles, Bryce assured the prime minister, as long as they knew that national security was at stake. With great pragmatism, Bryce reminded Diefenbaker that votes were not really an issue, because those who opposed nuclear weapons were unlikely to support the Conservatives anyway; they would vote for the newly formed NDP or for Pearson. In any event, Bryce concluded, the weapons the government planned to acquire were likely to be a temporary measure, given the rapidity of technological change.[16]

Diefenbaker agreed with Bryce but did not take his advice. The pro-nuclear forces dominated cabinet in early 1961,[17] and until cabinet decided otherwise, Canada's nuclear policy remained as Diefenbaker had explained it in the House of Commons on 20 February 1959.[18] While there was a difference of opinion within cabinet, it was not an equal division. Canadian public opinion reflected this imbalance. At the meeting of cabinet on 17 February, Harkness pointed out that a public opinion poll indicated that 46 percent of Canadians supported nuclear weapons for Canada's armed forces, 20 percent opposed them, and the remaining 34 percent were undecided.[19] That 46 percent were in favour was little comfort to Diefenbaker. With 34 percent undecided, it was reasonable for him to worry that opposition to nuclear weapons would increase as a result of the anti-nuclear movement's efforts. There was simply no way for him to predict the possible political damage.

In response to growing criticism that the government lacked a coherent defence policy, Diefenbaker decided to restate the government's position. Although he refused to make the strong public statement in favour of nuclear weapons that Bryce had suggested, he wanted to make it clear to Canadians that his government had a strategy for dealing with national security issues. The problem, as he saw it, was managing expectations. Disarmament talks were scheduled to resume in Geneva in March 1961, and he was afraid that growing interest in the talks "had weakened the public appreciation of the need to have nuclear weapons available."[20]

Diefenbaker likened the situation to that facing the British as they prepared for war against Adolf Hitler in the late 1930s. Given his reverence for Mackenzie King, Diefenbaker may have believed he could use the current international situation to his advantage. If Mackenzie King had been able to persuade Canadians that he had no other choice but to go to war in 1939 after the policy of appeasement had failed, perhaps Diefenbaker would be able to convince Canadians that he had no choice but to accept nuclear weapons. Once disarmament talks broke down irrevocably, Canadians would see that the government had accepted nuclear warheads with only the greatest reluctance.[21]

Distinguishing between public opinion and public protest, Diefenbaker noted with some trepidation an increase in correspondence from Canadians opposed to nuclear weapons in recent months. Yet the contents of his mailbag did not persuade him to forgo nuclear weapons for Canada's armed forces; he realized that only those against the government's position were likely to write to express their opinion.[22] But the growing volume of mail from opponents of nuclear weapons, particularly in view of the high percentage of undecided Canadians, indicated that there was a volatility to public opinion on the subject.

Diefenbaker's office was not alone in paying attention to correspondence from the public. The Department of External Affairs also kept track of correspondence related to nuclear issues, presumably as a way of persuading Diefenbaker to abandon his plan to acquire the warheads. In February 1961 department officials produced a report responding to Harkness's expressed skepticism about the state of public opinion. Since January 1960, the department had received 3,797 letters opposing Canada's acquisition of nuclear weapons, roughly divided between letters and petitions. While the department had received fewer than two letters a month in early 1960, the number had increased to double digits by June and July. But the level of correspondence was unpredictable, varying from month to month. For instance, although the department received almost thirty letters against nuclear weapons in both August and September, the numbers fell off dramatically in October (when the department received only four letters) but then increased steadily from November 1960 to February 1961. During the latter period, the numbers ranged from a high of forty-three in December 1960 to a low of twenty-one the following month. The total number of letters sent to the department by individual Canadians, written on their own behalf, was 307, while names on petitions sent in by individuals added up to a total of 301. Organizations represented the greatest source of anti-nuclear sentiment, sending in petitions with signatures totalling 3,189.[23]

The population of Canada was roughly 20 million at this time, and correspondence of this magnitude on a particular issue was not necessarily cause for concern. More to the point, the department's survey did not change Diefenbaker's mind about the advisability of accepting nuclear weapons for the armed forces. Rather, it reinforced his belief that the negotiations required adept handling and great secrecy. This meant that a big public statement on the subject was now out of the question. Diefenbaker needed an agreement in hand before he presented a decision to the public – and then only after Canadians believed the government had exhausted all possibilities for a disarmament agreement. Canadians, he decided, had to be presented with a nuclear *fait accompli*.

It is unclear whether Diefenbaker understood that most of this mail was not from "ordinary Canadians" but was the beginning of an organized campaign from a growing anti-nuclear movement in Canada. It would be surprising if this were the case, given the amount of literature Diefenbaker received as part of the various organizational drives. The various groups – the CCCRH, CUCND, and VOW – did not include membership lists in the packages they sent to the prime minister, so unless individual letter writers identified themselves as members of a particular anti-nuclear organization, Diefenbaker's office staff would have had no way of knowing whether their letters were part of an organized effort. However, the various groups had not been shy about their plans to set up letter-writing campaigns to pressure the government to forgo nuclear weapons, and they included this and other information about their pressure tactics in the newsletters they sent to the prime minister. For this reason, one could have deduced over time that the individual letters were part of an elaborate and well-planned campaign. That many of the letters followed the same format makes this abundantly clear.

In many respects, it would not have mattered that the letters and petitions were part of an organized campaign. In fact, an organized effort would simply have proved to Diefenbaker that Canadians could be rallied to support the anti-nuclear cause.

Regardless, his growing apprehension about correspondence from disarmament activists was part of the general atmosphere in which Diefenbaker and Kennedy first met in February 1961. It was a meeting that was fuelled more by a sense of competition than the need to be a good neighbour. After learning that the British prime minister Harold Macmillan was going to visit Kennedy in April, Diefenbaker announced to Parliament in early February that Macmillan was also invited to Ottawa. At the same time, he added that he too wanted to meet with the new president, ideally before the Commonwealth Conference in March.[24]

External Affairs officials were taken off guard; they had no inkling the prime minister had been contemplating a visit to Washington. At short notice, Arnold Heeney, Canada's ambassador in Washington, was able to arrange a meeting between the two leaders for 20 February.[25] The meeting was to be an informal one to discuss general impressions of international affairs and Canadian-American relations, as well as some finer points on NORAD and nuclear weapons.[26]

Diefenbaker had been thinking about Kennedy for weeks. Within days of the US presidential elections, Canadian officials had briefed him about the new president, whom they described as "aggressive, shrewd and tough-minded."[27] Diefenbaker's experience of a minority government meant that he might have sympathized with Kennedy about the narrowness of his victory over Nixon, which Canadian officials thought might serve to constrain his activities at home and abroad; and though the new president had visited Canada a number of times (he even had an honorary degree from the University of New Brunswick), he had no real knowledge of relations between Canada and the United States.

Regardless, as officials went through the list of bilateral matters, few items were obviously problematic. Issues between the two countries were such that the new administration was not expected to bring with it a substantial change in relations. Kennedy would likely review NATO's nuclear policy and American defence and disarmament policies, but nothing indicated that nuclear weapons would be any more contentious under the Kennedy administration than they had been under Eisenhower.[28]

Almost immediately, Diefenbaker was leery of the new president, so much so that Robinson noted in his diary that the prime minister had "formed an irrational prejudice against Kennedy and Rusk which could be a serious portent."[29] A number of little things exacerbated this "irrational prejudice." When the incoming secretary of state Dean Rusk met with Heeney in Washington, he asked the ambassador to "justify" Canada's special relationship with the United States. Rusk explained that he was concerned that the relationship might inspire jealousy among other American allies, though Heeney's response seemed to satisfy him.[30] But the request infuriated Diefenbaker.[31] There was also the president's slow response to his letter of congratulation in November. In addition, Diefenbaker's last official meeting with Eisenhower in January, one week after the Rusk interview, did little to improve his initial impression of Kennedy. Eisenhower did not have a "high opinion" of the new administration and, given Diefenbaker's respect for the outgoing president's opinions, the comment confirmed his suspicions.[32]

Quite apart from these irritations, the two leaders had little in common. The president was a Harvard-educated veteran of the Second World War from a wealthy and prominent Boston family. The prime minister was from a different time and place; he had served in the First World War and was a small-town Prairie lawyer to whom nothing had come easily. Yet they shared an important characteristic: both were outsiders. Kennedy was the first Roman Catholic president at a time when being an Irish Catholic was anything but an asset in national politics; it was the kind of prejudice that Diefenbaker could understand, having suffered similar treatment because of his German ancestry.

External Affairs officials had advised Diefenbaker that the new president would be thoroughly prepared for their first meeting,[33] and certainly Kennedy's briefing material was sweeping in scope and generally solid in its insight. State Department officials described Diefenbaker as "shrewd," a man who promoted Canadian nationalism "with evangelical fervor."[34] They emphasized that he had a flair for the melodramatic and was prone to using nationalism as a political tool. Canadians, they warned, always feared American absorption, which was at the root of Diefenbaker's brand of nationalism.[35]

State Department officials were equally accurate in their assessment of Green's influence on Diefenbaker. The minister was described as an old and loyal colleague of the prime minister, zealous in his promotion of disarmament, but inexperienced in his current portfolio. His attitude toward foreign affairs was labelled "almost pacifist" and described as "a naive and almost parochial approach to some international problems which was first attributed to his inexperience but which is now believed to be part of his basic personality."[36] Thanks to the State Department's assessment, the Kennedy administration had serious reservations about the minister of external affairs and his promotion of disarmament. For example, Green had proposed that a collection of non-nuclear nations assemble together in an ad hoc UN committee to determine how best to restart disarmament talks. This annoyed the Americans, who regarded these discussions as belonging solely within the purview of the nuclear nations. Green's proposal seemed to be but one instance of his naiveté on the subject of nuclear weapons and disarmament, and US officials came to believe that he was the most significant obstacle to concluding a nuclear agreement with the Canadians.[37]

Kennedy's briefing material also highlighted Diefenbaker's preoccupation with public support, pointing out the likelihood of a federal election in the next twelve to eighteen months. More importantly, Kennedy was told that, according to opinion polls, the Liberals were more popular with Canadians than the government. He was also warned about the small but growing anti-nuclear movement in Canada. The American officials were quick to blame the prime minister for most of this rising opposition, attributing it to his procrastination and inability (or unwillingness) to rally Canadians to support the acquisition of nuclear weapons. There was no other reason for public resistance as far as they were concerned. Similarly, they blamed Diefenbaker for allowing divisions within cabinet to get out of hand. In terms of continental defence, the Americans were afraid that the Canadians' reluctance to increase defence expenditures meant they were spending their way into neutrality. After all, in the event of a crisis with the Soviets, Canada was strategically located.[38]

Kennedy's advisers suggested several tactics the president could use to influence Diefenbaker. First, they suggested an appeal to the prime minister's preoccupation with consultation, speculating that Diefenbaker could be persuaded to support an American position or policy if the president consulted him personally about the matter. This was thought to be a particularly appropriate tactic when dealing with potentially contentious issues. The Canadians, the briefing material noted, "are favorably impressed when given friendly and intimate treatment by US government officials."[39]

More pointedly, Kennedy's advisers stressed the importance of concluding an agreement for the storage of nuclear weapons in Canada. They suggested that he reassure Diefenbaker about the feasibility of joint control, relying on the existing Anglo-American arrangement as a template. At the very least, they urged the president to ask the Canadian leader candidly about the specifics required to conclude an agreement between the two countries. All this was expected to be a straightforward exercise, and the American officials did not anticipate any obstacles to the joint control of nuclear weapons, whether they were for Canadian use or SAC storage in Newfoundland.[40]

As accurate and insightful as the briefing papers were, they completely ignored Diefenbaker's greatest weakness by failing to provide a full picture of his political pedigree. Kennedy was told of the Conservatives' landslide victory in 1958 and that Diefenbaker alone was responsible for it. He was also told about Diefenbaker's various leadership bids. However, the implications of Diefenbaker's repeated political failures were never mentioned. State Department officials similarly failed to recognize or appreciate the role that political vulnerability and personal insecurity played in the prime minister's formulation of nuclear policy, remarking that Diefenbaker was a "self-confident" leader.[41] Yet electoral success was Diefenbaker's most important consideration, especially with a federal election looming. He was bound to reject anything that could be construed as weakness in the face of American pressure, and this was as true for nuclear policy as it was for other areas of Canadian-American relations. Thus, for all their insight into Diefenbaker's strengths and weaknesses, Kennedy's advisers missed the most important element motivating his behaviour: the maintenance of his political position. Awareness of this would surely have tempered an American assessment of Diefenbaker as a self-confident leader.

When the two leaders finally met in Washington on 20 February 1961, the encounter was relaxed and covered a range of issues. Kennedy, Dean Rusk, and Livingston Merchant (the Eisenhower administration's ambassador to Canada until 1958, who returned to the position under Kennedy) represented the Americans. Diefenbaker, Green, and Heeney represented the Canadian government at the meeting. It was clear from the outset that both leaders wanted to maintain the close tie between the two countries, and after a brief discussion about the Congo, South Africa, and Laos, talks turned to China. Although relations between the Western bloc of nations and China had improved recently, Diefenbaker agreed with Kennedy that the Chinese were still difficult to deal with.

Despite this agreement, Canada's continued trade with China was a potential sore spot. On this subject, Diefenbaker reassured the president that Canada's trade with the People's Republic consisted solely of non-strategic goods, just like Canada's trade with other countries. Kennedy accepted this explanation and was even willing to consider the use of oil bunkers from US subsidiaries to assist the sale of Canadian wheat to China.[42] However, Kennedy was not as sympathetic when it came to Canada's trade with Cuba. He accused the Canadian government of permitting US companies to ship goods to the Caribbean island through Canada, an accusation that Diefenbaker vigorously denied. The American embargo had not turned into a trade boom for Canada, he said, and Canadian-Cuban trade was actually below the levels permitted for American exports.[43]

Over lunch, the discussion turned to continental defence. Kennedy adhered closely to his briefing material and offered the Canadians various incentives to persuade them to take on greater responsibility for the defence of North America. Diefenbaker agreed, pledging that Canada could be counted on to do its fair share and criticizing those who supported what he called a "bird-watching" role for the armed forces. But his promise came with a condition. Unless the Americans were willing to share in the production costs associated with North American defence, there would be no Canadian cooperation. In response, Kennedy offered to build the F-104G interceptor aircraft in Canada – a move which Diefenbaker saw as a show of good faith.[44]

Diefenbaker also took the opportunity to express his concern about nuclear weapons and disarmament. The president tried to accommodate him, asking point-blank what the Americans had to do to secure a nuclear agreement with Canada. As Diefenbaker explained Canada's nuclear policy, he emphasized that joint control was crucial, the key component in any agreement. The president was willing to negotiate and proposed an arrangement similar to the Anglo-American double key system. This was exactly what Diefenbaker had in mind, and the two leaders quickly agreed that the system would form the basis of a draft agreement between Canada and the United States, an arrangement that Sidney Smith had proposed in 1958.[45]

The two-key system was just a beginning, and Diefenbaker listed a few other obstacles to reaching a satisfactory arrangement. Canada was in an awkward position, he confided, because Canadian officials were negotiating to acquire nuclear stockpiles at the same time as they were promoting disarmament internationally. Diefenbaker explained his fear that Canadians would think the government's nuclear policy was contradictory or even hypocritical, and he cautioned Kennedy that his government could accept nuclear weapons only when the current round of disarmament talks broke down. Here there was conflict. The president agreed with the prime minister only on the importance of disarmament, noting his own support for some kind of test ban agreement. After much discussion, the two agreed to disagree about how best to approach what seemed to be the doomed disarmament talks. Both agreed that a disarmament agreement was unlikely, but Diefenbaker was more willing than Kennedy to make the effort to conclude an agreement with the Soviets for the sake of public opinion or, at the very least, public perception.[46] There the first meeting between the prime minister and the president ended.

Although the meeting did not end on a high note, Diefenbaker's first encounter with the new American president was an undeniable success, far surpassing his expectations. En route to the airport, Diefenbaker pronounced the meeting "excellent."[47] "The prime minister was jubilant on the way back," H.B. Robinson recalled in a letter to the Canadian embassy in Washington. He "told so many anecdotes that we had the greatest difficulty completing his statement for the House by the time we touched down at Uplands." Indeed, Diefenbaker had only four pages of his text with him when he rose to speak in Parliament, requiring that an aide deliver the final two to his desk while he was midway through his statement.[48]

Diefenbaker had been favourably impressed with Kennedy and Rusk, and was struck by the care with which the president had obviously studied Canadian-American issues.[49] "The [prime minister] described the president as having great capacity, a farsighted judgement on international affairs, and an attractive human quality in private exchanges," Robinson later recalled. "The meeting began, in the [prime minister's] words, 'stiffly,' but it closed on a note of cordiality which to the many newspapermen and others in attendance was obviously unforced."[50]

Diefenbaker was particularly happy about the discussion about nuclear policy, and he was pleased that he had taken the opportunity to clarify Canada's position for the new administration. As Diefenbaker recounted it, he had explained to Kennedy that "while disarmament was being pressed forward, no agreements would be signed but all the preliminaries in negotiation ... would be completed so that there would be no holdup should the need arise."[51] According to Diefenbaker's private notes of the meeting, the Canadians had told the Americans they were willing to negotiate a nuclear arrangement just short of implementation. There remained room to manoeuvre in this statement, for Diefenbaker referred to "should" the need arise, not "when." Of course, whether he meant the conditional phrasing to apply to the acquisition of nuclear weapons or the circumstances surrounding that acquisition is unclear. Most likely, he meant that he was uncertain when the inevitable breakdown in disarmament talks that would lead to the acquisition of nuclear weapons would occur. There was nothing to indicate that he had changed his mind about the overall merits of stockpiling nuclear warheads in Canada.

Diefenbaker placed particular emphasis on a comprehensive arrangement: "We do not intend to enter into any of these agreements or arrangements piecemeal – the whole thing is a package."[52] He described this initial meeting with Kennedy even more decisively in his memoirs. "We agreed," he wrote, "that detailed arrangements on all aspects of this matter should be worked out and embodied in agreements ready for immediate execution *when conditions made it necessary* ... So far as I was able to judge ... the new administration's policies on defence were not going to be fundamentally different from those of its predecessor."[53] Yet Diefenbaker's recollection of what occurred as given in his memoirs may have been more explicit than was actually the case. For example, the meeting was held in February, not January, as he wrote in his book, and the notes he made at the time of the meeting are not nearly as crisp as the account that appears in the memoirs. It is entirely possible that Diefenbaker said one thing and recalled another, while being understood to have meant a third.

What is clear is that the president and his advisers had a different impression of this first meeting between the two leaders. In his own mind, Diefenbaker may have been firm about a package agreement, but the Americans had not been left with that impression. Their account of the conversation noted, "In concluding this discussion [on nuclear weapons, particularly at Goose Bay and Harmon Field] the prime minister expressed the view that *all our defense arrangements, including both joint defense production sharing and nuclear storage problems*, should be settled at the same time."[54] The Americans understood that Diefenbaker wanted a package agreement, but they broadened the scope of the package to include defence production, something not noted by the Canadians and arguably not intended by the prime minister.

Perhaps because of the generally positive sentiments on both sides, the February meeting left both men with a false impression. In viewing the meeting as a success, Kennedy did not anticipate any problems in dealing with Diefenbaker, believing that he would be a staunch ally at the ready.[55] Moreover, he was convinced that Diefenbaker had promised to accept nuclear weapons, and to accept them soon. In contrast, Diefenbaker believed that Kennedy, like Eisenhower, would do nothing to pressure the Canadians to move forward with the nuclear negotiations. Given this glaring misunderstanding between the two men, it is hardly surprising that Kennedy grew rather impatient as Diefenbaker continued to take his time negotiating with the Americans for nuclear weapons. Ultimately, the meeting between Kennedy and Diefenbaker in February 1961 served to heighten Washington's irritation with the Conservative government in Ottawa when subsequent negotiations progressed at a snail's pace.[56]

When Diefenbaker spoke to the House of Commons about the success of his meeting with Kennedy, he announced that the president would visit Ottawa in the spring. In describing the meeting to cabinet, he focused on their discussion of nuclear policy, emphasizing that the president had understood and accepted the premium the Canadians placed on a package agreement based on the two-key system.[57] When Howard Green chimed in, it was as if he had attended a different meeting altogether. The minister of external affairs focused not on negotiations for nuclear weapons but on the discussion about the prospect of a disarmament agreement. While neither Kennedy nor Diefenbaker had thought that an agreement was likely (or even possible), it served both their purposes to allow the talks to continue. Green, however, either refused to concede the point or did not understand this, telling cabinet that the Kennedy administration was going to re-evaluate American disarmament policy before getting involved in the current round of negotiations.[58] By all accounts, Green's recollection mischaracterized the American position.

The minister of national defence Douglas Harkness had not attended the Washington talks and chose not to comment on Diefenbaker's discussion of nuclear policy at this cabinet meeting. Instead, he returned to his earlier investigation of public support for acquisition. Cabinet had discussed public opinion before Diefenbaker's departure for Washington, with some ministers commenting on a recent CBC poll that indicated 46 percent of Canadians supported acquisition of nuclear weapons, while 20 percent opposed possession. Others had countered that a new Gallup poll had produced entirely different results.[59] Harkness had been curious about this possible divergence in the state of public opinion and decided to look into it. What he found was that the most recent Gallup poll, conducted in January 1961 and published in the

Toronto Star, actually mirrored the findings of the CBC, reporting that 45 percent of Canadians supported the acquisition of nuclear weapons, 21 percent were opposed, and 34 percent were undecided,[60] as described earlier in this chapter.

Harkness reported these results to Diefenbaker on 23 February in an effort to persuade him to ignore External Affairs' survey of correspondence highlighting opposition to nuclear weapons. He was well aware of Diefenbaker's growing anxiety about public support and the possible political consequences of concluding a nuclear agreement with the Americans, so although his report indicated that the only potential problem was the 34 percent of Canadians who remained undecided, he focused his attention on the plurality of Canadians who supported the acquisition of nuclear warheads.[61]

In the weeks between Diefenbaker's visit to Washington and Kennedy's reciprocal trip to Ottawa in May 1961, the prime minister attended the Commonwealth Conference in London – one of the original reasons for requesting a meeting with Kennedy as early as February – and both he and the Department of External Affairs were busy preparing for the conference, which would be discussing the status of South Africa within the Commonwealth. Consequently, they turned their attention to the president's visit only in late April. Since the meeting in Washington in February, Kennedy had announced the reappointment of Livingston Merchant as US ambassador to Canada.

Merchant was happy to return to Canada, and Canadian officials were equally content with the appointment.[62] He understood both Diefenbaker and the Canadian political situation, and was a wise choice as US ambassador in Ottawa. Prior to his departure from Washington, he met with Kennedy to talk about various issues in Canadian-American relations, and nuclear negotiations topped the list. Kennedy confided that he was bewildered by Diefenbaker's apparent reluctance to conclude a nuclear arrangement with the United States, and he sought the ambassador's insight on the subject.[63]

Merchant explained that nuclear policy in Canada was overwhelmingly a political issue because it gave the Liberals an opportunity to criticize Diefenbaker's government for its dependence on the Americans, and political criticism was of importance because the government's support among Canadians was falling. To counter this problem, Merchant suggested that Kennedy frame defence agreements within a multilateral rather than bilateral context – NATO rather than

NORAD, for example. Diefenbaker valued individual contact, he said, adding that a short personal note from Kennedy would go a long way toward maintaining Canadian support when necessary. The president, thankful for the guidance, concluded the conversation by asking Merchant to offer his advice, at any time, about how best to handle the Canadian leader in a given situation.[64]

In seeking advice on how best to deal with Diefenbaker, Kennedy would have had no idea that the prime minister's initially positive impression of him had started to change. Kennedy's star began to lose its lustre after the Bay of Pigs fiasco in mid-April. The mission – dreamed up by the Eisenhower administration – was designed to remove Cuban leader Fidel Castro from power. The Americans had trained a group of Cuban exiles, whom they then helped to return to their native country. The object of their mission was to inspire the locals to rise up and overthrow Castro's government. The plan was ill conceived from the start, and when Kennedy withdrew air support, the landing turned into a disaster that tarnished the president's image among foreign leaders, including Diefenbaker.[65]

It was within this context that Kennedy travelled to Ottawa in the spring of 1961. Once again, he was well prepared for his meetings with Diefenbaker. Green's influence and his growing intransigence on disarmament was causing increasing alarm among American officials. His behaviour at a recent NATO meeting in Oslo was a case in point. There, Green had made a bad situation worse by telling reporters on the flight home that he would be happy to help the Cubans and Americans settle their differences. About the incident, Rusk wrote, "Green is obviously bemused by [the] great peace-making role which Canada (obviously usefully) plays in such situations as Suez, Congo and other affairs on which they have been asked to participate."[66] American officials wasted no time calling Heeney to complain.[67]

Green's interjection reaffirmed to State Department officials that he, not the prime minister, was the true obstacle in the conduct of Canadian-American relations. They also realized that Green's position was popular with Canadians, which meant he would have to be handled carefully.[68] Compounding this difficulty was the belief that Green was the most influential member of the Canadian cabinet when it came to disarmament and nuclear weapons.[69] To offset his influence, the American officials urged Kennedy to speak candidly to Diefenbaker on the subject.[70]

Kennedy's primary objective in Ottawa was "to promote a frank and working relationship with Prime Minister Diefenbaker" and to "impress upon him and his government our views and policies on global problems."[71] More importantly, he was determined to seek a solution to some of the more nagging bilateral problems, with defence-related issues among the most prominent.[72] In the days before the visit, Diefenbaker had asked Merchant not to broach the subject of nuclear weapons with the Department of External Affairs, promising instead to bring the matter before cabinet prior to Kennedy's arrival in Ottawa. Merchant complied and was hopeful that Diefenbaker would keep his promise too, though he was not entirely surprised when he did not.[73] In fact, few of Kennedy's advisers expected to make much progress on the subject of nuclear weapons. They reminded the president that the prime minister placed great weight on public opinion and was worried about the growing anti-nuclear movement in Canada. With an election call imminent and Diefenbaker in a precarious position politically, the nuclear issue was likely to be banished from the agenda for the near future.[74]

Kennedy's mid-May visit to Ottawa was a great public success. Press reports of the visit glowed with enthusiasm for the president and the first lady,[75] and enormous crowds turned out to see them. US Embassy officials regarded the entire visit as a positive one; the media coverage was "extensive and universally friendly," and Kennedy was thought to have made a "deep and favorable impression" on Diefenbaker and his advisers.[76]

The two leaders talked about a range of issues: Cuba, Canadian membership in the Organization of American States (OAS), development aid, the sale of aircraft, Southeast Asia, disarmament, NATO, and nuclear weapons. US officials were still irritated about Green's offer to mediate between the Americans and the Cubans, and said so. Diefenbaker reassured his American guests that neither he nor his minister would intervene in the dispute. The reason was simple: Canadians were not very interested in what was going on in the Caribbean island, and there was thus no reason to get involved. Indeed, it was because of this lack of interest in the region that Canada did not become a member of the OAS, despite Kennedy's rather pointed request that Canada join the organization. Public opinion, Diefenbaker countered, would not support it. The president was undaunted and tried again. Perhaps in an effort to allay

Diefenbaker's wariness, he pledged that he would talk to the Canadians about any military intervention in Cuba "before such actually took place."[77] Significantly, although he promised to talk to Diefenbaker, he did not promise to consult him.

When the discussion turned to nuclear weapons, Kennedy sought agreement from the Canadian leader on several related issues. Diefenbaker, however, repeatedly balked. Whether the discussions involved warheads for NATO, NORAD, or US bases in Canada, he returned to his concern about the state of public opinion in Canada. He said that Canada's armed forces should and would be equipped with nuclear weapons, but it was a question of timing; it was not politically expedient to commit formally to such an arrangement at present. It was "politically impossible today," Diefenbaker explained.[78] With the Canadian anti-nuclear movement growing, the government could not risk adopting such a potentially contentious policy.[79]

The problem, he told Kennedy, was that the anti-nuclear movement was not restricted to communists and radicals. It was broadly based, "including a very high percentage from mothers and wives."[80] Worse still, it was credible. Therein lay the political threat. With exaggeration, Diefenbaker told the president that he was so worried about the state of public opinion that he doubted he would even be able to convince his own cabinet to accept nuclear weapons from the Americans. Nonetheless, he reiterated that he was still committed to acquiring nuclear warheads, and pledged to "make an effort to change public opinion on this question this summer and fall."[81]

Diefenbaker repeated the same concerns (and same reassurances) to Kennedy when the talks turned to the Bomarc missile and disarmament. During these talks, he expressed his pleasure that the negotiations for nuclear warheads "had gone a long way" and said "it would not be too difficult to go a little further – but not just at the moment."[82] As before, he promised to do his best to convert public opposition to Canada's acquisition of nuclear weapons, echoing his earlier doubts about his ability to secure the support of his cabinet.[83] There was also Parliament, particularly Pearson and the Liberal opposition, to consider.

Kennedy remained unconvinced. He laughingly chided the prime minister for his concerns about the political influence of the anti-nuclear movement, remarking that "he could get a parade in Boston at any time on nuclear weapons, but it would not be serious."[84] Diefenbaker was equally unmoved, telling the president that "he did not normally trust the Gallup poll but that it revealed strong public feeling against nuclear weapons." The "hope of disarmament" was at the root of this anti-nuclear sentiment, he argued, stressing again the credibility of many individuals who were opposed to nuclear weapons.[85] Diefenbaker said that he had proof that anti-nuclear sentiment was growing, having seen the evidence with his very own eyes. There were letters, lots of letters. Hundreds of Canadians who were against Canada's acquisition of nuclear warheads had taken the time to write to him, he stressed; and significantly, this correspondence "was not the lobby type of mail." [86]

Diefenbaker must have known that his comments about public support were misleading. He knew from his discussions with Harkness that recent Gallup polls indicated that a plurality of Canadians supported the acquisition of nuclear weapons. Only the level of uncertainty, not outright opposition, should have been cause for concern. As for the source of the opposition to nuclear weapons, by mid-1961 Diefenbaker knew that the anti-nuclear groups had organized formal campaigns to persuade the government to forgo nuclear weapons. Similarly, he knew that anti-nuclear activists were responsible for most of these letters. External Affairs' report on the subject of anti-nuclear correspondence had indicated as much.

Why, then, did Diefenbaker take this approach? Possibly, he thought Kennedy would be more sympathetic if he believed the correspondence had come from ordinary Canadians, unaffiliated with any of the anti-nuclear organizations – in other words, that there was a groundswell of public opposition. Political support was something that a president who had only narrowly won the White House should have understood.

Diefenbaker was probably reacting to the volatility of the nuclear issue. He continued to worry that the public would not support his decision to accept warheads from the Americans, a preoccupation that stemmed from the anti-nuclear movement's increased level of activity in the first half of 1961 and the level of uncertainty indicated in opinion polls. Yet groups raised awareness by drawing greater public attention to themselves, not all of which was positive. Harkness, for one, commented that the anti-nuclear movement was "pacifist, neutralist and dangerous."[87] Others were even more critical, insisting that communism was rife within the movement.

The accuracy of the charges depended very much on the group involved; while CUCND had been plagued by well-founded accusations of communist infiltration since its inception,[88] the same could not be said about the CCCRH and VOW. The CCCRH escaped most red-baiting because of Van Stolk's efforts to maintain a restrictive membership policy, but the VOW was not as fortunate, and for good reason. Although its organizers understood how important it was to avoid even the hint of communist sympathies, the lengths to which they went to screen their members were minimal. Moreover, the decision to exclude only *known* communists from "high-profile" positions within the organization, rather than excluding them altogether, left the VOW vulnerable to attack.

Because of its lax membership policy, the newly formed women's group had to stave off some particularly hostile allegations by early 1961. In January of that year, Marjorie Lamb's "Alert Service" newsletter included the VOW on its list of communist organizations. Created in 1957 to assist Hungarian refugees in Canada, the newsletter regularly published lists of communists, both organizations and individuals. Lamb's allegation was subsequently repeated by the Imperial Order Daughters of the Empire (IODE), a women's organization founded in 1900 to promote imperialism in Canada that had since transformed itself to promote traditional values. As a credible if conservative association with the weight of longevity behind it, the IODE's opposition, while not out of character, nonetheless hurt VOW's efforts to become a national organization that represented the views of women from across the political spectrum.[89] To compound the problem, a number of honorary members left the association at this time, specifically because of the allegations of communist infiltration.[90] By the time Kennedy came to Ottawa in May 1961, the VOW was more active than credible, a distinction that Diefenbaker of all people must have appreciated.

Notwithstanding his obvious anxiety about popular support for nuclear weapons and his repeated references to public opinion in his talks with Kennedy, Diefenbaker remained willing to accept the weapons. Acquisition was still subject to the provisions agreed to in February, but Diefenbaker wanted Canada's armed forces to be equipped with nuclear warheads. Joint control remained an absolute necessity, something all too clear when talks in Ottawa turned to the proposed SWAP agreement. This was a triangular arrangement of some complexity. In exchange for the RCAF's willingness to assume the maintenance of sixteen radar stations on the Pinetree Line, the Americans agreed to transfer sixty-six F-101B interceptors to Canada. Completing the triangle, the US government would then order $200 million worth of F-104Gs from Canada to be assigned as Mutual Aid to NATO allies, of which the Canadians agreed to pay 25 percent.

Ambassador Merchant had approached Diefenbaker about the proposal prior to the president's visit and anticipated his reaction.[91] The sticking point, once again, was whether the F-101Bs would carry missiles with nuclear warheads. In discussions with Kennedy, Diefenbaker proposed that the Canadians would accept the aircraft and then negotiate an agreement for the warheads. Kennedy refused, and Merchant was left to try and settle the matter. He attempted to persuade Diefenbaker that the Americans needed something to justify placing orders for military material outside the United States. Strengthening continental security was just the sort of explanation that would fit the bill. But Diefenbaker would not budge; he said that the nuclear requirement would make the exchange appear to be little more than an American diktat.[92] Kennedy, too, was undeterred and tried another tactic, the threat to Canada's national security. There would be no time in an emergency, he warned Diefenbaker, to retrieve the warheads required for use with the interceptors; and he proposed – once again – an arrangement along the lines of the Anglo-American double-key system.[93]

The problem from the Canadian point of view, it seemed, was not the basic principle underpinning the acquisition of nuclear warheads. The difficulty was making it palatable politically as a federal election loomed. Anything that seemed to undermine Canadian autonomy or sovereignty would be a political disaster for the Diefenbaker government, particularly given the Conservative Party's own harsh criticism of the Liberals on this very subject in the previous two elections.

Diefenbaker raised two important points that were subsequently excised from the Canadian account of the meeting: the importance of secrecy and the political implications of Pearson's position on nuclear weapons. He had suspended earlier nuclear negotiations with Eisenhower when rumours of the talks appeared in the newspapers, and he warned that he would not hesitate to do the same thing with Kennedy.[94] He wanted to be able to announce an agreement, not simply that negotiations were underway, he explained.

He had tried the latter in the past, and the only response was an increase in the outpouring of anti-nuclear sentiment, which he was determined to avoid. The two men then discussed the Liberal leader's stand on the nuclear issue.[95] In January 1961, Pearson had reaffirmed his opposition to nuclear weapons at the Liberal Party's National Rally in Ottawa, the rally that had been called to launch the party's platform for the next federal election. The party's defence policy had focused on the importance of collective security, pledging to re-evaluate Canada's role in NATO. "Unilateral disarmament," the foreign policy brief read, "is not the solution to the problems of peace."[96]

If the Liberal's foreign policy did not contain much to worry Diefenbaker, its defence proposals certainly did. The Liberals were now willing to accept nuclear weapons in NATO provided two conditions were met. First, the warheads had to be subject to collective control and thus unanimous approval by the NATO Council before they could be used. Second, the weapons were to be used for defensive purposes only. The Liberals criticized the government's involvement in NORAD, promising that they would withdraw from Canada's "present interceptor role." Instead, "the Canadian role in such defence should be that of detection, identification and warning." In no circumstances was the party willing to accept nuclear weapons on Canadian territory. Nuclear warheads in Canada, under any arrangement, would constitute proliferation. Not only would Canada become a nuclear nation, but its efforts to achieve a disarmament agreement would be ruined.[97] In short, Pearson and the Liberal Party rejected Diefenbaker's pursuit of nuclear weapons for Canada but accepted at least the possibility of a nuclear role within the North Atlantic alliance.

By the time Kennedy met with Diefenbaker in Ottawa, the prime minister still had every reason to believe that Pearson would make Canada's nuclear policy into a political issue. He confided to Kennedy that Pearson knew better than to oppose the government's nuclear policy.[98] Kennedy's advisers had told him the same thing: "Even in matters where the government position has shifted in the last two years, e.g., in its increased reluctance to acquire nuclear weapons, the Liberal Party position has moved in the same general direction and at roughly the same pace, partly through conviction, partly through domestic pressure. It is unlikely, therefore, that the return of the Liberal Party to power would occasion any sharp turns in Canadian policy."[99] From the Americans' perspective, then, Canada's nuclear policy would not be any more agreeable under a Liberal government. In fact, it might be worse. And while the US officials disliked the Liberal Party's pledge to reduce Canada's role in NORAD, they thought there was at least the potential for nuclear weapons under NATO and stockpiles for US forces in Newfoundland.[100]

The State Department officials were no more enthusiastic about Pearson than they were about his party's nuclear policy. They reminded Kennedy that Pearson had won the Nobel Peace Prize for his work at Suez and had vast experience in the conduct of foreign affairs. They were not, however, impressed by his leadership skills. As a politician, Pearson was said to be "clumsy" and his campaign skills "uncertain." The American officials held him personally responsible for the party's poor showing in the 1958 election and equally accountable for the Liberal Party's defence policies. Here, the US officials agreed with Diefenbaker that the Liberal defence strategy was politically motivated. "In his search for political issues," they emphasized, "Pearson has flirted with propositions which are disturbing from a United States point of view ... The public impression he has given has been encouraging to groups advocating neutralism and unilateral disarmament."[101] Pearson may have been the more personable of the two major political leaders in Ottawa, but when it came to nuclear policy the Liberal leader was not much more palatable to the Americans than Diefenbaker.

While the press in both Canada and the United States celebrated Kennedy's stay in Ottawa, all was not as pleasant as it appeared. The visit gave rise to difficulties that undermined the relationship between the two men. The first was an unexpectedly contentious speech that Kennedy made to Parliament. Well aware of Canadian sensitivities, the president's staff reviewed the speech to make sure that comments were warm and solicitous. So did advisers from the State Department. And Theodore White, a journalist who had chronicled Kennedy's 1960 campaign and later became the president's speechwriter, had carefully crafted the speech. The writers had even decided to modify a reference to increases in NATO's conventional forces, fearing it might cause confusion within the alliance, with members clamouring for nuclear arrangements with the Americans.[102] The advisers were so cautious that they had gone so far as to vet the speech with the Canadian ambassador in Washington.[103]

Everyone missed the problem: a reference to the possibility of Canadian membership in the Organization of American States (OAS). Kennedy had raised such a possibility privately with Diefenbaker during their talks, and the prime minister had firmly rejected the invitation. When Kennedy said in his speech to Parliament that the Americans would appreciate it if Canada joined the OAS, Diefenbaker saw it as a heavy-handed tactic. He thought the subject had been laid to rest in their private meeting and was livid that the president would try to pressure the Canadians publicly to accept what had already been rejected behind closed doors.[104]

Diefenbaker did little to demonstrate his displeasure to the Americans at the time of the speech, suffering in silence to the extent that one US official later concluded that the "president's forthrightness startled but did not offend Canadians who have been given much to think about."[105] Although the reference did not seem to offend Canadians, it certainly offended the prime minister, who later remarked, "I was not about to have Canada bullied into any course of action. This was the first of a number of occasions on which I had to explain to President Kennedy that Canada was not Massachusetts, or even Boston."[106] Kennedy, however, was not to blame for the reference to Canadian membership in the OAS. Ambassador Heeney had reviewed Kennedy's speech and had apparently seen nothing wrong with the reference.[107]

Diefenbaker's irritation with Kennedy grew over the course of the visit. On the evening of 17 May, just after the president's address to Parliament, a document entitled "What We Want from Ottawa" was discovered in the Prime Minister's Office. It had been left behind accidentally, though Diefenbaker later claimed that Kennedy had deliberately left it in his wastebasket intending him to find it.[108] Written by W.W. Rostow and later dubbed the "Rostow Memo," it urged Kennedy to "push" the Canadians to increase their interest in Latin America, join the OAS, increase foreign aid, and support the Americans at Geneva and on the International Control Commission (ICC) for Indochina.

These were talking points for the president; they were not meant to be used to bully the Canadians. There was nothing overly contentious on the list and, interestingly, no reference to nuclear weapons. H.B. Robinson interpreted the memorandum as the kind of document he routinely gave to Diefenbaker before a meeting. It was nothing more than a briefing document, designed to serve as a reminder to stress or focus on a particular point.[109] Diefenbaker did not see it this way. He literally underlined his fury by marking the word "push" on his copy of the memorandum,[110] and he refused to return the document to the State Department (which would have been in accordance with diplomatic protocol). As with Kennedy's presentation to Parliament, Diefenbaker saw the Rostow Memo as evidence that the Americans would resort to browbeating the Canadians in order to get their way. The final straw came when the president had a very long conversation with Pearson at a dinner hosted by Ambassador Merchant. Diefenbaker had no way of knowing how the Americans regarded Pearson and took the lengthy discussion between the two as a personal snub.[111] He could not have known that Kennedy was demonstrating a personal preference, not a political one.

The Ottawa visit made a lasting impression on Kennedy. It was his first visit to a foreign country as president. It was also an occasion in which he re-injured his back during a ceremonial tree planting at Rideau Hall.[112] After Ottawa, Kennedy returned to Washington to prepare for his highly anticipated summit in Vienna with Nikita Khrushchev. Held in early June, the summit was another foreign policy fiasco for the Kennedy administration. The Soviet premier renewed his demands over Berlin, which undermined relations between East and West. This increased international tension in the summer of 1961 provides the context of the next round of nuclear talks between Canada and the United States.

5

Nuclear Negotiations and the 1962
Federal Election

Although the Rostow Memo changed forever Diefenbaker's attitude toward Kennedy, he was still willing to deal with the Americans on nuclear matters. Indeed, following the talks with Kennedy in the spring of 1961 until the federal election in June 1962, Diefenbaker never wavered in his desire to arm Canada's military with nuclear weapons. What changed was his perception that nuclear weapons could damage his political standing.

Meanwhile, the Canadians and Americans concluded the SWAP agreement. Having notified the Americans that Ottawa would reject the arrangement outright if nuclear weapons were required,[1] Canadian officials were pleased when the Americans acquiesced.[2] On 15 June 1961 representatives of the two countries signed an agreement that allowed the Canadians to accept the F-101BS without the nuclear tips, at least until arrangements were made to accept them more generally in accordance with the prime minister's preference for a "package deal."

The SWAP agreement was, in fact, a simple arrangement: the Canadians agreed to operate, staff, maintain, and finance sixteen Pinetree line stations, and the Americans agreed to give Canada sixty-six F-101B interceptors, which were to be fitted with conventional warheads for the RCAF component of NORAD. As well, they agreed to purchase F-104GS from Canada with their support equipment and spare parts. The total cost of the F-104G purchase was $200 million, with the Americans contributing $150 million and the Canadians paying the balance. Deliveries were expected to begin in mid-1963 and to continue at approximately forty-eight aircraft per year until the $200 million was spent.[3] Although the

F-101B required significant reconfiguration in order to use conventional weapons, the Americans were willing to make this change. But the Canadians made it clear to them that this was unnecessary. Presumably, it was unnecessary because the Canadians expected to reach an agreement with the Kennedy administration on the acquisition of nuclear weapons in the very near future.[4]

Ambassador Merchant spoke to a number of Canadian officials about the likelihood of concluding an arrangement for nuclear weapons, though one conversation stood out in particular. At the end of May, Merchant had a conversation with George Ignatieff, the assistant undersecretary of state for external affairs, who had pleaded his minister's case. "Green is not soft-headed or pacifist-minded," Ignatieff seemed to apologize, "but very clear on the matter of the Soviet threat and where Canada's basic interests lie."[5]

In his report to Washington, Merchant noted some of the more general concerns of Canadian officials. "There is a general and curious confusion in Canadian thinking over the acceptance of defensive nuclear weapons in Canada under joint control but under U.S. custody, and the problem of the proliferation of nuclear powers in the world," he wrote. "This," he explained, "combined with a desire self-righteously to abjure a dirty weapon of warfare, and a failure to distinguish between the protection of our deterrent power as an essential element in that power and a futile defense of the U.S. against nuclear attack with all the fallout dropping in their garden, renders most discussions of this subject peculiarly frustrating."[6] Merchant's sentiments capture nicely the Diefenbaker government's position and the resulting confusion. The Canadians had led the Kennedy administration to believe that the remaining details for nuclear stockpiles would be settled as quickly and as easily as the SWAP agreement,[7] but soon after the deal had been completed, trouble in Berlin led cabinet to reconsider its position.

In mid-1961 the Soviets threatened to cut off Western access to the city, which was located in the heart of East Germany. The threat necessarily resurrected the nuclear issue, and a lengthy cabinet discussion on 24 July 1961 highlighted the entrenched division within cabinet, primarily between Howard Green, minister of external affairs, and Douglas Harkness, minister of defence. Diefenbaker proposed that the Canadians renew negotiations with the Americans for the SAC bases in Newfoundland in the light of "present circumstances."[8] Green disagreed. Although there were indications that he was coming to accept the inevitability of nuclear weapons,[9] he argued that the Americans had gone beyond mere defensive measures and were now preparing for all-out nuclear war. On this point, Green gave his most dramatic statement to date opposing Canada's acquisition of nuclear weapons. "One must recognise how high the stakes were in nuclear war," he said. "It was an issue that might determine whether or not Montreal, Toronto, Hamilton, Ottawa, Vancouver and other Canadian cities might be blotted off the map. It was not just a question of losing some troops but rather one of the future of Canada and of civilization." He concluded dramatically that "if the present situation gave rise to a nuclear war, the United Kingdom might be blotted out entirely and most of Canada as well."

Harkness disagreed vehemently. He argued that the Bomarc, with its range of 400 to 500 miles, could not start a nuclear war, and he soundly rejected Green's assertion that Canada's mere acquisition of nuclear warheads for the Bomarc system would transform the nation into a nuclear power. Appealing to his cabinet colleagues' sense of pragmatism, he stressed the vital importance of an agreement with the Americans; there would be no time to waste in the event of an emergency.[10]

Diefenbaker sided squarely with his defence minister. He agreed with Harkness that joint control of nuclear weapons would not constitute proliferation, and he took pains to distinguish between the situations in NORAD and NATO.[11] This exchange within cabinet leaves little doubt that Diefenbaker still supported the acquisition of nuclear weapons for the use of Canada's armed forces in both North America and Europe. Even Green reluctantly conceded that the government ought to allow the Americans to store nuclear weapons in Newfoundland. He refused to budge, though, on his position that Canadian forces at home and abroad should not go nuclear.[12] There the debate seemed destined to rest within cabinet.

The truce reached in cabinet on 24 July was a temporary one, and the nuclear issue returned to the fore on 3 August, when Kennedy sent a secret letter to Diefenbaker explicitly asking to resume nuclear negotiations.[13] The president and his advisers had every reason to expect the request would be well received. After all, they knew from their visit to Ottawa that Diefenbaker wanted nuclear weapons, and he had promised to convince Canadians of their strategic importance. As well, the looming possibility of a conflict with the Soviet Union over Berlin underscored the need for a strong Western defence. Finally, they knew that Canadian public opinion, notwithstanding Diefenbaker's comments to the contrary, was on their side.

Their assessment of public opinion was based on the CBC television program "Close Up," which had aired an episode in mid-June dedicated to the nuclear issue. Opening the discussion with the assertion that all Canadian weapons systems required nuclear warheads for optimum effectiveness,[14] the moderator oversaw a debate on the question "Should We Join the Nuclear Club?" Although a small number of people spoke in favour of Canada's acquisition of nuclear warheads,[15] most spoke against it. Among this group of opponents were Lester Pearson (who argued that nuclear weapons were "morally and politically" wrong), Hazen Argue, Rabbi Abraham Feinberg of the Toronto Campaign for Nuclear Disarmament (TCND), and General Macklin and H.L. Keenleyside of the Canadian Committee for the Control of Radiation Hazards (CCCRH).[16]

In his report to Washington about the broadcast, Livingston Merchant concluded that the CBC debate was an accurate depiction of Canadian opinion. "Program reflects continued growth Canadian nuclear weapons controversy," he wrote, "[but it] supports Embassy's opinion anti-nuclear sentiment in Canada much less than petitions and pickets lead some government leaders to believe."[17] For this reason, by the time Kennedy wrote to Diefenbaker in early August 1961, he could be confident that there was no logical reason for the prime minister to worry about public support for nuclear stockpiles in Canada. There was bound to be some opposition, but it was not broadly based and was certainly not likely to undermine the prime minister's political support. Widespread or not, American officials overlooked the possibility that vocal protest, no matter how small, might still lead Diefenbaker to fear political repercussions.

Nevertheless, Diefenbaker responded to Kennedy's initiative on 11 August pledging to lead a working group that included Green and Harkness to "consider whatever decisions may have to be taken in order to initiate these discussions with your representatives."[18] With that letter, nuclear negotiations were resumed. A few days later, in a speech to the Canadian Weekly Newspapers Association in Halifax, Diefenbaker took a stab at openly promoting Canada's acquisition of nuclear weapons and the resumption of negotiations with the Americans. "There are some in Canada who

advocate we should withdraw from NATO in the event that nuclear
weapons are made available for the possession and control of
NATO," he began. "I believe that to follow that course would be
dangerous to the survival of the forces of NATO that are there now,
should war begin. And it would be dangerous for the survival of
freedom itself. Would you in 1961," he asked the crowd, "faced by
the overwhelming power of Soviet might in East Germany close to
West Berlin with large divisions fully armed, would you place in the
hands of those who guard the portals of freedom nothing but bows
and arrows?"[19]

Alas, no one seemed to notice the prime minister's rallying cry.
Diefenbaker was disappointed by the media's decidedly weak
response to his speech; he had hoped Canadian journalists would
begin to debate the merits of a nuclear defence for Canada. "In ret-
rospect," Robinson later wrote, "I am reasonably certain that ... the
Halifax speech ... was intended to be the first real public step in ful-
filling his promise to Kennedy that he would try to move Canadian
public opinion towards acceptance of nuclear weapons."[20] But try
as he might, Diefenbaker did not seem to be able to get his message
across to Canadians. He had promised Kennedy that he would
work to "educate" anti-nuclear activists about the importance of
nuclear weapons for Canada's defence. However, far from launching a national campaign to educate Canadians, the speech in Halifax seems to have been Diefenbaker's only attempt to influence
opinion on this subject. It is unclear whether this was because he
was frustrated by the media's lack of interest in the issue or because
he simply lacked the will to offer more than a token effort to
explain why Canada needed its own nuclear weapons. What is
apparent is that he did not consider that the lack of response to his
speech might have been an indication that in the summer of 1961
Canadians generally supported the acquisition of nuclear weapons.

As the working group began to meet, it quickly ran into difficulties. While Bryce believed that Green was coming round to the inevitability of nuclear weapons for Canadian forces,[21] Harkness took a
far more cynical view. He believed that Green was actually trying to
sabotage the talks with the Americans.[22] Whatever the reason,
Green impeded negotiations by assisting in the decision-making
process no more than was necessary.

As political tensions grew in Europe, the Americans and NATO
command increased their pressure on the Diefenbaker government

to make a decision about whether Canadian forces in NATO would arm their Honest John missiles (the rockets held by the army in Europe) with nuclear warheads. Within this context, Green submitted a draft proposal to cabinet in late August. The memo and draft proposal on stockpiles reflected Green's general disdain for the acquisition of warheads. Echoing the government's earlier emphasis on consultation, he agreed that the Canadian government approve use of the warheads but proposed a new cumbersome security arrangement that involved a double perimeter around the stockpiles. American personnel would be responsible for guarding the inner circle, while Canadians would control the outer ring. The proposal also took consultation to an extreme, recommending that Canadian officials be required to give their permission to move the weapons anywhere for any reason.[23]

Proposed side agreements complicated matters further. Ordinarily, American officials negotiated agreements with theatre commanders and national military representatives, but Green pronounced such an arrangement unacceptable. Any agreement had to involve government-to-government talks only. In no circumstances was he willing to accept the delegation of authority to NORAD commanders or Canadian military representatives.[24] In truth, though Green's suggestions were complicated, they were a natural extension of his earlier focus on civilian control and government consultation.

The overarching difficulty with Green's plan was that it required three-tiered negotiations. The first would involve a general agreement between Canada and the United States to govern the provision of nuclear weapons by the Americans. The second would entail a set of more specific supplementary technical agreements involving the different weapons systems, such as the Bomarc and the Honest John, each set of agreements being subject to ministerial approval. Only after these two sets of agreements were concluded would the entire package be presented to cabinet for its approval, "at which time the government would be in a position *to determine what action it wished to take.*"[25]

In essence, Green was willing to enter negotiations with the Americans, but no more than that. As he told his cabinet colleagues, "The decision of the Canadian government to enter negotiations should not be interpreted to mean that Canada had decided to acquire nuclear warheads but rather that it wished to place itself in a position to do so rapidly if at any time in the future such action should be deemed necessary."[26] The implication was clear. The minister of external affairs was willing to allow an agreement for nuclear weapons that covered the terms of acquisition, but he still refused to concede the underpinning necessity of those weapons. No wonder Harkness found Green to be obstinate.

The cabinet discussed draft agreements at a number of meetings in late August and early September. Throughout, Diefenbaker's overriding concern was the need to keep secret the renewed nuclear talks. "If negotiations were started with the US," he cautioned cabinet, "the fact that they were taking place would almost certainly become known and would be interpreted as meaning that Canada had taken a decision in principle to obtain stockpiles of nuclear warheads for the Canadian forces. It was important that the remaining draft Schedules should be prepared for cabinet consideration without delay and that the negotiations should begin."[27] Meanwhile, Diefenbaker remained committed to acquiring nuclear warheads and told cabinet that he was willing to meet with Kennedy personally to conclude an agreement if that was what was necessary.[28]

If Diefenbaker was convinced that his government ought to acquire nuclear weapons from the Americans, what explains his caution in handling the negotiations? He does not appear to have been worried that the public would realize his government was close to accepting nuclear warheads per se. Rather, what he seems to have feared was the possibility that anti-nuclear activists would come out of the woodwork and stir up controversy for the government just as the Conservatives began to prepare for what was bound to be a difficult election campaign.

As members of cabinet debated the merits of negotiations with the Americans in late August, a number of issues were raised. Some ministers focused on Canada's relative importance in world affairs and the international situation more generally. Others were more specific, stressing the pressing need for nuclear weapons. After all, the Bomarc was scheduled to arrive in North Bay at the end of October, and there were no conventional warheads that could be used with the system. Appealing to Diefenbaker's concerns about public opinion, several ministers reminded him that polls indicated Canadians generally supported the acquisition of nuclear weapons.[29]

The debate dragged on and on, going around in circles at meeting after meeting. Then, on 31 August the Soviets dealt a setback to

Green and other disarmament advocates when they announced their intention to resume nuclear testing.[30] The announcement made the possibility of a disarmament agreement more remote than ever, and even Green now conceded that nuclear weapons would be the government's only option if the disarmament talks broke down irrevocably. As summer turned to autumn, nuclear policy was a priority for the government for other reasons too. A parliamentary debate on defence estimates was scheduled for mid-September, and as Diefenbaker prepared for the debate he became increasingly unsure whether he could maintain the support of his cabinet ministers and the Conservative Party caucus. This led him to survey members of both groups on whether Canada ought to acquire nuclear weapons from the Americans.[31] He fretted that although Canadians supported acquisition, the tide might turn, particularly when the Americans responded in kind to the Soviet resumption of nuclear testing.

In Parliament, the defence debate went about as well as could be expected. The government emerged, as one observer commented, "bloody but unbowed."[32] More importantly, at least from Diefenbaker's perspective, he managed to avoid a contentious exchange on nuclear policy. However, it turned out that the debate in Parliament was only the beginning of a renewed public interest in Canada's nuclear policy. Some newspapers began to speculate that the government's policy was about to change. Others demanded that the government clarify its position. What they shared was their criticism of the government's behaviour. To Diefenbaker's chagrin, the newspaper commentaries were nothing at all like the campaign to educate the Canadian public that he had envisioned when talking to Kennedy about nuclear policy in the spring.

Now, in mid-September, the members of cabinet agreed that something had to be done to stem the tide of criticism, and they proposed that Harkness – not the prime minister – should clarify the government's nuclear policy. Harkness agreed, promising to speak out about Canada's acquisition of nuclear warheads, adhering to the template set by Diefenbaker in February 1959 and reiterated in January 1960.[33] All signs, then, pointed to the Canadian government concluding an agreement with the Americans, and despite the government's growing public reticence, US officials continued to believe that Diefenbaker intended to accept nuclear weapons for Canada, and in the near future at that.[34]

However, several events in late September and early October made a significant impression on Diefenbaker, exacerbating his fears about political support. Canadian officials seemed to be in the last stages of the negotiations with the Americans, and External Affairs was working on a final draft agreement[35] when Harold Morrison of Canadian Press wrote an article reporting the state of nuclear negotiations with amazing accuracy. "JFK Presses Canada on Nuclear Warheads," screamed the headline of the Montreal *Gazette* on the morning of 20 September. Morrison's source was an article, set to appear in the 25 September edition of *Newsweek* magazine, speculating that Kennedy had taken the lead in promoting the current round of nuclear talks between Canada and the United States.

The White House, rather than declining to comment on the rumour, confirmed that talks were going on at the highest levels between the two governments, at Kennedy's instigation.[36] Given Diefenbaker's fears that Canadians would criticize the government for any hint of weakness in the face of American pressure, this article made a huge impression on him. That headline, with its emphasis on US pressure, made it virtually impossible for him to accept nuclear weapons without appearing to bow to American pressure. Diefenbaker had warned Kennedy that he would suspend talks in the event of a leak to the media. The question was whether the president could take the prime minister at his word.

Diefenbaker quickly went on the defensive. When asked in the House of Commons about the newspaper article, he responded that there was no agreement for nuclear weapons between Canada and the United States. He did not, however, deny the existence of negotiations. "Speculation which has been going on in the last few weeks" he claimed with great irritation, "is based on nothing more than the views of those who, desiring one final stand to be taken, are not taking into full regard the international situation nor in the event that it should worsen, the welfare, the future and the safety of Canadians." Yet there was to be no opportunity for Parliament to debate the merits of any agreement in advance. Diefenbaker was willing to concede that "in any stand it takes the government must ask for the support of the House," but that did not mean "that the decision would first be tentatively placed before the House. That would be a denial of responsible government."[37] Apparently, his earlier concerns about whether to consult with the leader of the opposition had evaporated.

After Diefenbaker addressed Parliament, he appeared on "The Nation's Business," a CBC political affairs program. Once again, he emphasized the current state of international affairs. "The world situation has deteriorated rapidly during the recent months," he stated ominously. Pointing out that Canadian officials had taken a leading role in disarmament and test ban talks, Diefenbaker addressed the recent speculation reported in the press: "There will always be rumours and predictions as to what the government intends to do in its defence and other policies. Sometimes for political purposes they are started. Be not alarmed by such rumours. I can say this to you, that as always I shall be frank with you and give you the facts. There will always be criticism. When any course is decided upon in defence or other areas of international or national problems, I will take you, the Canadian people, into the confidence of the government."[38] Focusing as he did on the absence of a formal agreement, not the existence of negotiations (which he never denied explicitly), his message seemed clear.

It was equally clear from Diefenbaker's reaction that he was furious about the leak, and it did not take long for American officials to realize their error. The *Newsweek* piece had undermined all the progress they had made in the negotiations in recent weeks. Far from encouraging the Canadians to conclude an agreement with the Americans, the article had increased their caution. Now US officials feared that only an explicit Soviet threat to the West would allow the Canadians to accept nuclear weapons without appearing to succumb to American pressure. Their earlier optimism about reaching an agreement began to wane.[39] And then it got worse.

In Kennedy's debut speech before the United Nations General Assembly on 25 September, he emphasized a "new" American disarmament policy, one that focused on non-proliferation.[40] Green, for one, was delighted. Having argued all along that arming Canada's military with nuclear weapons would constitute nuclear proliferation, he took Kennedy's statement to mean the same. Nuclear talks were now done as far as the minister of external affairs was concerned. In the House of Commons, replying to a question about proliferation from Liberal MP Lionel Chevrier, Diefenbaker reiterated the government's support for disarmament but failed to

respond to the apparent contradiction between containing the
nuclear club and accepting nuclear weapons from the United States,
even if under joint control.[41] Of course, Kennedy's speech had been
directed not at Canada but at the Soviet Union, in an effort to keep
East and West Germany nuclear free and encourage Khrushchev to
begin a dialogue on disarmament. But it gave Green yet another
opportunity to call for an end to the nuclear negotiations between
the United States and Canada.[42]

And then there was the peace movement. By September 1961,
after a summer spent on mobilization and organization, the Voice
of Women was eager to proceed with its efforts to prevent the proliferation of nuclear weapons. The poor attendance at the parliamentary debate on defence estimates (which only 90 of 264 MPs
attended), along with weak press coverage, inspired the vow's
leaders to mobilize for action. In a special newsletter to members,
Helen Tucker urged them to undertake individual campaigns to
increase awareness of the coming nuclear crisis. Tucker stressed the
importance of public opinion, since many MPs knew so little about
any given subject, especially nuclear weapons. At the same time, she
encouraged members to support MPs who opposed acquisition. In
this way, disarmament activists would reinforce positive behaviour
under the auspices of representing the views of ordinary Canadians.
There was no better way to demonstrate their opposition to nuclear
weapons than to undertake a letter-writing campaign, Tucker told
members. In such a campaign, quantity, not quality, mattered most
when it came to influencing politicians. "Every party at its monthly
caucus," she remarked, "counts the letters it receives and makes an
analysis of public opinion."[43]

More formally, the vow's executive arranged a series of meetings
with each of the party leaders to discuss the future of Canada's
nuclear policy.[44] They met with Diefenbaker on 25 September, the
same day as Kennedy's speech to the United Nations and a few days
after the rumoured nuclear negotiations were reported in Newsweek. The meeting proved to be anticlimactic for everyone
involved. Diefenbaker responded to the vow's brief by listing his
government's efforts to secure a disarmament agreement. In particular, he stressed everything Canada had done to support a nuclear
test ban, assuring the women that his government had been working diligently in this area. Yet Diefenbaker said nothing that put

them at ease about the prospect of Canada acquiring nuclear weapons or their more general concerns about nuclear proliferation. Diefenbaker's impression of the meeting was lukewarm in large part because he no longer viewed the VOW as a credible political threat. A Soviet group was now using the VOW name (about which he informed the women, to their great dismay), and the group had been investigated for communist infiltration.[45] Although Diefenbaker was moderately interested in the women's proposed "World Peace Year," forwarding the idea to the Department of External Affairs for comment,[46] there is little evidence to indicate that he took their other suggestions seriously, though he did keep a copy of the women's brief (alongside the rest of the material sent by the VOW over the years). The brief was long on rhetoric, short on new information, and Diefenbaker's preoccupation was whether the acquisition of nuclear weapons would undermine his political support, not whether there was an ethical or technological reason to eschew the weapons. For this reason, a brief submitted by a small group of women did not persuade him that there would be dire political consequences in response to a nuclear agreement with the Americans.

Diefenbaker's next encounter with the anti-nuclear movement came on 6 October when activists staged a number of events. First, CUCND organized a 73-hour protest on Parliament Hill, with between 500 and 800 demonstrators in attendance. More importantly, the CCCRH delivered a massive petition to the government. The number of signatures on the petition is unclear, but estimates range from 140,000 to 180,000.[47] It marked the culmination of months of activity by approximately thirty local organizations, each affiliated with the National Committee in one capacity or another.[48] Planning had begun in the spring of 1961, when the executive of the CCCRH mobilized to respond to what they believed was the government's imminent acquisition of nuclear weapons.

The campaign came on the heels of some major changes within the organization which had transformed the group into a more radical grassroots movement – the very opposite of what Van Stolk had originally intended. In March, the organization's head office had formally moved from Edmonton to Toronto as F.C. Hunnius replaced Van Stolk as executive secretary of the National Committee. An excellent organizer, Hunnius now served as a bridge between the CCCRH and the CUCND. His appointment signalled a

new willingness to embrace the more radical elements of the disarmament movement, and even though Van Stolk became vice-chair
of the organization, her influence began to wane.

In July Dr James S. Thomson replaced H.L. Keenleyside as chairman of the National Committee.[49] Thomson had impressive credentials, but Keenleyside had been better placed to deal personally
with government officials.[50] Moreover, Thomson was less interested in the day-to-day running of the organization, leaving much
of those details to Hunnius and the executive committee.[51] To be
fair, even though Keenleyside had a better relationship with government officials than his successor, there is little evidence that it translated into substantive political influence. His relationship with
Green was solid, but he never developed the necessary rapport with
Diefenbaker to influence nuclear policy.[52]

Personal appeals had proved futile in the past for the CCCRH, but
its leaders now decided to try to influence Diefenbaker by appealing
to his greatest concern – political support. The National Petition
was born from this idea, and was a collaborative effort with CUCND
and VOW. Although there was never an explicit reference to political
consequences in the petition[53] (there was not, for example, a threat
that the signatories would work to defeat the government in the
next election),[54] – the result was implied by the very fact that this
was a mass petition opposing nuclear stockpiles in Canada.

The original deadline for the petition was 15 June, but the organizers decided to extend the campaign over the summer to gather
more signatures after the minister of defence had implied that there
was still time to make a difference.[55] Harkness had stated publicly
that the government still had time to make a decision about nuclear
warheads because NATO had yet to resolve the issue, and the government might have to wait until these talks were concluded. In
addition, the Bomarc bases in North Bay and La Macaza, originally
expected to open in the autumn of 1961, were running behind
schedule and were not expected to be operational before 1962. This
delay provided the anti-nuclear movement with a window of
opportunity that could be used to full advantage.[56]

To lend credibility to their current campaign, the organizers
included the names of forty-five high-profile supporters alongside
the many signatures of ordinary Canadians on their petition. But
fewer than half of these high-profile Canadians had originally been
supporters of the National Committee (namely, Brock Chisholm,

Pierre Dansereau, Dr H.C. Dion, H.A. Dyde, Jean Louis Gagnon, Saul Hayes, J. Gordin Kaplan, Yousuf Karsh, H.L. Keenleyside, Walter C. Koerner, André Laurendeau, J.H. MacDonald, Hugh MacLennan, Robert Nielsen, Ivan Rand, W.C. Smalley, Mary Van Stolk, James S. Thomson, J.T. Thorson, and Dr J. Weijer).[57] To make up for this shortfall, the organizers sought new honorary sponsors, securing the support of Helen Tucker from vow, Dimitri Roussopoulos from CUCND, Rabbi Abraham Feinberg from the Toronto CND, and Pierre Trudeau, then a law professor and journalist in Quebec. Certainly, the first three names would have attracted attention from those in the anti-nuclear movement, but all would be seen as problematic by politicians because of their communist sympathies, and none was the sort of person who would bring the credibility to the movement that Van Stolk had worked so hard to create.

The list of prominent supporters was intended to encourage people to sign the petition, as well as to give it credibility.[58] Volunteers were advised to seek signatures in every conceivable location – in shopping centres, on street corners, at church gatherings and union meetings – and to emphasize the prominent Canadians who had lent their support to the petition.

Seeking a large number of signatures was a marked change of approach. It was necessary because of declining elite support, which was illustrated by some notable absences from the list of honorary sponsors, namely, John Bassett, Eugene Forsey, Claude Bissell, Henry Borden, and Oakley Dalgleish. These omissions have two possible explanations. First, the petition may have suffered from the same general organizational difficulties encountered by the CCCRH. Given the original time and trouble that Van Stolk had taken to secure the support of honorary members, one would have expected that every effort would have been made to keep them involved in the activities of the CCCRH. But this did not occur after the original flourish of activity. Although Van Stolk had realized the importance of credible signatories to assist in the launch of her organization, she had failed to recognize that they had to be kept involved in the movement. The other possible explanation is that many of the original sponsors did not support the organization's change of focus. The CCCRH's original mandate had been to promote awareness of the hazards associated with radioactive fallout; it was not to oppose nuclear weapons. Although one may seem a logical extension of the other, it was possible to oppose nuclear testing but not the acquisition of nuclear weapons. In some instances, this may have made the difference between support in 1959 and 1961.

Ultimately, the honorary supporters of the 1961 National Petition were a less notable group of Canadians than those assembled to launch the National Committee in early 1960. But this mattered little, for the petition attracted a great deal of attention, including an article in *Maclean's* magazine that praised the efforts and personalities of the disarmament movement in Canada.[59] What mattered most about the petition was its ability to influence political leaders. It certainly got Diefenbaker's attention. By all accounts, it was a credible appeal. Cabinet discussed Diefenbaker's meeting with Dr Thomson and representatives of the CCCRH the same day the petition was presented. It was the only time that cabinet really discussed a meeting with anti-nuclear activists, but the ministers' overarching concern was whether there were any communist influences within the organization. According to Minister of Justice Davie Fulton, to whom the RCMP reported communist activities in the anti-nuclear movement, the CCCRH was not one of the groups identified as cause for concern; there was, Fulton noted, no reason to believe that the CCCRH was a communist front.[60]

After meeting with the prime minister to present the petition, the activists triumphantly told reporters that they had a promise that Canada would not accept nuclear weapons unless there was a war. This, however, was not what Diefenbaker recalled about the meeting when he talked about it with his advisers. He reassured them that he had made no such promise. Rather, he had told the activists that he supported Kennedy's statement to the United Nations and agreed that there should be no expansion of the nuclear club. When asked about the implications of this policy in terms of the Bomarc missiles, which were just arriving at North Bay, he was firm in his response that the missiles were ready for use if ever it became necessary. Asked again whether this meant the missiles would be fitted with nuclear warheads, Diefenbaker declined to comment. He referred only to his earlier statements, which did little to clarify the matter.[61]

Robinson, for one, worried about the implications of Diefenbaker's replies to the activists. When he spoke to the prime minister about the meeting, he raised the possibility that Diefenbaker had not actually meant what he said about proliferation. But Diefenbaker was adamant that Kennedy's statement entailed a change in American policy. "The public position now taken by the president," he complained to Robinson, had "killed nuclear weapons in Canada." As Robinson later recalled, Diefenbaker "said that more and more it was becoming clear that we would not be having nuclear weapons in Canada unless there was war."[62]

Diefenbaker's conclusions both horrified and confused Robinson, who pointed out that the US disarmament plan included a provision whereby the Americans could supply nuclear weapons to other countries as long as ownership remained with the United States. Moreover, joint control – what the Canadians had been seeking in their negotiations with the Americans – would still conform to Kennedy's proposal. Perhaps more importantly, there was nothing really new about Kennedy's statement to the United Nations; much of what he told the General Assembly in New York echoed what he had told Diefenbaker at their meeting in May.[63] Robinson tried to appeal to the prime minister's logic. He told Diefenbaker there was simply no way that Canada's acquisition of nuclear weapons from the United States could constitute nuclear proliferation because there could be no proliferation unless the Americans relinquished ownership of the warheads, something that had never been part of the negotiations between the two countries.

Robinson had every reason to believe his argument would be persuasive. Diefenbaker had made the very same argument to cabinet only weeks earlier. But now, in October, Diefenbaker rejected the position as unacceptable semantics, extending the argument to include NATO: if Canadian forces had national control of the warheads, this would constitute proliferation even if the Americans continued to maintain ownership of them. However, nuclear warheads within NATO, Diefenbaker continued confusingly, would constitute proliferation only if each of the individual members of the alliance had national control of the stockpiles stored on its territory; there would be no proliferation if NATO as a whole were responsible for control of the warheads. [64] The final point sounded suspiciously like Pearson's stand on nuclear weapons, which Diefenbaker had criticized as a diminution of Canadian sovereignty.

Thus, by the middle of October the only clarity in Canada's nuclear policy was the prime minister's new-found determination to suspend nuclear negotiations with the Americans for the foreseeable future. The decision was not a fleeting change of heart, and it was confirmed in a conversation he had with Bryce.[65] With a federal election looming, Diefenbaker did not believe he could risk his

political future on such a controversial subject. Kennedy's actions –
first confirming the story in *Newsweek* and then his statement to
the United Nations – marked the beginning of the end of the most
promising nuclear negotiations between Canada and the United
States. There were two not entirely compatible reasons for
Diefenbaker's decision. On the one hand, he feared that in view of
the *Newsweek* story, acquiring nuclear weapons would make it
appear that he had succumbed to American pressure. On the other,
he feared that Kennedy's statement at the United Nations might
strike a chord with Canadians and encourage opposition to the government's acquisition of nuclear weapons. It was the latter that
caused Diefenbaker the greatest anxiety.

The National Petition, with well over a hundred thousand signatures in opposition to nuclear warheads, reinforced Diefenbaker's
intuition that public support for nuclear weapons was unpredictable, and it sealed the fate of the talks. The petition was tangible
proof – much more so than the brief delivered by the vow or
CUCND's demonstration on Parliament Hill – that there would be
electoral consequences for concluding a nuclear agreement with
Kennedy. This alone was sufficient to persuade Diefenbaker to suspend negotiations with the Americans until after the next election.[66]
Now, nothing could alter his conviction that the acquisition of
nuclear weapons was a politically dangerous issue. He had assurances from Boeing that it could manufacture conventional warheads for the Bomarc, so nuclear weapons were no longer necessary
to make the Bomarc system fully functional.[67] In addition, the eas-
ing of tensions over Berlin and general improvement of the international situation by the end of 1961 removed the broader impetus
for Canada's acquisition of nuclear weapons.

While Diefenbaker decided to abandon the issue until after the federal election, Harkness was not willing to forget about nuclear weapons as Bomarc missiles arrived at North Bay and La Macaza and as
the Canadian army received its Honest John missiles in Europe.[68]
Harkness continued to promote nuclear weapons in cabinet, focusing almost exclusively on the state of public opinion in his attempt to
persuade Diefenbaker to renew talks with the Americans. Gallup
polls, Harkness argued shrewdly, revealed that 61 percent of Canadians now supported nuclear weapons for Canadian forces, with only
31 percent opposed and only 8 percent undecided.[69]

The poll indicated clearly that Canadians were becoming more certain in their views on the subject. The number of "undecided" had dropped considerably in the past six months, just as those in favour had risen to a clear majority, even though the number of Canadians opposed had also increased. Yet the numbers were encouraging, particularly in the light of Diefenbaker's preoccupation with political support. What Harkness failed to appreciate was that Diefenbaker had a new concern as a result of the *Newsweek* article – that the acquisition of nuclear weapons might be construed as subservience to American pressures.[70]

Harkness was relentless and continued privately to insist that the prime minister ought to renew negotiations with the Americans.[71] In public, he was more circumspect. When he spoke to the Air Industries and Transport Association in November, he commented, "We must face the fact that we lie between the world's two greatest protagonists, and, if war comes, we will be in the middle of it whether we are neutralists, isolationists or active supporters of the West; and whether we are unarmed or are armed with conventional or nuclear weapons." He ended his address on a less ambiguous note: "The government is doing its utmost in the United Nations and other councils to find the key to arms control with security. Until our statesmen and those of other nations can find the key, we can best serve the cause of democratic nations by assuming our share of the responsibility for preserving the peace."[72] When asked about the fate of the Bomarc, Harkness replied simply that there was not yet the need for a decision because the bases in North Bay and La Macaza were not operational.[73]

In Washington, officials were surprised by what they viewed as a change in Canada's nuclear policy. Kennedy, for one, was completely taken aback. Officials at the US Embassy in Ottawa were worried that the president's address to the United Nations might alter Canadian public opinion, so much so that they encouraged the administration to clarify what was meant by the "nuclear club." Someone had to make it clear that the "nuclear club" referred only to nations with *independent* control of nuclear weapons. Such a definition clearly excluded Canada, which could not have independent control of the warheads acquired from the United States. However, the embassy officials were pragmatic. They understood that Diefenbaker needed time to let passions cool, and they advised

Kennedy to give him that time before returning to the issue of nuclear stockpiles.[74]

Notwithstanding this new sensitivity to public opinion, some senior officials in the US Embassy remained hopeful that Harkness could influence Diefenbaker to make nuclear weapons a priority.[75] When there was still no movement on nuclear negotiations by November, the president intervened. Perturbed that the matter had not yet been settled, he turned to Ambassador Merchant for assistance. Merchant confessed that he, too, was at a loss to explain Diefenbaker's position. Yet he cautioned Kennedy not to expect a settlement any time soon, certainly not before the next election.[76]

The Ambassador's discussion with Norman Robertson confirmed his assessment of the situation. Robertson claimed to be unaware of the status of nuclear talks between the two countries.[77] Major General C.V. Clifton, the president's military aide, also tried to find out why Diefenbaker was behaving in such an unreasonable manner. When Clifton spoke with Heeney's military attaché, Colonel H.W. Sterne, at a party, he remarked that relations with the prime minister had been good, and he was now puzzled by the state of affairs. The visit to Ottawa had gone well, and he could not understand the lack of contact between the two governments. Kennedy knew that something was wrong but had no idea what it could be.

Heeney, who knew nothing about the Rostow Memo, suspected that the report in *Newsweek* was the source of the problem. He had attended the meetings when Kennedy was in Ottawa and understood the premium Diefenbaker placed on secrecy. Heeney speculated in a letter to Diefenbaker that Clifton's queries were likely Kennedy's way of apologizing for the administration's confirmation of the leak. "I suppose," he wrote, "that Mr. Kennedy was taking this roundabout way to reassure you of his desire for the continuance of a personal relationship to which I feel sure he does attach a great importance."[78]

Heeney's words did little to comfort Diefenbaker's bruised ego. The Rostow Memo was problematic, but by itself had not stalled the nuclear negotiations. It was only when it was combined with the leak to *Newsweek* that Diefenbaker's faith in Kennedy was undermined: the memo had hurt Diefenbaker's pride, but the leak contravened his explicit request for secrecy. There is no question that Diefenbaker was overly sensitive, but it was a sensitivity compounded by Kennedy's disregard for the Canadian leader's political priorities.

Aside from Liberal sniping and anti-nuclear protests, it was easy for the government to defer all nuclear matters for the time being. Negotiations in NATO were going nowhere, and as 1961 ended, the alliance seemed no closer to acquiring nuclear weapons than Canada was. At its meeting in early December, NATO was preoccupied with other matters. Members of the alliance worried about Khrushchev and his involvement in Berlin. The Berlin Wall, erected in August 1961, had seemed to stabilize the situation, but the North Atlantic alliance was divided over what policy to pursue. Apart from France, the member countries wanted to maintain NATO's military strength while promoting negotiations with the Soviets whenever possible. The French position was that NATO should not negotiate with Khrushchev as long as the Soviet Union was a threat to the West. When Green presented the NATO situation to cabinet, his concluding comments about Canada's role in the alliance that it had helped found were not encouraging. "Canada," he remarked, now amounted "to very little in the NATO picture."[79]

By early 1962, the nuclear issue had not captured the attention of the Canadian people as a whole, though the polls indicated that most felt positively about the possibility of acquiring nuclear weapons from the Americans.[80] Still, Diefenbaker had to reconsider his government's nuclear policy before he could turn his attention to an election. In response to the opposition's accusations of indecisiveness, he decided to portray his nuclear policy as flexible, adaptable to changing needs and circumstances.[81] With this direction in mind, he asked the Department of External Affairs to investigate how other nations balanced technological innovation and defence priorities. Ignoring the request, department officials argued that the evolving strategic doctrine within the Western alliance made it impossible for Canada to move forward with its own defence policy.[82] Such a response did little to help the prime minister with his electoral strategy.

In late January, as part of his attempt to clarify his government's nuclear policy, Diefenbaker addressed Parliament. Once again he reiterated his statement of February 1959: "We made our enunciation of policy as far back as 1959 clearly, definitely and absolutely. Since that time we have continued in that policy, and when the debate takes place on international affairs we shall deal with this matter and point out at the same time the tremendous cleavage and schism which exists on this subject within the ranks of the opposition despite the fact that in this regard the advertising represents the Liberals as having the answer."[83]

The Liberal Party challenged Diefenbaker's statement, with Paul Martin accusing the government of concluding a secret agreement with Kennedy during his visit in May. Again, Diefenbaker pondered publicly whether the Americans had leaked confidential information, this time to the Liberals. In view of previous indiscretions, Diefenbaker's concern was not unreasonable. Merchant called Diefenbaker and promised him that the Americans were not to blame. During the conversation, Diefenbaker acknowledged that the most likely source of the leak was the civil service, not the Americans.[84] His assessment was correct; Pearson had learned of the exchange between Diefenbaker and Kennedy through Douglas Le Pan, a former assistant undersecretary with External Affairs. It was Pearson who had passed on the information to Martin.[85]

Of course, there was no "secret agreement" for the use of American warheads in an emergency. However, by late 1961 and early 1962 Diefenbaker began to acknowledge that Canadian systems would be armed with nuclear warheads in the event of an emergency, notwithstanding his public support for a disarmament agreement.[86] There was but one difficulty with Diefenbaker's pledge to act in a crisis. There was no formal arrangement between Canada and the United States to transform this promise from theory into practice. Nor was there an impending agreement or even the possibility that talks would resume before the next election.

In truth, Diefenbaker seemed to revel in attributing his nuclear woes to the Americans, blaming them for refusing to allow joint control and thus scuttling any possibility of a nuclear agreement between the two countries.[87] This approach was not only unfair but was inaccurate. Eisenhower may have been reluctant to permit joint control, but Kennedy was only too willing to allow such an arrangement. In fact, the Kennedy administration had always been willing to conclude an agreement based on joint control, and Diefenbaker knew it. But he hoped that by holding the Americans accountable for his own nuclear shortcomings, he would reap benefits at the ballot box.

On 18 April Diefenbaker dissolved Parliament, setting the election date for 18 June. From then on, nuclear negotiations took a back seat to electioneering, though Canadian-American relations moved to the forefront of the issues Diefenbaker had to deal with in the midst of the campaign. Kennedy's efforts to improve his relationship with Diefenbaker had been fruitless, and the prime minister's resentment toward the president grew throughout the spring of 1962. Several incidents contributed to this feeling, which was exacerbated by his declining political fortunes.[88]

In early April, Kennedy had invited American Nobel Prize winners to a reception at the White House, an invitation that was extended to all Nobel Prize recipients in the Western Hemisphere. This meant that Pearson attended a White House dinner during the election campaign, which sent Diefenbaker into a rage. He worried that the Liberal leader would use the dinner to his advantage politically,[89] and he believed the invitation was a clear indication that the Americans were interfering in the Canadian election. Why else, he wondered, would the president invite Pearson to dine at the White House if not to indicate that his preference was for the Liberals to win the spring election? Canadians adored Kennedy, and Diefenbaker feared that the president's "endorsement" of Pearson would add to the Liberal's growing lead in opinion polls.

Nothing could be further from the truth. There is no question that Kennedy's personal preference was for Pearson, but the Liberal Party's nuclear policy was no more appealing to American officials than Diefenbaker's was.[90] As far as the Americans were concerned, Diefenbaker was unlikely to be defeated in the June elections, and they fully expected he would resume negotiations after the election. Yet the fact that the lengthy dinner conversation between Kennedy and Pearson was reported in the Canadian press infuriated the prime minister, reducing even further the chances that he would be willing to renew negotiations if he won the election.[91]

Ambassador Merchant learned first hand about Diefenbaker's irritation with Kennedy when Merchant met with the prime minister in May 1962. The meeting was supposed to last a brief fifteen minutes, but Diefenbaker ranted and raved about the president in "what can be only described as a tirade" for almost two hours.[92] Robinson had warned Merchant, who was leaving his post in Ottawa to return to Washington permanently, that the prime minister was furious about Kennedy's conversation with the Liberal leader, harping on the "political capital" of such a discussion. Merchant was left to explain to Diefenbaker that there was nothing sinister about the invitation to Pearson. There was certainly nothing untoward about the president discussing foreign policy with a man such as the Liberal leader who was so obviously distinguished in that field.

The departing American ambassador could not mollify Diefenbaker, who accused the president of meddling in the election and threatened to make Canadian-American relations into a campaign issue. To prove he was serious, Diefenbaker did the unthinkable. He threatened to reveal the existence and contents of the Rostow Memo. That revelation, he warned, would show the Canadian people that only he would protect Canada from American domination. Merchant was shocked; it was the first he had heard of the mysterious memo, and the prime minister's behaviour greatly disturbed him. Charitably, he attributed much of the outburst to campaign fatigue.[93] Yet the reference to the lost memo caused Merchant great anxiety. He thought the document sounded like an unofficial memo advising the president on foreign affairs, and said so. He also warned that revelations about the memo would have negative consequences for the prime minister only. People would wonder how he had come to possess a confidential document and why it had not been returned to the US government.[94]

After the meeting, in spite of the prime minister's histrionics, Merchant felt he had convinced Diefenbaker not to use the memo in any capacity during the campaign. But he was not absolutely certain and advised the White House "that we take out any available insurance against the worst."[95] Discussions followed in Washington about how best to deal with the irate northern neighbour and his threat to embarrass the administration. Merchant suggested that the president contrive a reason to meet with Diefenbaker in some neutral location. That way, any public perception of American interference could be laid to rest. He cautioned the president about the importance of secrecy; there could be no leaks about the possibility of such a meeting. Although he hoped a face-to-face discussion between Kennedy and Diefenbaker would mend relations between the two leaders, Merchant was pragmatic enough to know there were no guarantees. "Needless to say," he concluded in a memo to George Ball, the US undersecretary of state, "I am distressed to bring this problem to your and the president's attention. Its implications are so serious, however, as, in my judgment, to require the president's consideration and prompt effort to forestall what could be a very damaging development in relations between Canada and the United States."[96]

McGeorge Bundy, Kennedy's national security adviser, quickly responded. He told the ambassador to speak to Diefenbaker personally and to make sure that he understood how unwise it would be to do anything that could be construed as a threat to the United States. Bundy advised Merchant to point out that the memo was a personal paper, not to be used for political purposes. He underscored that the Americans had their own set of records of the conversations between Diefenbaker and Kennedy, and there was not even a hint of pressure in those documents. Even the suggestion that the memo might be made public would have a negative impact on the administration's perceptions of Diefenbaker and his government.[97] The president was more understanding than his advisers were. He was willing to disregard Diefenbaker's temper tantrum, attributing it, as Merchant had done, to the typical strains of an election. Kennedy encouraged Merchant to "show real sympathy with Diefenbaker on this one point."[98]

Because Diefenbaker was busy campaigning, Merchant did not see him until a week later, on 12 May. He followed Bundy's advice, stressing that there would be incalculable harm done to Canadian-American relations if the prime minister tried to use the memo to inflame anti-American sentiment for political purposes. Diefenbaker was much calmer than he had been during their last encounter, and he reassured the ambassador that he had reconsidered his earlier comments and did not intend to use the memo.[99] Merchant was greatly relieved by this change of heart, concluding in a memorandum to Rusk, "Notwithstanding [the] fact [the] PM [is] nervous and in my judgment on verge of exhaustion, I believe storm has passed and that chances are now minimal that he will embark on all-out anti-American line using reference memo in process. At end of conversation we both lowered our voices and with complimentary close he bade me warm good night."[100] With that, the Rostow Memo was put to rest.

Personnel changes also did little to smooth the ruffled feathers between the two countries. In February, Diefenbaker had decided to replace Arnold Heeney with Charles Ritchie as Canada's ambassador to the United States. Ritchie, who was Canada's permanent representative to the United Nations in New York, took over the post in mid-May, right in the middle of the election campaign. However, Heeney had departed from Washington at the end of April, leaving a vacancy at an important time, especially as there was no American ambassador in Ottawa. He had been an able intermediary between the two governments, softening some of the sharper edges in many of Diefenbaker's statements.

When Ritchie arrived in Washington, although the president understood that the Conservative government was preoccupied with its election campaign, he nonetheless took the opportunity to press the new ambassador on several issues when he presented his diplomatic credentials. On Merchant's advice, Kennedy had spoken to Heeney about the possibility of a meeting between the two leaders after the election to talk about nuclear negotiations.[101] Not surprisingly, nuclear weapons remained at the top of the list of things to discuss with Ritchie in mid-May, even if the president and his officials were clearly impatient with Diefenbaker and his government on the subject.[102] Kennedy remained only too willing to allow joint control over the use of nuclear weapons. All that remained was for Diefenbaker to approve the agreement in cabinet.[103]

A change closer to home also had an impact on the prime minister. Robinson was anxious to move on to more interesting (not to mention less stressful and volatile) working conditions, and he accompanied Ritchie to Washington to become the new Canadian ambassador's second in command. Robinson was keenly aware of the deterioration in Canadian-American relations and wanted to help remedy the situation.[104] It was, however, a significant loss for Diefenbaker in Ottawa.

The Conservatives had their work cut out in the 1962 election, and the Liberals had every reason to be optimistic, given Diefenbaker's vulnerability. There was an economic downturn and high unemployment; and, of course, Canadians had reason to think the government had handled defence policy ineptly. The Liberals intended to emphasize the government's shortcomings in addition to their own strengths, counting on a new generation to return the party to power. Keith Davey, a thirty-five-year-old former radio executive, relied heavily on polling data and the Kennedy campaign for inspiration, using Theodore White's *The Making of the President, 1960* as a type of political handbook.[105] Walter Gordon, J.W. Pickersgill, Mitchell Sharp, Tom Kent, and Paul Hellyer joined Davey in running the Liberal campaign, which emphasized two things: the Liberal "team" and the "solutions" that the party offered to the various ills attributed to Diefenbaker. Polls indicated that Canadians still liked Diefenbaker, so the Liberal organizers advised candidates to avoid direct attacks on the prime minister or his government and instead focus on their own party's agenda.[106] The Conservative Party's campaign focused on Diefenbaker and his record.[107] As one campaign document boasted, "John Diefenbaker has brought to the Conservative Party *both* leadership *and* policy. Pearson brought neither to the Liberals."[108] Once again, Dalton Camp and Allister Grosart were the key organizers behind the government's campaign. The emphasis on Diefenbaker had reaped huge rewards for the party in 1958, and officials hoped to duplicate this success in 1962.[109]

The dynamics of the 1962 campaign were odd in that the Liberals campaigned as if they were still the government party, and the Conservatives, never comfortable with the trappings of power, campaigned as the perennial party of opposition, oblivious of their historic majority in Parliament. The Liberals were well organized, with campaign "colleges" for candidates and information on the finer points of running for election, which put the Conservative practices to shame. And they had a solid election platform, based on policies that had emerged from the National Rally of January 1961.[110]

By contrast, the Conservatives focused on how best to deliver their message to the Canadian people, with plenty of advice on advertising strategies as well as basic campaign and rally techniques. There were few policy documents and only a few select members of the party (brought in specifically to help run the election) who were responsible for developing campaign issues. Neither caucus nor the party at large determined the party's platform, a marked contrast to their Liberal opponents.[111] Yet for all the differences in organizational structure and approach, both parties focused on similar issues: the economy and unemployment. Defence and nuclear policy were not prominent issues.[112] If nuclear policy could have played any role in the 1962 election, it would have been for the Liberals to highlight the government's shortcomings in handling its defence policy. This was not their approach, however.

Only anti-nuclear activists sought to make nuclear policy a campaign issue. They understood that Diefenbaker was vulnerable politically and hoped to capitalize on his insecurities. They looked to the National Petition for inspiration in this regard, since it had aroused interest in the media, and they hoped to be able to build on that interest.[113] But the odds were against them for they suffered from a lack of organization, money, and time.[114]

For the good of the movement, disarmament groups such as the CCCRH (now reborn as the Canadian Campaign for Nuclear Disarmament (CCND), CUCND, and VOW agreed to work together.[115] In April the executive secretary of the National Committee, F.C. Hunnius, prepared an assessment of each party's nuclear policy. The NDP, Social Credit, and the Communist Party of Canada all earned high marks for their opposition to nuclear weapons for Canadian forces; the Conservative and Liberal parties offered considerably less hope to the anti-nuclear movement. Compounding this lack of mainstream political support was the growing realization that the press no longer seemed to be on side. The media may have been interested in the National Petition, but this attention did not translate into support for the movement's opposition to nuclear weapons. Indeed, most of the English Canadian press supported acquisition, not the position of the peace movement.[116]

The activists had tried to devise a multipurpose strategy, one that could be used in the period leading up to the election call as well as during the campaign itself. Their first goal had been to approach members of parliament, and some of the CCND's more prominent supporters vowed to meet personally with the various leaders.[117] Thomson wrote to several members of parliament requesting an interview.[118] The activists met with parliamentarians on 16 April, their meetings held in conjunction with a series of nation-wide peace demonstrations in honour of Easter. As well as being an exercise in public relations, this was a dress rehearsal for the election campaign, and delegates were well prepared for their meetings, peppering parliamentarians with a host of defence-related questions. The topics included the DEW line, multilateral disarmament, the test ban agreement, Canada's role in NORAD and NATO, and whether Canadian forces should have nuclear weapons.[119]

The activists believed their meetings were successful,[120] though there is no evidence that this was so. Diefenbaker could not spare time away from election preparations and sent Howard Green in his place. The delegates must have appreciated Green's support, but there was little value in preaching to the converted. For the same reason, it was no great loss when the delegation could not meet with NDP leader T.C. Douglas, who was already an ardent opponent of nuclear weapons and a reassuring figure for the movement.[121] The leaders of the Liberal and Social Credit parties also met with delegates, though they were not nearly as supportive on the matter as the New Democrats.[122]

Once the election was called, the movement turned its attentions to the candidates,[123] forgetting about raising public awareness at the grassroots level. The strategy was well intentioned but problematic, because the movement was too small to accomplish such an enormous endeavour. Communication with each candidate from each party in each riding required tremendous resources. Even in Ontario, where the movement had the greatest number of supporters and volunteers, the members could muster only a weak effort. Organizers quickly learned that it was one thing to coordinate a letter-writing campaign or petition drive, but it was quite another thing to raise a tertiary issue to the level of significance required to merit notice in a federal campaign where more pressing concerns predominated.

There was also not enough time; the election was called on 17 April, but organizational memoranda and candidate lists were not available to volunteers until the second week in May, leaving the movement some four weeks to contact approximately three hundred people.[124] The delay was not solely the fault of the disarmament groups, since both the NDP and Social Credit took their time in nominating candidates. Although it is understandable that organizers wanted to wait for complete lists before distributing them, they could have started their campaign with what they had; instead, they did nothing but wait.

Two examples in the Toronto area illustrate why the movement failed to make nuclear policy a campaign priority. As one organizer bemoaned, "We have already interviewed a few candidates (including Basset [sic]), and the ignorance on the part of the candidates has been appalling. We are afraid that detailed questions would result in candidates not replying at all."[125] The problem, of course, was that John Bassett, publisher of the *Telegram* and one of the original sponsors of the CCCRH's National Committee, was now running for the Progressive Conservatives in the Toronto riding of Spadina. If the CCND could not educate an original supporter, there was little hope it would be able to raise awareness among the general public. Bassett was precisely the kind of sponsor the CCND could have used in the 1962 election – a candidate for the governing party with access to the prime minister and editorial control of a major Toronto newspaper. The loss of his support underscored how much the movement suffered because of its inability to keep original high-profile supporters involved.

The second example involves the nearby riding of Eglinton, where Diefenbaker's minister of finance, Donald Fleming, had won the riding by more than eighteen thousand votes in the last election. Now, he was vulnerable. As the finance minister during an economic downturn, he was a crucial member of an unpopular government. This status within the government also meant that Fleming was away from the riding a good deal and thus unavailable to campaign there. More generally, Toronto was no longer the Conservative stronghold it had been in the last election.[126] When the Liberals nominated Mitchell Sharp, who had risen to prominence within the party by organizing the Kingston Conference, many in the media turned their attention to the riding. Sharp was expected to make the race a close and exciting one, having chosen to run in Eglinton as an expression of opposition to the government's handling of the economy.[127]

The New Democratic Party was uncertain about whether to nominate any candidate in Eglinton, fearing that the party would siphon votes away from Sharp and thus contribute to Fleming's re-election.[128] But the 1962 campaign was the first for the NDP since the party had transformed itself from the CCF, and the decision was made to nominate as many candidates as possible. Ultimately, the NDP nominated David Gauthier, a thirty-year-old lecturer in philosophy at the University of Toronto. Gauthier had been an anti-nuclear activist since the late 1950s, and he hoped to use his candidacy to promote disarmament.[129] But although he had been involved in some of the pre-election efforts to ready the peace movement for the upcoming campaign,[130] he was able to do very little to make nuclear policy an issue in the riding. In Eglinton as elsewhere, the 1962 campaign focused on the economy, and Gauthier's focus on the perils of nuclear weapons missed its mark.[131] Neither nuclear weapons nor the NDP stood a chance in the riding,[132] and Fleming defeated Sharp by a margin of 760 votes, with a count of 18,648 to 17,888.[133] Gauthier won 4,113 votes, which could have changed the outcome if even one-quarter of them had gone to Sharp.[134]

One of the most surprising aspects of the Eglinton campaign was the weak showing of the anti-nuclear movement. Gauthier had to conduct his campaign with just four people.[135] Only a small fraction of the one thousand anti-nuclear supporters who had marched en masse just weeks earlier in the Easter peace march were available.[136]

Several factors explain their absence. Many anti-nuclear activists, particularly the more active ones, were also New Democrats, so volunteers who might have helped out with an anti-nuclear campaign concentrated their energies on working with NDP candidates; and while the party opposed nuclear weapons, not all of its candidates were devoted anti-nuclear activists. Similarly, not all anti-nuclear activists were New Democrats; there were those who traditionally supported the Liberals or the Conservatives and had no intention of doing anything different in the 1962 election. Still other disarmament activists were involved in an awareness campaign waged by the Canadian Peace Research Institute.[137] Moreover, students – who had been a numerical asset when the CCCRH became the CCND earlier in the year and agreed to a formal affiliation with CUCND – were unavailable because they had either left Toronto or were too busy with summer jobs.[138] Finally, and most basically, there was too much ground to cover. The Toronto branch of the CCND had forty ridings to cover, many requiring extensive travel.

On 18 June the Conservatives won 116 seats, the Liberals 100, Social Credit 30, and the New Democrats 19. It was a staggering change from the election four years earlier when the Tories had swept to power with 208 seats. Diefenbaker continued to preside over the government, but it was deeply weakened. He had embodied the party's victory in 1958, leading its sweep into office, but in 1962 much of that support had vanished and he barely remained prime minister. Both the leader and his party needed time to collect themselves for the autumn session of Parliament and, in all likelihood, to prepare for another federal election before too long.

The Liberals were equally upset about the election results.[139] They had expected to win and win big, and their organizers were stunned when they did not.[140] As late as 9 June, Gallup had predicted a Liberal majority, indicating that the party had a plurality of the popular vote across Canada, with 44 percent compared with the Tories' 36 percent. The Liberals led the Tories in Ontario and Quebec, while the Conservatives continued their hold only in the western provinces.[141]

Although the Liberals had been confident about their chances in 1962, there were trends that are apparent with hindsight. For instance, in mid-April they had 45 percent of the popular vote, dropping one point by mid-May. A further decline came in June as support dropped from 42 percent on 6 June to 38 percent on 13

June. The final election result was 37 percent of the popular vote, which translated into just 100 seats. And while the party gained 51 seats over its 1958 showing, there were major disappointments, particularly in Quebec. There, the Social Credit Party made huge gains, winning 26 of its 30 seats, generally at the expense of the Liberals. The Conservatives had been far more consistent. In April the party stood at 38 percent, dropping to 36 percent in mid-May and mid-June. The final result was 37.5 percent of the popular vote. That the Liberals failed to win the 1962 election was as much an indication of Pearson's weakness as a campaigner as it was a testament of Diefenbaker's skill in that area.

As Diefenbaker tried to figure out what had gone wrong, his weakened government encountered other problems. Within days of the election, Canada faced a monetary crisis, causing the new minority government to announce an austerity program on 23 June.[142] The trials and tribulations facing the prime minister were more than just public and political, for he faced several personal challenges that summer. In July, Senator William Brunt, one of his few close friends, died in a car accident. Diefenbaker had just recently offered him the speakership of the Senate, and the news of his death hurt as much as his electoral setback. Then he cracked his ankle, and he took time to nurse his broken bones and battered ego, slipping into a brief depression for the remainder of the summer.

With a reduced government, Diefenbaker had to worry not only about the next election but the composition of his new cabinet. Although the election presented Diefenbaker with an ideal opportunity to resolve the nuclear issue with a cabinet shuffle, he chose to leave the two most contentious positions unchanged: Harkness and Green remained in their respective portfolios. He was also worried about maintaining his leadership of the party. In early 1962, well before the election, Grosart had gathered party organizers together in Montreal to talk about the coming campaign, and some time had been spent discussing the prime minister's dwindling ability to lead.[143] The June election results hastened calls for Diefenbaker's resignation, rumblings of which he was well aware.[144]

While the results of the 1962 election had little to do with nuclear policy – which ranked well down the list of concerns for most Canadians – Diefenbaker still viewed the issue as potentially controversial. With well over one hundred thousand signatures, the National Petition had underscored to Diefenbaker the political dangers of acquiring nuclear weapons. It was the anti-nuclear move-ment's greatest success to date, having made the prime minister take notice. With such a show of force, organizers viewed the petition as the beginning of a large-scale campaign to persuade the government to reject nuclear weapons, but this massive effort never materialized during the election campaign. Afterwards, the activities of the anti-nuclear movement were quickly overtaken by world events.

6

To the Brink and Beyond: The Cuban Missile Crisis and Canada's Nuclear Policy

By the fall of 1962, Canadian political parties had decided that nuclear policy was best left alone. After a certain amount of introspection over the summer months, both major parties had settled into a holding pattern, just waiting for the next election. The Conservatives, now a minority government, returned to the nation's business – though in truth there was little on the legislative agenda – with one eye on the House of Commons and the other on future election plans. The Liberals were also firmly focused on domestic issues, not defence policy.

The most public element of Diefenbaker's nuclear policy was his government's support for a United Nations resolution in favour of an unverified moratorium on nuclear tests. This left the Americans so dissatisfied that Kennedy sent a letter to the prime minister on 18 October.[1] At the same time, despite his electoral setback, Diefenbaker agreed to renew nuclear negotiations with the Americans. If the prime minister had fretted about the impact of nuclear negotiations on his electoral fortunes when he had a majority in Parliament, those worries were even stronger now. Undeterred, Harkness continued to try to persuade cabinet to resume nuclear negotiations. By the beginning of October, he seemed to be making some progress, and there were clear indications that cabinet ministers wanted to renew talks with the Americans. Robinson, recounting a conversation with Ross Campbell, an assistant undersecretary at External Affairs, summarized the state of Canada's nuclear policy in mid-October 1962:

> A national defence memorandum was now on the cabinet agenda and that it related particularly to armaments for the

F-104GS [SWAP agreement] to be delivered to the RCAF in Europe. Some thought is also being given to nuclear weapons for continental defence and in this sector the minister claims to have the PM's support for the idea of standby arrangements which would provide for weapons being held in the US for transfer on short notice to Canada in the event of an emergency. What will happen to all this cannot yet be foreseen but Campbell expected that decisions, or at least cabinet discussion, could be expected shortly.[2]

Two days later, the same day that Kennedy wrote to complain about the Canadian position on the UN moratorium resolution, Pearson rose in the House of Commons to ask the prime minister about the status of Canada's nuclear policy.

While Diefenbaker tried to dodge the question and stall for time,[3] Campbell's comments to Robinson revealed a new wrinkle in Canada's nuclear policy. The prime minister was willing to conclude arrangements for nuclear weapons, but the warheads themselves (the only nuclear component) would be stored outside Canada. This was Howard Green's idea, and it meant the government could legitimately claim there were no nuclear warheads in Canada. This was the general state of Canada's nuclear policy when the Cuban Missile Crisis occurred.

On 16 October 1962, McGeorge Bundy told the president there were Soviet missiles in Cuba. It was two days after the first inklings of trouble on the island, though Kennedy had been concerned for weeks about Fidel Castro and the possibility that the Soviets might store missiles there.[4] Most Canadians, however, were unprepared for the crisis. Despite the US embargo on Cuba, Canada had continued to pursue relations with Castro's regime – which was yet another source of irritation for Kennedy when dealing with Canada and Diefenbaker.[5]

Nevertheless, despite tensions at the highest political level, Canadian-American relations were steady in the autumn of 1962. Officials from each country continued to get along well enough with one another that officers from External Affairs occasionally met with American intelligence officials, which is what happened the weekend of 20 October. It was at this meeting that Canadian officials learned about the crisis brewing in the Caribbean, information they passed on to Norman Robertson and R.B. Bryce, who in turn told the prime minister. The Americans formally contacted

Diefenbaker about the crisis on 22 October, and then only to indicate there was important news that would be delivered personally
by former ambassador Livingston Merchant. By the time Merchant
arrived in the Canadian capital late that afternoon, Diefenbaker
had already known about the trouble in Cuba for twenty-four
hours. Kennedy, by contrast, had known about the increasingly
dangerous situation for a week.

Merchant and two intelligence officers met with Diefenbaker,
Harkness, Green, Bryce, and Air Chief Marshal Frank Miller. Robertson had been expected to attend the meeting but did not. Merchant, who had not yet been replaced at the US Embassy,[6] had been
an excellent ambassador, understanding Diefenbaker as much as
anyone. Yet even this solid relationship did not help him soothe the
prime minister's wounded ego. Diefenbaker was upset that he had
not been genuinely consulted, and he convinced himself that Kennedy's decision to send a retired ambassador to deliver such an
important message was a personal insult.[7]

When Merchant read the president's statement to the Canadian
officials, Diefenbaker objected to only a single sentence, which was
changed to his satisfaction.[8] Without a doubt, he believed the evidence brought to his attention, and he promptly promised Merchant that Canada would honour its NATO and NORAD obligations
if the missiles stationed in Cuba attacked the United States.[9] It is not
clear, however, whether Diefenbaker meant that Canada would
support the Americans *only* if the United States were attacked or if
this was a more general pledge of support in view of the current
threat. Diefenbaker also promised not to make a public statement
about the crisis until the following day.

At Pearson's suggestion, he changed his mind and addressed Parliament immediately after the president's television broadcast to the
world on the evening of the twenty-second. He spoke eloquently,
with only a handful of notes jotted on a slip of paper indicating the
points he had to make: "A sombre and challenging speech";
"Offensive IRBMs in Cuba constitute a threat against all Canadian
cities"; and "Have a group of 'neutral' nations perhaps 8 non
aligned members of 18 Nations Disarmament Committee conduct
an on site inspection to ascertain if offensive nuclear weapons are
installed."[10] Diefenbaker stuck to these notes. He urged Canadians
to remain calm and appealed for political unity. "Above all," he
remarked, this was "a time when each of us must endeavour to do

his part to assure the preservation of peace not only in this hemisphere but everywhere in the world. The existence of these bases or launching pads is not defensive but offensive." No one nation should have to deal with such a threat, he said and suggested that "the United Nations should be charged at the earliest possible moment with this serious problem."[11]

Diefenbaker had meant what he said to Merchant about waiting to make a formal statement until 23 October, but Pearson's intervention had persuaded him to do otherwise. Although he disliked Pearson, he trusted his views on foreign affairs. Of course, there was more than a bit of pragmatism to Diefenbaker's decision in that he was afraid Pearson would make a statement if he did not. The problem with his statement was the proposed UN mission, which was taken by some to call into question the veracity of Kennedy's allegation of Soviet missile sites in Cuba.[12]

The proposal, however, was not Diefenbaker's. Most likely, it came from Norman Robertson; it definitely originated in the Department of External Affairs. Both Robertson and Green supported a United Nations approach to solving the crisis, and the former encouraged the latter to promote this proposal as he prepared to appear on the CBC to discuss the crisis on 24 October. The undersecretary explained to his minister that the introduction of an "international element" might persuade the Soviets to withdraw or cease shipments of warheads to Cuba, thereby removing the need for the naval blockade deployed by the Americans. He was worried that world opinion, which favoured Kennedy's action, might not hold. Some Western nations, he observed to Green, were already beginning to question the American response. Some even hinted that domestic politics in the United States (the mid-term elections were just around the corner) might be at play in the crisis.[13] Even after it was apparent that the Americans were against the proposed UN role, Robertson continued to urge Green to promote the idea. Perceptions that the Canadians were less than enthusiastic about endorsing the American blockade were only strengthened by Green's presentation to the CBC when he portrayed the government's position as a matter of obligation within the context of an alliance, not one of simple conviction.[14]

Cabinet discussed the situation in Cuba at great length on 23 October. The day before, as Diefenbaker had prepared for his statement in Parliament, Air Marshal Miller had told Harkness that

American armed forces had gone on alert, moving to DEFCON-3.[15] Harkness was willing to give Miller permission to move Canada's armed forces to the same increased level of readiness, but the air marshal reminded him that as minister of defence, he did not have the authority to implement such a measure because cabinet had not yet approved the new War Book. Until cabinet approved it, Harkness lacked the authority to order troops on alert without the consent of cabinet.[16] Harkness had no choice but to discuss the matter with Diefenbaker.[17] This was the context within which cabinet discussed the crisis on 23 October. Some ministers favoured immediate action; others supported a more cautious position.[18] Harkness raised the issue of the War Book. Cabinet responded by referring the matter "urgently" to the CDC in order to obtain the committee's opinion of the proposed revisions. Diefenbaker preferred to take a "wait and see" approach, a position that Harkness later attributed to "a pathological hatred of taking a hard decision."[19]

Harkness was outraged by cabinet's response. He met with Defence staff after the cabinet meeting and ordered them to implement all measures required for alert status, despite cabinet's decision. No personnel were allowed to go on leave, though no one was recalled from leave either. It was, essentially, an alert in all but formal declaration. Not willing to give up so easily in his attempt to secure cabinet's approval of the alert measures, Harkness persuaded Diefenbaker to put the issue before cabinet again, holding another meeting on the morning of 24 October. After a heated exchange, Diefenbaker once more rejected the recommendation that Canada's armed forces be placed on alert. It was only after the meeting, when Harkness had learned that US forces had stepped up their alert to DEFCON-2, that Diefenbaker finally agreed to act.[20]

The authorization was too little, too late. When Diefenbaker addressed Parliament on 25 October to proclaim that Canada stood by the Americans in support of the quarantine, the statement had a hollow ring to many US officials, given the delay. Three days later, on 28 October, Kennedy announced to the world that Soviet Premier Khrushchev had agreed not to keep nuclear warheads in Cuba.

What, then, to make of Canada's involvement in the Cuban Missile Crisis? Canada, like other American allies, had been left in the dark until 22 October. But while other allies had been quick to reassure the Americans of their firm support in the crisis, Diefenbaker had not done so. Angered by Kennedy's failure to consult with him as the crisis unfolded,[21] Diefenbaker viewed the episode as confirming his worst fears: the Americans would never confer with their northern neighbour in the event of an emergency. Instead, they would present their allies with a plan of action without genuine consultation.

The Americans saw things differently. Their behaviour during the crisis had not been meant to snub their allies; it simply recognized that there was not the luxury of time to consult in an emergency. It was the price that leaders, whether Charles de Gaulle or John Diefenbaker, paid for being allied with – and protected by – the United States. But Diefenbaker saw Canada as being different from other US allies. For all his apprehensions about the Americans, he believed that Canada and the United States had a special relationship. Canada was not only an American ally in NATO but also its partner in NORAD. Diefenbaker and his advisers mistakenly believed that this relationship should count for something extra.

The Cuban Missile Crisis crystallized the nuclear debate in Canada. On 30 October, just two days after the president had declared victory in Cuba, cabinet discussed Green's proposal to store the warheads in the United States for shipment to Canada in the event of an emergency. Finally, cabinet agreed to renew nuclear negotiations with the Americans. With the Cuban crisis so fresh in his mind, even Green now believed that Canada's national security required an agreement covering nuclear weapons. But whereas the earlier negotiations had focused on the provision of nuclear warheads for various theatres of use – whether NORAD, NATO, or Newfoundland – now any agreement would cover the provision of nuclear weapons for emergency situations only. The state of international relations, not the location of use, would be the determining factor. Still adamant that the government should not allow nuclear weapons on Canadian soil, Green proposed (much as he had done before) that Canadian officials negotiate agreements whereby nuclear warheads were "earmarked" for Canadian forces. These warheads would be stored on American soil and shipped to Canada in an emergency, requiring "standby" agreements for Canadian forces in NORAD and NATO.[22]

Cabinet approved talks based on Green's complicated proposal, creating an interdepartmental group to deal with the issue. Assigned the task of drafting the agreements for cabinet's approval, the group included representatives from External Affairs, National

Defence, and Finance. Once the group drafted the agreements, cabinet would have to approve them. Only then would they be sent to the US Embassy to form the foundation of a nuclear arrangement between the two countries.[23] So, for the time being, negotiations remained on hold. Harkness was not enthusiastic about Green's proposal. He accepted that it was better than nothing but was annoyed with his cabinet colleague. For his part, Diefenbaker once again insisted that the talks be kept secret, failing which he would suspend them as he had done in the past.[24] With that, the negotiating team of Harkness, Green, and Gordon Churchill, the minister of veterans affairs, got to work.

Arrangements for NATO were reasonably straightforward, but the negotiations involving NORAD were more complex because of the limited time available to respond to a North American nuclear emergency. There would be only two to three hours' notice of such an attack, and the warheads would have to arrive in Canada within that timeframe. This fact alone called into question the feasibility of Green's proposal to store Canadian nuclear components on American soil. It did not take long for Harkness to grow weary of Green's attempts to convince other members of the committee that the plan had real merit. Green kept going over and over the details – the times, the number of men, and so on. This effort led Harkness to conclude there could be but one possible rationale for a plan so costly and impractical: Green wanted to be able to claim there were no nuclear warheads on Canadian soil. Harkness had no time for what he viewed as a game of semantics.[25]

At the same time, Harkness tried to convince Diefenbaker to approve the NATO proposal on its own. Diefenbaker refused, once again insisting on a complete nuclear package.[26] With a minority government, he remained preoccupied with the political feasibility of nuclear weapons and was thus cautious about how best to negotiate a nuclear arrangement with the Americans. The Americans, for their part, remained intent on concluding an agreement, political consequences be damned.[27]

In the weeks that followed the crisis, Diefenbaker continued to fret in cabinet about such implications. He even went so far as to contemplate making the next election a de facto referendum on the subject. Most ministers disagreed. However, although they did not think nuclear policy should be the sole issue of the campaign, they were more than willing to make acquisition one of several major points in the Conservative Party's platform. Not surprisingly, Green and a few others adamantly opposed the idea.[28]

Bryce, as before, reassured Diefenbaker that the electorate did not share Green's views. In the wake of the missile crisis, he noted, Canadians were more in favour of the government's plans to accept nuclear weapons than ever before.[29] By contrast, Harkness was now so angry with the prime minister that he refused to cajole him, expressing nothing but contempt for his musings about public support.[30] One can sympathize with Harkness's sense of frustration, but Diefenbaker's concern about public support is also understandable, given the precarious nature of his political position, even though the acquisition of nuclear warheads was not the divisive issue he thought it was.

Even the anti-nuclear movement could not generate opposition to the acquisition of nuclear weapons in the weeks following the missile crisis. In many respects, the Cuban Missile Crisis was a missed opportunity for the activists. Before the crisis, the VOW, CCND, and CUCND all had scheduled meetings with government officials to follow up their electoral efforts. As well, they all had plans to launch a new round of lobbying.[31] During the crisis itself, anti-nuclear groups sent a flurry of telegrams to Diefenbaker and other leaders, urging them to "do the right thing" and reject all things nuclear for Canada.[32] But they did not then capitalize on the fact that the world had been brought to the brink of nuclear disaster, a danger completely dependent on mass nuclear holdings and entirely avoidable as a result. Instead, they chose to direct their attentions to the highest levels of government, working to persuade them of the perils presented by nuclear weapons. This was probably the wrong tactic. The resolution of the Cuban Missile Crisis had not made a nuclear arsenal appear to be more dangerous. Indeed, a nuclear arsenal now seemed to be something that could be managed quite nicely through international negotiation and diplomacy.

Unless anti-nuclear groups could show the prime minister that the acquisition of nuclear warheads would undermine his already vulnerable political position, their appeals were likely to be ignored even more than before. To make an impression on Diefenbaker, a show of strength, something like the National Petition, was required. Even though most activists regarded the crisis as the most basic proof that the Canadian government should eschew nuclear weapons, a majority of Canadians did not agree.[33] In the end, the activists presented no new evidence to convince Diefenbaker to reject nuclear weapons. There was thus no compelling reason for him to do so.[34]

In early November, members of the Voice of Women took a "Peace Train" to Ottawa to deliver their brief to party leaders. The brief contained little that was new. The women urged the government to reject a nuclear role and encouraged it to support a test ban treaty. They also suggested that Canada withdraw from alliances that required it to take on a nuclear role.[35] The VOW missed an ideal opportunity to expand upon the fears created by the missile crisis, to which there were only minor references. The brief had been written before the crisis, and organizers had not thought they had sufficient time to include a full discussion of the missile crisis and its implications.[36]

The CCND and CUCND faced similar problems when they tried to promote disarmament. The two groups met with ninety members of parliament, including several cabinet ministers, on 8 November.[37] Few supported the activists' stand on nuclear policy.[38] Like the VOW brief, the CCND-CUCND effort contained nothing that would have changed the minds of those who had already decided that the Canadian government ought to acquire nuclear weapons.

The CCND meeting illustrates the general atmosphere in the weeks following the missile crisis, one in which there was a surprising lack of interest in the debate about Canada's nuclear policy. For example, in addition to their meetings with politicians, organizers had hoped the crisis would inspire supporters to join in a march against nuclear weapons on Parliament Hill. It did not. Nor were ordinary Canadians motivated to join the movement as they had been after the U-2 incident. More surprising still was the lack of participation from actual members of the two groups, who turned out to be more inclined to offer financial support than to make the trip to Ottawa.[39] That anti-nuclear activists could not even maintain their existing support to protest against the acquisition of warheads confirms Bryce's reassurances to the prime minister that Canadians favoured the acquisition of nuclear weapons.

Timing certainly did not help the anti-nuclear movement; most MPs were absent from Ottawa during the CCND-CUCND meeting, for any number of reasons.[40] There was the meeting of the United Nations General Assembly in New York, a NATO conference in Paris, and a meeting of the Commonwealth Parliamentary Association conference in Lagos, Nigeria, all of which kept many MPs otherwise occupied.[41] Worse still, it was the members most interested in defence, disarmament, and foreign affairs who attended these meetings.

Even if activists had met with those MPs involved in the formulation of Canada's nuclear policy, it is unlikely that they would have been able to change the course agreed to by cabinet in the days following the crisis. Yet the road to acquiring nuclear weapons remained a bumpy one in late 1962, and Diefenbaker soon faced the consequences of his behaviour during the missile crisis. His hesitation had destroyed the remnants of his credibility within the Kennedy administration, something American officials made clear to the Canadians.

Merchant and Robinson met for lunch in early December. When the conversation turned to the missile crisis, Robinson commented that Diefenbaker was both upset and concerned about the administration's failure to consult with its allies. Merchant was unmoved, responding that the prime minister's statement to the House of Commons on 22 October "surprised and disappointed me," as had Green's interview with the CBC two days later. Robinson defended the prime minister, pointing out that Kennedy had put him in an awkward position by presenting him with a done deal. But Merchant had little time for such an explanation. If anyone, he retorted, should have been upset about the president's lack of prior information and consultation, it was the British prime minister, Harold Macmillan, "who had comparably short advance notice."[42] He added that he "didn't think Canada had earned, by its actions and by certain non-actions, the right to the extreme intimacy of relations which had existed in years past." Furthermore, it was unrealistic to expect broad consultation when secrecy was of the utmost importance. In an international crisis, secrecy took priority over consultation.[43]

The exchange between Merchant and Robinson made clear the damage done to Canadian-American relations by Diefenbaker's behaviour during the missile crisis. To be sure, the failure to reach a nuclear agreement had already created tension between the two governments, as had the trouble Diefenbaker had caused over the Rostow Memo, but the missile crisis exacerbated them in a dangerous way.

Diefenbaker was wrong to think that everything would be fine now that he had resumed nuclear negotiations with the Americans.

Although the missile crisis had caused the government to renew talks with the Americans, it also had inspired the Liberals to re-examine their nuclear policy. On 12 January 1963 Pearson unveiled the Liberal Party's new defence policy. In a speech delivered to the Liberal riding association in Scarborough, Ontario, he promised that he would "honour Canada's international obligations" and accept nuclear weapons if Canadians elected him as their next prime minister. The speech marked the end of a transition period for the Liberals that had begun at the end of October, and several factors contributed to this dramatic change in policy.

Paul Hellyer, the party's defence critic, had played a significant role in changing Pearson's attitude. He had missed the CCND's November lobby because he was attending the NATO conference in Paris, a conference that had changed his views on the country's nuclear policy.[44] Hellyer was struck by how Canada's position within the alliance had changed in the seven years since he last attended a NATO conference. "In 1955, Canadian airmen had been on top of the world because their souped-up F-86 Sabre aircraft could fly rings around the Americans," he recalled. "Now the government was refusing to arm the F-104s it had purchased for the strike role, and pilots were so ashamed they avoided bars frequented by their NATO colleagues."[45]

Hellyer's discussions with General Lauris Norstad, the supreme allied commander of NATO, and George Ignatieff, Canada's ambassador to the alliance, were also influential. Norstad showed Hellyer maps and battle plans that included Canadian forces, telling him that while Canadian forces formed a major component of his battle plans, those forces were unreliable without nuclear warheads. Talks with Ignatieff revealed similar frustrations. The ambassador explained that the NATO Council was losing patience with the Canadian government and had even talked about passing a resolution expressing its concern, though alliance officials had been persuaded to postpone the motion for the time being. Although no one indicated the extent of these deliberations or speculated about the chances that a resolution would be introduced at a later date, it was clear that the Americans were not the only ones losing patience with Diefenbaker's procrastination.[46]

Upon his return from Paris, Hellyer reported his observations to both the Liberal caucus and its leader. His conclusion was straightforward: the acceptance of nuclear weapons for Canada's armed forces in Europe would not threaten the balance of peace, nor would it hinder disarmament talks. And if the Canadian government accepted nuclear armaments for its NATO forces, there was no logical reason to refrain from accepting them within NORAD. For Hellyer, it was a matter of honour and obligation more than nuclear strategy. "I have not changed my opinion about the usefulness of the Bomarc missile," he wrote, "but if there is one thing that is more useless than an armed Bomarc it is an unarmed Bomarc."

Hellyer also considered the potential political implications of reversing the party's nuclear policy. "The great majority of the Canadian people," he wrote, "would want their country to fulfil its obligations." The party would be fine politically. "We have consistently recommended a different course at a time when a different choice was feasible." The difficulty, he added, was that "our choice is limited by the circumstances," though "we are not bound by the present circumstances for all time. If we wished to play a different role this could be negotiated and implemented over a period of years in a responsible way. Now, however, we must uphold the honour and integrity of our word as a nation."[47] In addition to his written attempt to persuade Pearson to change the party's nuclear policy, Hellyer spoke with him personally, but he saw "no indication" that Pearson was about to change his mind. Nevertheless, Hellyer continued to be an outspoken proponent of Canada's acquisition of nuclear weapons, urging the government to conclude an agreement with the Americans that would allow for warheads in the event of an emergency.[48]

Pearson may not have been immediately responsive to Hellyer's suggestion, but his attitude began to change during the first week of January. By mid-January, he had accepted that Canada ought to acquire nuclear weapons. Why did he change his mind at this time? Although some have argued that Pearson decided to accept nuclear warheads on New Year's Day 1963 as a result of a series of memos that he received before that date, the record is less clear.[49]

At the end of December, John Gellner, a Toronto publisher and former wing commander, had delivered a brief on defence recommendations to Hellyer, writing, "I now believe that we should make good on our commitments to NORAD and NATO until we can change them through renegotiation. I still believe, of course, that the sooner we start renegotiating them the better."[50] The Gellner brief was circulated to various Liberal advisers, including J.W. Pickersgill, Walter Gordon, C.M. Drury, and Tom Kent.[51]

Pickersgill's was the most detailed response. His primary concern, like Diefenbaker's, was the political implications that might follow such a dramatic change in policy. Style was as important as the substance of the issue, and he urged Pearson to be decisive above all else: "The public condemns the government for vacillation. This is the one subject on which a wrong course could sink our prospects without a trace." [52] Pickersgill had written his memo to Pearson on 3 January before leaving for Paris, and he returned to Ottawa two days after Pearson's Scarborough speech. He later recalled that Hellyer had told him that neither he nor Gordon had learned of Pearson's change of view until Pearson made his speech at Scarborough on 12 January. "My notes to Pearson on January 2nd and 3rd," wrote Pickersgill, "make it apparent that Pearson has already indicated to me that he had decided what our position must be on the existing commitments. I was, therefore, not trying to change his mind, but merely to get him to express his position clearly and without qualification."[53]

Richard O'Hagan, Pearson's press secretary and adviser, also had sent him a memorandum. The text leaves some room for doubt about whether Pearson had firmly decided to accept nuclear weapons. "It is obvious of course that in elementary political terms the whole question revolves on nuclear weapons, simply and starkly," O'Hagan wrote. "Will we accept them, and on what basis? I agree entirely with Jack [Pickersgill] that the answer you give the country must be a model of simplicity and decisiveness, even – and I say this advisedly – at the risk of some over-simplification. We will be hailed or censured not on the subsidiary refinements, however important they may be, but on the central position we adopt, or at least what that position appears to be."[54] This memorandum, then, dealt with *whether* the Liberals would accept nuclear weapons, not *when* they would be accepted, an important distinction.

O'Hagan's memo was written on 7 January, a few days after Pickersgill's notes. Several things occurred in between that probably influenced Pearson's decision. On 3 January, General Norstad, who was retiring as NATO's supreme commander, visited Canada as part of his farewell tour. In response to a question from a reporter in a televised scrum at the airport, he indicated that Canada had not been living up to its commitments within the alliance, just as he had told Hellyer in November.[55] The fact that Air Marshal Frank Miller, the Canadian chief of staff, was standing beside Norstad and agreed with his comments would have made the American general's remarks all the more convincing.[56] This public rebuke was another factor that contributed to Pearson's decision to accept nuclear weapons.[57]

Yet not all of Pearson's advisers wanted the party's nuclear policy to change. Kent, in particular, argued against the acquisition of nuclear weapons, calling Pearson's decision "the nuclear error."[58] By late 1962 Kent was an indispensable adviser to Pearson as well as his chief speechwriter.[59] Having helped to plan the party's strategy for the 1962 election, Kent was ready for the challenge of preparing for another election campaign. Immediately after the missile crisis, Pearson had still been reluctant to accept nuclear weapons, and Kent had hoped this would remain his position.[60] His own view was that the Liberals ought to push the government to clarify its nuclear policy, for he believed that Diefenbaker intended to accept the weapons before too long.[61]

Kent helped Pearson with the Scarborough speech, taking into consideration both O'Hagan's memo and Pickersgill's notes. His draft focused on the importance of a full and frank discussion of defence policy, suggesting the creation of a select committee on defence policy to determine the extent of Canada's international obligations.[62] The government's failure to honour its obligations and responsibilities within NATO and NORAD was central, though the draft intimated that these were not commitments carved in stone. Instead, it encouraged the government to consider expanding Canada's conventional forces.[63]

The draft speech was not the straightforward statement that Pickersgill and O'Hagan had envisioned, and Kent's memoirs give the impression that there was little change between the draft notes of 7 January and the speech Pearson gave on 12 January. But this is not the case. At Scarborough, Pearson proposed to reassess Canada's defence policy and renegotiate its commitments, but only after he had honoured the nuclear obligations of the Diefenbaker government. He was precise and explicit about accepting these commitments, pledging to accept nuclear weapons based on the Anglo-American agreement that had served so many times as a model for negotiations between Canadian and American officials. As Pearson explained, this arrangement meant that "a US finger would be in the trigger; but a Canadian finger would be on the safety catch."[64]

In his memoirs, Pearson attributed the policy change to the Cuban Missile Crisis and Hellyer's memo.[65] However, it is inconceivable that opinion polls did not also influence his change of heart. One poll indicated the Liberals had a decisive lead over the governing Tories – 47 percent to 32 percent.[66] Another addressed the nuclear issue explicitly, reporting that 54 percent of Canadians believed Canada's armed forces should have nuclear weapons, 32 percent opposed acquisition, and only 14 percent remained undecided.[67] Notwithstanding the Cuban crisis, however, this poll did not differ significantly from one taken in March 1962, which indicated that 56.5 percent of Canadians wanted Canada to accept nuclear arms, compared with 34 percent opposed, and 9.1 undecided.[68] It is difficult to imagine that external polls alone, given the similarity of results, had a profound effect on Pearson in January 1963 but not in March 1962. It is more likely that internal Liberal polls were the decisive factor.

Pearson and the Liberals had employed President Kennedy's pollster, Lou Harris, for the 1962 election. Despite the less than stellar results, Keith Davey and other organizers decided to keep using him and his firm, Penetration Research Ltd. Harris produced a study entitled "A Survey of the Political Climate of Ontario and Quebec" that arrived in the Liberal Party offices on 10 January 1963.[69] This internal poll was the final factor to influence Pearson's decision to accept nuclear weapons.

The introductory summary of the survey praised the Liberals for their clear and concise criticism of Diefenbaker's government but raised concerns about its tone. Criticism of the government had the tendency to make the party and its leader appear more intent on obstruction than constructive participation in debate. As for the issues, the report revealed that nuclear weapons were now the number one concern for Canadians whereas they had not even registered on the list of significant concerns in the survey that Penetration Research had delivered in September 1962. In Ontario, 70 percent now favoured nuclear weapons; in Quebec there was 58 percent support.[70] Ontario was crucial to a Liberal victory in the next election, and its voters' support for nuclear weapons was hard to ignore. Furthermore, the expectation was that public support for acquisition was only growing.[71] The survey ended by stating that there were two issues – old age pensions and the acquisition of nuclear weapons – that would guarantee a Liberal majority in the next election.[72] Such a conclusion, with these kinds of numbers, was important to a party that had narrowly lost the previous election. It was also personally vital for Pearson, who needed to find a winning issue to retain his position at the helm of the party.[73]

The Penetration Survey findings were precisely what the party leadership wanted to hear, particularly after organizers decided to push the government into an early election that would exploit public opinion in the party's favour.[74] Yet Kent was later adamant that Pearson accepted nuclear warheads out of a sense of honour, not political expediency: "Mike took the position he did because he was utterly dedicated to the co-operation of the Western nations as a group; he could not bear the thought of Canada failing to carry out an agreement with them ... He was completely sincere in believing that in these matters there should be as little partisanship as possible. He was no more capable of taking the position he did as a matter of political calculation than he was of murdering his mother."[75] When questioned about the possible role of political polling in this decision, Kent repeated that it had nothing to do with Pearson's decision to accept nuclear weapons.[76] However, the evidence suggests otherwise. Historian John English has noted a conversation between Pearson and Denis Smith in 1972 when the Liberal leader recalled that his nuclear statement "was when I really became a politician."[77] The results of the Penetration Survey were such that political considerations must have been the final factor that led to Pearson's change of policy.

The response to Pearson's statement was swift. The Americans were pleased to see that he was now on side.[78] The press generally supported his statement, as did the general party membership. There were, however, some notable exceptions. Pierre Trudeau, who had been expected to run under the Liberal banner in the next election (though he was not yet an actual member of the party), harshly criticized Pearson, calling him the "unfrocked priest of peace."[79] Trudeau was so opposed to the decision that he refused to run for the Liberals in the 1963 election. Another future Liberal notable, Lloyd Axworthy, wrote less colourfully to express similar disappointment.[80]

Canada's anti-nuclear activists were horrified. They felt abandoned by a politician who had led them to believe he supported their objectives. It was, one activist recalled, the "blackest betrayal."[81] The outpouring of outrage was such that Mary Macdonald, Pearson's assistant, prepared two versions of a form letter (long and short) to respond to the many complaints that streamed into the office in the days following the Scarborough speech.[82] In his memoirs, Pearson recalled the reaction, noting with great understatement that "some very bitter letters were sent to me, accusing me of shameless immorality."[83] As anti-nuclear forces moved quickly to denounce Pearson, they turned to embrace Diefenbaker. In their eyes, the prime minister was their saviour with his "decisive" opposition to nuclear weapons.[84]

If activists thought Diefenbaker was on their side, members of the Conservative Party certainly did not approve. They thought Pearson's speech would inspire Diefenbaker to clarify his own nuclear policy and come out expressly in favour of acquisition of the weapons. If not, perhaps the party's membership could persuade him to do so. The party's annual general meeting, held in the days that followed the Scarborough speech, presented just such an opportunity.

Diefenbaker's leadership and the party's nuclear policy were the source of much discussion at the meeting.[85] Eddy Goodman, a leading Conservative organizer and chair of the policy resolution committee for the 1963 annual general meeting, thought that the discussion of nuclear policy surrounding Pearson's speech presented the ideal moment for the party to clarify its policy. When Goodman learned that Pearson was going to announce his willingness to accept nuclear warheads, he went to see the prime minister. Diefenbaker was incredulous when he learned that Pearson would make such a change, remarking that it would surely undermine the Liberal leader's credibility. "We've got him now!" Diefenbaker shouted with glee. Goodman disagreed, pointing out that the Liberals were only promising to fulfil the Conservative government's existing obligations.[86]

The differences between the two men reflected the party's growing dissatisfaction with its leader on the nuclear issue, and Goodman was not the only one who urged Diefenbaker to follow Pearson's example. What they failed to appreciate was that the very fact that the Liberal leader was willing to accept nuclear weapons now made it impossible for Diefenbaker to do the same. Diefenbaker had worried that Pearson would attack the government for accepting nuclear weapons, but he had never anticipated that their roles would be reversed. Worse still, Diefenbaker was in the midst of negotiations with the Americans and had even considered making the acquisition of nuclear weapons a major issue in the coming election campaign. By allowing Pearson to make the first clear statement in favour of nuclear weapons, Diefenbaker had backed himself into a corner. If in the past he had feared succumbing to American pressure for nuclear weapons, he certainly could not now turn round and appear to follow Pearson's lead. Diefenbaker had no choice but to take the exact opposite position of the Liberals. For this reason it was Pearson, not Diefenbaker, who determined the government's nuclear policy in early 1963.

At the Conservatives' annual general meeting, Diefenbaker opposed the introduction of a resolution in favour of nuclear weapons and did everything in his power to prevent its acceptance. The party had accepted suggestions for resolutions from riding associations, and the missile crisis, twinned with Pearson's Scarborough speech, made nuclear policy the most pressing concern for party members.[87] Diefenbaker did not see it this way.

Initially, Diefenbaker advised Goodman that he would accept a pro-nuclear resolution only if Howard Green approved. Not one to ignore an opportunity, Goodman talked to the minister of external affairs and agreed to modify the resolution to give the government more time to continue the current round of negotiations. Green was amenable, but Diefenbaker was not, rejecting the new resolution altogether. He was so determined to avoid the resolution that he prohibited Flora MacDonald from making copies of it so that it would not be available for delegates. Goodman retaliated, scheduling a press conference before the meeting to announce the resolution. Not to be outdone, Diefenbaker and Grosart rescheduled the speaking order at the conference to make sure the prime minister spoke before Goodman could make his announcement.

In the end, a modified resolution was introduced, with a further amendment that the government – not the party at large – would merely consider the resolution.[88] When asked by reporters if he would resign, Goodman was good-natured about being outmanoeuvred by the prime minister, remarking that if the defence minister could live with the party's nuclear policy, so could he.[89] The consequence of the amendment, however, was more serious, precluding any real discussion of nuclear policy by the party membership.

With the House about to resume sitting, Conservatives thought they would finally be able to get Diefenbaker to clarify the government's policy in a statement to Parliament. Once again they were mistaken. The government was on the verge of self-destruction, with Harkness leading the charge. As an ever-growing number of ministers sided with Harkness over Green, Diefenbaker refused to budge, proposing to cabinet on 20 January, the day before Parliament returned, that the government postpone making a decision about nuclear policy until after the anticipated election.[90]

Cabinet met several times to discuss this issue in the days that followed. On 22 January, Diefenbaker created a subcommittee consisting of Harkness, Green, Churchill, and Donald Fleming to examine the government's nuclear policy. With the exception of Fleming, these were the men who had been charged with drafting the nuclear agreements following the missile crisis. After much wrangling, primarily between Harkness and Green, the subcommittee agreed unanimously to continue negotiations with the Americans. Diefenbaker, however, rejected the committee's recommendations. The committee persevered, and when its proposal was submitted to the rest of cabinet on 24 January everyone but the prime minister approved its recommendations. Harkness's exasperation finally got the best of him, and he decided to resign from cabinet, though some of his cabinet colleagues persuaded him to wait until the next day to submit his resignation, on the off chance that the prime minister's statement to Parliament would address his concerns.[91]

Diefenbaker's long-awaited statement to Parliament on 25 January proved to be his most baffling on nuclear policy. In it, he tried to be all things to all people. He spoke about recent talks between British Prime Minister Macmillan and President Kennedy in Nassau, to which he had invited himself. He also implied that Canada could not accept nuclear weapons from the Americans, even under joint authority, without contributing to nuclear proliferation. Switching gears, he concluded his remarks with a rough rendition of the nuclear subcommittee's report to cabinet – the report he had rejected but now seemed to support.[92] Initially, Harkness was delighted. He thought Diefenbaker had finally come out publicly in favour of acquiring nuclear weapons. Others, particularly those in the press, were not as certain. They thought he had endorsed Green's position on nuclear policy. This confusion led Harkness to issue his own "clarification" on 28 January.[93]

If Diefenbaker's statement to Parliament ultimately disappointed Harkness, it appalled officials at the State Department in Washington. Diefenbaker had revealed the existence of negotiations to secure nuclear weapons for Canada's armed forces "if and when" they were needed. These talks, which had broken down in late December, had been secret. Neither Diefenbaker nor anyone else had asked the State Department whether the prime minister could reveal their existence to Parliament. Diefenbaker, for one, should have known better, given his own previous concerns about secrecy. There is, of course, the possibility that he was being vindictive, based on a sense that turnaround was fair play. If this was the strategy, it backfired.

Whatever Diefenbaker's motivations, his statement made American officials think he was now determined to avoid clarifying his nuclear policy at all costs, for all time.[94] Moreover, attitudes had changed in Washington as a result of Pearson's Scarborough speech. Officials in the administration believed that it had transformed the political situation in Canada. Now that the Liberals were willing to accept nuclear weapons, there was no incentive for the State Department to resume negotiations with Diefenbaker.[95] The US Embassy in Ottawa suggested the State Department might want to make its own clarification. George Ball, the undersecretary of state, agreed and issued a press release on 30 January.

The press release denied Diefenbaker's claim that negotiations with the Americans were underway, blaming the Canadians for the lack of an agreement. Furthermore, it said there was no obstacle to Canada's acquisition of nuclear weapons, nor would Canadian acquisition constitute nuclear proliferation. In essence, the press release called Diefenbaker a liar. State Department officials knew that they had to live with Diefenbaker, at least for the time being, and thought their efforts to clarify his nuclear policy would inspire his respect for the Americans.[96] Nothing could have been further from the truth.

Whether the State Department press release was a legitimate clarification of policy or an untoward allegation of deceit, Diefenbaker was enraged. He met with his cabinet the following day, 31 January, and proposed calling a snap election based solely on the issue of American interference in Canadian affairs. Green was sympathetic; the press release had greatly disturbed him. He commented that the Canadians had been in the midst of "good faith" negotiations with the Americans, and he could not understand why the State Department would do something that would so obviously undermine these efforts. More.sinister was his concern that Pearson had played a role in the State Department's press release – he wondered whether there was any coincidence in the fact that Pearson had made an about-face in policy just a couple of weeks earlier. This, to Green, was tantamount to American intervention to defeat the government.[97] Harkness and other ministers disagreed, staunchly opposing Diefenbaker's proposed election tactic. Instead, cabinet agreed to issue a formal protest to the United States.[98]

In both Parliament and the Canadian press, criticism of the US press release was tempered by the belief that the government's policy had been so unclear that the American response was understandable even if it was not entirely appreciated.[99] Although the Canadian Embassy in Washington was informed that the State Department press release had been carefully phrased so as not to preclude further nuclear talks, it was clear that there would be no talks between the Diefenbaker government and the Kennedy administration any time soon.[100] The Americans had to bide their time, waiting for another election and, hopefully, a Liberal government.

The government and Conservative Party had been in turmoil in the days following Pearson's Scarborough speech, and Diefenbaker's fortunes worsened in early February. On 3 February, after cabinet rejected the prime minister's offer to resign, Harkness made good on his oft-repeated promise to abandon his post as minister of defence. "The failure to get rid of Diefenbaker at this time," Harkness later wrote, "was a failure in human courage."[101] Perhaps. More importantly, it was a missed opportunity for the government to save itself from certain defeat at the polls.

The government was defeated on a non-confidence motion two days later, on 5 February. Parliament was formally dissolved the following day, and the chaos continued when George Hees and Pierre Sévigny followed Harkness out of cabinet on 9 February. Diefenbaker now had to face the electorate with a fragmented cabinet and a deeply divided party. Still others were lost during the course of the 1963 campaign: Davie Fulton decided to seek the Conservative leadership in his home province of British Columbia and did not run; Donald Fleming left politics altogether; and George Hees, having resigned from cabinet, spent much of the campaign skiing in Europe.[102]

The 1963 campaign began in earnest on 28 February, and nuclear policy was the dominant issue. Diefenbaker was unwilling to accept this and refused to believe his defence policy was in any way responsible for the defeat of his government.[103] Indeed, only when Pearson began to equivocate on his own nuclear pledge did the prime minister's position take shape. Over the course of the campaign, Pearson increasingly emphasized renegotiation rather than acceptance. This waffling over nuclear policy was precisely what strategists had warned him against, fearing that the public would construe any hesitation as a sign of weakness.[104] With every tentative step away from the acquisition of nuclear weapons, the focus was less on honouring Canada's international obligations and more on the possibility of reworking that commitment. Such a stance emboldened Diefenbaker to criticize Pearson's position.

By the beginning of March, Diefenbaker saw that Pearson was on the defensive about his new policy and moved in for the attack. The Conservatives produced a pamphlet targeting the Liberal leader's vacillation with a tag line that read "Lester Pearson and Nuclear Warheads – a Riot of Indecision." It chronicled the Liberal Party's flip-flop on nuclear policy, complete with a caricature of Pearson in various contorted stages of the twist.[105]

The Liberal Party was vulnerable on other fronts too. Its strategists had expanded their use of gimmicks from the previous campaign, few of which were a success. There were homing pigeons, an Election Colouring Book, and a Truth Squad. Each was a disaster, hurting the party far more than it helped. The homing pigeons got lost.[106] The colouring book,[107] inspired by a similar novelty in President Kennedy's 1960 presidential campaign, was another blunder. It was a bit funny, but also cruel. Not everyone shared the creators' sense of humour[108] as a series of line drawings and accompanying text sought to capture Diefenbaker's indecisiveness: "This is a Prime Minister. / He is at breakfast. / Should he have orange juice or a grapefruit? / It is a hard decision. / He dreads decisions. / Perhaps he will never have breakfast. / Colour him hungry." On nuclear policy, the colouring book jabbed: "This is a Canadian fighter pilot. / He flies for NATO. / All the other NATO pilots have planes that fight good. / The Canadian pilot doesn't. / Colour him highly embarrassed."[109]

The Truth Squad was also a flop. Composed of Judy LaMarsh, Jack Macbeth, and Fred Belaire, the squad was supposed to tag along after Diefenbaker on the campaign trail, pointing out the prime minister's errors and errors of omission to the gathered crowd.[110] Rather than demonstrating that Diefenbaker had a problem with the truth, it only served to remind voters that he was faster on his feet than Pearson was. Where the Liberal leader would have been mortified and distracted by hecklers, the prime minister was in his element. He quickly turned the Truth Squad against the Liberals by putting it on display. At each event, a table and chair were set up for LaMarsh to make her notes in full view of an assembled crowd of Conservative supporters. It was a very public embarrassment for a would-be government. Announced 12 March, the Truth Squad made its first appearance on the fifteenth, only to be scrapped a mere two days later. Keith Davey told Pearson that while many people opposed Diefenbaker, they were also looking for reasons not to vote for the Liberals. "Unfortunately," he wrote, "a great many of our key people seem to think we have provided such a reason with our Truth Squad."[111]

The Tories had more than Liberal antics to use to their advantage. The Americans also proved to be an easy target for the prime minister. In mid-February, *Newsweek* – the source of the leak that had helped to undermine the nuclear talks in September 1961 – was once again the subject of Diefenbaker's fury. The magazine's editor, Benjamin Bradlee, was a friend of the Kennedys, which did little to endear the publication to the prime minister. Then the 18 February edition appeared. Diefenbaker's jowled grimace graced the cover, and as John English has written, "the story was nastier than the cover."[112]

The article provided a spiteful description of the prime minister. "Diefenbaker in full oratorical flight is a sight not soon to be forgotten," it began. "The India-rubber features twist and contort in grotesque and gargoyle-like grimaces; beneath the electric gray V of the hairline, the eyebrows beat up and down like bats' wings; the agate-blue eyes blaze forth cold fire." It continued, "Elderly female Tory supporters find Diefenbaker's face rugged, kind, pleasant, and even soothing; his enemies insist that it is sufficient grounds for barring Tory rallies to children under 16."[113]

By ridiculing Diefenbaker, the *Newsweek* article gave the prime minister more ammunition to use in his allegations of American interference with the election. The magazine staff denied the accusation,[114] but the article and its cover cast a pall over the campaign, one that Diefenbaker could have exploited even further had he learned that Kennedy had offered to assist the Liberals with their election campaign. When Pearson learned of the overture, which came in mid-March, he responded, "For God's sake, tell the president to keep his mouth shut."[115]

There were also renewed concerns about the Rostow Memo, rumours of which surfaced in the Canadian press.[116] In the wake of these rumours, there was a fraudulent letter from the American ambassador congratulating Pearson for his stand on nuclear weapons.[117] Forgery or not, the letter sent shivers of fear through the Liberal team in view of the president's earlier suggestion. Finally, there was Defense Secretary McNamara's testimony before Congress, released at the end of March, in which he stated that the Bomarc missiles were valuable if only to draw enemy fire to the north.[118] Such a statement added to Diefenbaker's arsenal, primed as it was, to mock the Liberals and their pledge to acquire nuclear weapons.

The 1963 election campaign ended with a whimper, to the frustration of everyone involved. On 8 April, the Liberals won 129 seats, just 3 shy of a majority government. The Progressive Conservative Party was reduced to 95 seats in Parliament, while the NDP was reduced to 17, and Social Credit to 24. But Pearson's triumph was bittersweet: the Liberals had started the campaign with an enormous lead in the polls, and anything short of a majority was a great disappointment. The Conservatives had made it a close race, denying a majority to the Liberals, but they suffered great losses in the process. Cabinet ministers Richard Bell, Ellen Fairclough, and Raymond O'Hurley were all defeated, as was Howard Green, whose efforts to promote global disarmament were not rewarded by the voters of Vancouver-Quadra. While the local Liberal candidate defeated Green, the minister on the other side of the nuclear debate did not suffer the same fate: the voters of Calgary reaffirmed their support for Harkness, returning him to Parliament quite handily. Both outcomes met with American approval.[119]

The electoral impact of Pearson's new nuclear policy is debatable. While Kent has argued that Pearson's about-face was a major obstacle to the party securing a majority government, Hellyer is equally adamant that it was the only reason the Liberals won even a minority in Parliament.[120]

On 17 April, the Diefenbaker government resigned, and on 22 April, Pearson became Canada's fourteenth prime minister, just one day before his sixty-sixth birthday. After almost six years in opposition – the party's longest period out of office since Laurier's leadership in the First World War – the Liberals were back in power. While the party with Lester Pearson at its helm was not the mighty "Government Party" of William Lyon Mackenzie King and Louis St Laurent, a minority government was better than being the opposition. All the most prominent Liberal candidates had been elected: Lester Pearson, Paul Martin, J.W. Pickersgill, Lionel Chevrier, Paul Hellyer, C.M. Drury, Walter Gordon, Mitchell Sharp, Maurice Lamontagne, Maurice Sauvé, and Judy LaMarsh. Pearson's cabinet held great promise after the 1963 election, and commentators noted the array of talent.[121] Veterans from the St Laurent years assumed the two most contentious portfolios amid the nuclear debate. Paul Martin succeeded Green as secretary of state for external affairs, and Paul Hellyer replaced Harkness as the minister of national defence. For how long this new Liberal government would last, no one could be sure. One thing, however, was definite: Pearson had promised to accept nuclear weapons if elected, and now it was time for him to honour his own commitment, never mind Diefenbaker's. At long last, nuclear weapons were coming to Canada.

Conclusion

The Americans were as relieved to be done with Diefenbaker in the spring of 1963 as they were enthusiastic about dealing with the new Canadian government of Lester Pearson. They knew nothing would be resolved automatically because of the change in government, but they now had great confidence that outstanding bilateral problems, including the nuclear issue, could be settled with relative ease.[1] The first opportunity to test this confidence came in mid-May when the two leaders met at the president's summer home in Hyannisport, Massachusetts. It was Pearson's second foreign visit as prime minister, having first made the traditional trip to London to meet with his British counterpart. US officials had a single overarching objective for the meeting in Hyannisport – to establish a solid relationship with the new government and the new prime minister. Less important was their desire to brief Pearson on the general direction of American policy on an array of subjects.

In preparation for his meeting with the new Canadian prime minister, Kennedy had been advised not to push Pearson on any issue, especially as Parliament had not yet met, because the last thing the Americans wanted was to seem overly aggressive or too eager to reach an agreement on any of the outstanding issues. But while his advisers cautioned the president to proceed slowly, Kennedy's personal approval of Pearson was such that he was far more willing to accommodate the prime minister's domestic political priorities than he had ever been when dealing with Diefenbaker.[2]

Such a cautious approach to the meeting reaped great benefits, and by all accounts the get-together was a great success.[3] Pearson's ability to talk baseball with Kennedy and his advisers has become the stuff of legend, but the president had been impressed with the Liberal leader, at least on a personal level, long before this first formal visit. Indeed, Pearson was precisely the sort of person with whom Kennedy was naturally friendly,[4] and by 1963 the two men already knew each other quite well.

To everyone's relief, Pearson expressed his willingness to resolve the nuclear issue. Kennedy had been briefed not to expect a formal agreement that weekend,[5] but the Americans were prepared to conclude one on the spot if that was what Pearson wanted, so much so that a contingency plan was in place to fly a "plane load of appropriate people" to the meeting at a moment's notice.[6] Despite these preparations, Pearson did not announce a formal nuclear arrangement. This much was reflected in the rather circumspect joint communiqué that was issued following the meeting. The announcement did, however, provide a clear indication that Pearson intended to honour his campaign promise to accept nuclear weapons for Canada. It stated, "The Prime Minister confirmed his government's intention to initiate discussions with the United States Government leading without delay towards the fulfilment of Canada's existing defense commitments in North America and Europe consistent with Canadian parliamentary procedures."[7]

In private, Pearson was far more candid and explicit, reassuring Kennedy and his aides that his government fully intended to acquire nuclear warheads and that a draft agreement, based on the American proposals of the autumn of 1962, had already been prepared in Ottawa. Some modifications had been made, he cautioned, but these were "largely a matter of wording for domestic political reasons" and were changes that would be entirely acceptable to the Kennedy administration.[8]

But nuclear policy was not the only delicate topic discussed at Hyannisport. There was also the Rostow Memo. News of the memo had surfaced in Canadian press reports at the end of March and throughout the first week of April there was a flurry of activity in the White House as the president considered how to deal with the allegations of American interference in the Canadian election that were sure to follow verification of the document's existence. Kennedy's aides, convinced that Diefenbaker was going to try to use the memo to his political advantage as one last desperate effort to secure re-election, decided that their approach would be a simple denial. They had a copy of the memorandum and knew that it contained nothing untoward or embarrassing. But the formal contents of the memorandum were not the real source of concern; more pressing were the repeated rumours that something derogatory had been scrawled in its margin,[9] and worries about this were exacerbated when an article on the subject appeared in the *Washington Post*.

In early April, Kennedy had asked Benjamin Bradlee of *Newsweek* (which was owned by the same family as the *Post*) if he had ever told him the story of "the stolen document," which he considered to be "the incident at the root of all US-Canadian problems." When Bradlee replied in the negative, the president had promised to give him an exclusive story, but only if Diefenbaker lost the election. True to his word, Kennedy delivered to Bradlee "a fat file" on 10 April, just two days after the election, that contained all the memoranda exchanged on the subject. Shortly thereafter, the story appeared in the *Washington Post*. In response to Bradlee's question about whether he had indeed written anything, let alone the alleged "s.o.b." in the margin, Kennedy replied that he had not. Besides, he explained, "at that time I didn't think Diefenbaker was a son of a bitch. (Pause, for effect) I thought he was a prick." He added that the whole situation was difficult to fathom and he wondered why Diefenbaker "didn't do what any normal, friendly government would do ... make a photostatic copy, and return the original."[10]

This, then, was the background that led to Kennedy's decision to ask Pearson if he had seen the document, but before the president could ask for its return, Pearson confessed that he did not have it – indeed, he had never even seen the memo. As a result, he was unable to confirm – or deny – that an unflattering comment about Diefenbaker had been scrawled in the margin. In fact, the location of the document baffled him, and the document was never returned to the American government. It remains to this day, without a single comment in the margin, in the collection of Diefenbaker's papers housed at the Diefenbaker Centre in Saskatoon. Ironically, Diefenbaker had made a "photostatic copy," which can also be found in his papers and is the only copy to bear any markings – the word "push" underlined in his own hand.[11]

Upon his return from Hyannisport, Prime Minister Pearson set to work sorting out the details for Canada's acquisition of nuclear weapons. By mid-July a final agreement was reached, and diplomatic notes were signed 16 August. Four and a half months later, at long last, the first nuclear warheads entered Canada.[12] Having made the decision to accept nuclear weapons, Pearson took no action in response to the predictable opposition of the anti-nuclear movement. It was easy for him to ignore the outrage of these activists, since Canadians overwhelmingly supported his decision to acquire the warheads. Thus, although anti-nuclear activists protested the arrival of the warheads at North Bay and La Macaza at the end of 1963, few Canadians were converted to the cause. The result was that the anti-nuclear movement became a movement in search of a mission; for those who remained involved in the peace movement, the growing conflict in Vietnam proved an appealing alternative to nuclear weapons.[13]

In many respects, Pearson's handling of nuclear policy was an indication of the type of government that he would lead. Although he viewed his decision to accept nuclear weapons as the moment he became a true politician, Canadians were not entirely sure they liked what they saw in the former diplomat. His handling of the issue seemed to be hesitant and overly cautious, notwithstanding his bold announcement of 12 January. Much like Diefenbaker, Pearson seemed to wither in response to the slightest opposition on the nuclear issue, and while he remained committed to "honouring Canada's international obligations," he did more than his fair share of back-peddling on the campaign trail, reminding Canadians that these were commitments that could be renegotiated. He governed with two successive minority governments, a majority always just beyond his reach, and the manner in which he handled the nuclear issue seemed to be reflected in his rather tentative style of governance from 1963 to 1968. Pearson's faith in polling data may have been well placed for the formulation of his nuclear policy, but it seemed to reap few political rewards in other areas.

Similarly, Diefenbaker never regained his authority within the Progressive Conservative Party after the nuclear fiasco, and the years that followed the 1963 defeat were filled with turmoil for him. He fought off a series of attempted political coups, finally succumbing in September 1967, when a messy leadership convention led to Robert Stanfield's election as party leader. Despite the humiliation of this defeat, Diefenbaker remained in Parliament, doing what he loved until his death in August 1979. It was just long enough to see the Progressive Conservatives returned to power with a minority government led by Joe Clark.

Ultimately, Diefenbaker was defeated by his own shortcomings; he was, in fact, the architect of his own demise. Throughout his tenure as prime minister he remained more preoccupied with maintaining his political position than in actually governing, so much so that he lost sight of his parliamentary majority, a majority so large that policy formulation on even the most contentious issues would have been possible if only he had had the courage and the will. As this book has illustrated, Diefenbaker's contemplation of nuclear policy was overwhelmingly a matter of political calculation, not national security. The same could be said of Pearson's approach. To be sure, different theatres of use and different alliances complicated the formulation of Canada's nuclear policy, but this complexity was exacerbated by political hesitation and Diefenbaker's preoccupation with maintaining his political position. Most of Diefenbaker's difficulties with nuclear policy were problems of his own making.

From the moment the Cabinet Defence Committee began to discuss nuclear negotiations with the Americans in April 1958, Diefenbaker had worried about the potential political liability and the possibility of an outspoken anti-nuclear movement. Neither Pearson's opposition to nuclear weapons nor poor relations with the United States deterred Diefenbaker from negotiating with the Americans to acquire nuclear weapons. Only the anti-nuclear movement, and only when it mustered a show of force with its National Petition, made Diefenbaker pause. Yet while he continually worried that disarmament activists would be able to persuade Canadians to oppose nuclear weapons, the fact remains that the Canadian anti-nuclear movement did not even exist when Diefenbaker first became anxious about their ability to influence public opinion. Nor is there any indication that the movement ever managed to garner much support among the Canadian public beyond the petition that the CCND presented to the prime minister in October 1961. But even the petition should not have represented a political threat to Diefenbaker. While it is true that a petition containing more than a hundred thousand signatures was an impressive feat, it should not have caused him to balk at the thought of acquiring nuclear weapons from the Americans.

As a self-styled populist, one who owed much of his electoral success to the support of the grassroots of the Conservative Party, Diefenbaker paid particular concern to letters from ordinary Canadians. He came to use these letters, which were actually from anti-nuclear activists, as a substitute for more formal opinion polls (which he did not trust) to tell him about the true volatility of the nuclear issue. Although he understood that the movement did not represent popular sentiment, he nonetheless viewed it as a political threat. It was a threat because he understood that political support could be unpredictable. This was a particular concern during his early years in office, when the number who did not know whether Canada should acquire nuclear weapons remained high. And when the number of Canadians opposed was combined with the number of undecided, it represented a majority. Diefenbaker's early caution, then, was reasonable within this context. The same is not true as the level of uncertainty dwindled and a majority of Canadians came to support acquisition. By late 1961, the strength of popular support was such that even as the number of Canadians opposed to nuclear weapons grew, the number of undecided was so low that even in combination they were a minority. Clearly a majority of Canadians wanted the government to acquire nuclear warheads. Moreover, Diefenbaker never came to terms with the fact that the number of undecided Canadians was never higher than (or the same as, for that matter) the number who supported the acquisition of nuclear weapons.

Diefenbaker's promise to Kennedy that he would educate Canadians about the necessity of nuclear weapons was a similar paradox because it was largely unnecessary. In any case, he made only a half-hearted effort, giving just a single speech on Canada's nuclear policy in the months that followed the pledge, and then giving up because of the media's failure to take notice. Although he could have regarded the muted reaction to his speech as widespread approval of the government's nuclear policy, he did not.

While his approach to the nuclear problem was reminiscent of the tactics used by Mackenzie King and Franklin Roosevelt to ready their respective nations to enter the Second World War, Diefenbaker was dealing with an entirely different situation from the one faced by the wartime leaders. There was plenty of evidence to suggest that Canadians and Americans were divided about entering the Second World War, but there was no such evidence to suggest that Canadians felt the same way about the acquisition of nuclear weapons. Diefenbaker's self-proclaimed need to persuade and educate the

Canadian public was a figment of his imagination, spurred on by the contents of his mailbag, more than a realistic reaction to public opinion. Opinion polls, throughout his tenure as prime minister, demonstrated that more Canadians than not supported acquisition. It is plausible to suggest that if Diefenbaker had acted swiftly to acquire nuclear weapons, he would have been able to avoid the perceived political difficulties entirely. After all, if he had concluded a nuclear arrangement in 1958 or 1959, there would have been at least three years left in his mandate – more than enough time for any outrage among the electorate to subside.

Pearson was similarly moved by considerations of public opinion and political gain, but the internal polling data upon which he relied was put to better use than the contents of Diefenbaker's mailbag. Like the polls that were shown to Diefenbaker, the Liberal Party's data indicated that a majority of Canadians supported the acquisition of nuclear weapons. The added incentive for the Liberal leader was the promise of a majority government based on the presumption that support for the acquisition of nuclear weapons would translate into electoral support. Ultimately, Pearson turned out to be the better of the two men at gauging the weight of public opinion on the subject.

By the same token, Pearson was almost as uncertain as Diefenbaker in his approach to nuclear policy. Despite his pledge to honour Canada's international obligations and then renegotiate them, he did no more than acquire the warheads. Even Pearson's successor, Pierre Trudeau – the man who had called him the "unfrocked priest of peace" – was slow to remove the offending warheads from Canada. It was not until his final year in office, 1984, that Trudeau banished nuclear weapons from Canadian territory.

That both Pearson and Diefenbaker were governed by the consideration of politics rather than national security is not meant to be a critical observation. There is nothing inappropriate about a politician worrying about how a particular issue might influence his or her electoral support. The problem was the manner in which both leaders handled the formulation of policy in the light of their political considerations. That said, the Americans did little to give Diefenbaker reason to trust them. Whether it was Operation Sky Hawk or the Cuban Missile Crisis, successive administrations illustrated that Diefenbaker was quite right to be skeptical of promises that the Americans would consult with the Canadian government in the event of an emergency so grave as to warrant the use of Canada's nuclear arsenal.

Perhaps, then, it is fair to adjust a well-known adage: just because one is paranoid does not necessarily mean that one is unreasonable. In the end, history has remembered Canada's thirteenth prime minister as an indecisive leader, a paranoid populist, whose misplaced faith in letters he thought were from ordinary Canadians served to secure his downfall. This characterization is a bit of a caricature. Rather, a preoccupation with political security, and a belief that the nuclear issue would threaten his tenure of office were the essence of Diefenbaker's indecision. It was, however, an indecision that was largely of his own making and one that was ultimately avoidable.

Notes

INTRODUCTION

1 *Newsweek*, 18 February 1963.
2 Bundy, *Danger and Survival*, 256.
3 See Maloney, *War without Battles* and "Canadian Shield"; Richter, "'Strategic Theoretical Parasitism' Reconsidered" and *Avoiding Armageddon*; and Simpson, NATO *and the Bomb*.
4 English, *The Worldly Years*, 251.

CHAPTER ONE

1 Gallup poll, February 1957, Progressive Conservative Party (PCP) papers, vol. 415, file: The Canadian Liberal, 1957–1961, Library and Archives Canada (LAC).
2 Spencer, *Trumpets and Drums*, 28.
3 Kidd, "Memorandum to All Campaign Staff," 16 May 1957, H.E. Kidd Papers, vol. 5, file 16: Memoranda 1957 election, May–June 1957, LAC.
4 Pickersgill, *Seeing Canada Whole*, 474.
5 Granatstein, *Canada, 1957–1967*, 26.
6 Pickersgill, *Seeing Canada Whole*, 474.
7 Granatstein, *Canada, 1957–1967*, 26.
8 English, *The Worldly Years*, 157. Gordon Churchill also commented that it was a "black day in Canada's history" (Granatstein, *Canada, 1957–1967*, 14).
9 Bothwell and Kilbourn, *C.D. Howe*, 303–4.
10 See English, *Worldly Years*, 156, and Thorburn, "Parliament and Policy-Making."

11 Ibid.

12 Thomson, *Louis St. Laurent, Canadian*, 483. See also Eayrs, "Canadian Policy and Opinion during the Suez Crisis," 103.

13 English, *The Worldly Years*, 141–2.

14 Grosart was Diefenbaker's national director in 1957 and a former journalist, having worked for the *Toronto Star* in the early 1930s before forming the Canadian Publicity Bureau in 1932, Canada's second public relations firm. Grosart also had political experience, having run George Drew's leadership campaign in 1948, which was waged and won against Diefenbaker. Known to carry a grudge and reluctant to trust past adversaries, Diefenbaker nonetheless allowed Grosart a great deal of leeway when it came to running the 1957 campaign. It was Grosart, for example, who decided to use the Bible as the basis of the Conservatives' campaign focus on vision: "Where there is no vision, the people perish." See Marketing, *Ottawa Sun*, 27 June 1958, Allister Grosart Papers, Vol. 8, file 13: Conservative Campaign Manager, Clippings: 1936–1974, LAC.

15 Granatstein, *Canada, 1957–1967*, 22.

16 Spencer, *Trumpets and Drums*, 24–7.

17 "We Can Win with John," n.d., PCP papers, Vol. 371, file: Election 1957, Advertising.

18 Ibid.

19 Spencer, *Trumpets and Drums*, 26.

20 "General Guide to Candidates," n.d., PCP papers, file: Election – Canada, Memoranda.

21 "We Can Win with John," n.d., PCP papers, vol. 371, file: Election 1957 – Advertising.

22 "One Canada and Canada First," n.d., ibid.

23 Thomson, *Louis St. Laurent, Canadian*, 486.

24 For more on the characterization of the Liberal Party as the "Government Party," see Whitaker, *The Government Party*. For a characterization of the Progressive Conservatives as the perennial party of opposition, see Perlin, *The Tory Syndrome*.

25 Thomson, *Louis St. Laurent, Canadian*, 518.

26 Douglas Harkness to Arthur Beaumont, 13 June 1957, Douglas S. Harkness Papers, vol. 64, file: Election 1957 (2), LAC.

27 Thomson, *Louis St. Laurent, Canadian*, 523–6.

28 Granatstein, *Canada, 1957–1967*, 28.

29 Thomas Delworth, interview with author, 18 May 1999.

30 Memorandum, 8 August 1957, John G. Diefenbaker Papers, vol. 2, MG 01/XII/A/19, Cabinet Documents, August 1957–1959, Diefenbaker Canada Centre.

31 Hilliker, "The Politicians and the 'Pearsonalities,'" 152–67.

32 Robinson, *Diefenbaker's World*, 7–8.

33 Ibid., 34.

34 Granatstein, *Canada, 1957–1967*, 29–30.

35 Granatstein, *A Man of Influence*, 324

36 Robinson, *Diefenbaker's World*, 14.

37 Ibid., 16.

38 Ibid., 17.

39 Immerman, *John Foster Dulles and the Diplomacy of the Cold War*, 17.

40 For detailed assessments of the NORAD negotiations, see McLin, *Canada's Changing Defense Policy, 1957–1963*; Jockel, *No Boundaries Upstairs*; and Granatstein, *Canada, 1957–1967*.

41 Granatstein, *Canada, 1957–1967*, 103.

42 The memo providing the list of representations on defence bodies had not been updated since 1954. See "List of Department of External Affairs Representations on Defence Bodies," 17 June 1957, H.B. Robinson Papers, vol. 1, file 1.3: April 1957 to 28 August 1957, LAC.

43 Moreover, the new prime minister did not much care for cabinet committees, and his decision not to work within the cabinet committee structure for the creation of NORAD was only the first sign of things to come. See Hilliker and Barry, *Canada's Department of External Affairs*, 2:236–7.

44 Granatstein, *Canada, 1957–1967*, 104.

45 Ibid.

46 Ibid., 103.

47 "List of Department of External Affairs Representations on Defence Bodies," 17 June 1957, Robinson Papers, vol. 1, file 1.3: April 1957 to 28 August 1957.

48 Granatstein, *Canada, 1957–1967*, 103–4.

49 Ibid., 105.

50 Hilliker and Barry, *Canada's Department of External Affairs*, 2:236.

51 McLin, *Canada's Changing Defense Policy*, 39–41.

52 Hilliker and Barry, *Canada's Department of External Affairs*, 2:236.

53 Jockel, *No Boundaries Upstairs*, 111.

54 Cabinet Conclusions, 7 July 1958, Privy Council Office, RG 2, LAC.

55 Jockel, *No Boundaries Upstairs*, 109.

56 Cabinet Conclusions, 11 April 1958, paras. 4–7. Note in particular that Sidney Smith states "that the terms of reference could not become effective until the note was negotiated. The prime minister [absent from this meeting] had seen the note and agreed that a draft of this general nature might be taken up with the US authorities." See also Cabinet Conclusions, 8 May 1958, paras. 4–6.

57 Granatstein, *Canada, 1957–1967*, 105.

58 Robinson, *Diefenbaker's World*, 37.

59 Undersecretary of State for External Affairs to Chair, Chiefs of Staff, 6 September 1957, Robinson Papers, vol. 8, file 8.1.

60 There is an extensive body of literature on the Avro Arrow. See, for example, Russell Isinger and Donald C. Story, "The Plane Truth: The Avro Canada CF–105 Arrow Program," in Story and Shepard, eds., *The Diefenbaker Legacy*, 43–55.

61 The Americans and the British might have encouraged the Canadians to continue production of the Arrow, but they were equally firm with the Canadian government and A.V. Roe (the Arrow's manufacturer) that no orders for the interceptor would be forthcoming. See Cabinet Defence Committee (CDC) minutes, 115th Meeting, 19 September 1957, Diefenbaker Papers, vol. 3, MG 01/XII/A/45: Defence – CDC, 1957–1959.

62 Goodman, *Life of the Party*, 54, 79, 80, 85; E.A. Goodman, interview with author, 8 April 1999.

63 Goodman *Life of the Party*, 92, and Goodman interview.

64 Cabinet Conclusions, 29 October 1957.

65 Bryce to the Prime Minister, "Cabinet item – atomic weapons at Goose Bay," 3 October 1957, Diefenbaker Papers, vol. 3, MG/01/XII/A/52: Defence – Nuclear Weapons – Goose Bay, 1957.

66 A.R. Crepault to Diefenbaker, "NATO Stockpiling of Nuclear Weapons," 26 July 1957, Robinson Papers, vol. 8, file 8.1: Nuclear Weapons Policy, 1957–1958.

67 Ibid.

68 Ibid.

69 "Leading Planks in Progressive Conservative Party Platform in 1957 General Election as Interpreted by Donald M. Fleming (Toronto-Eglinton)," n.d., Donald M. Fleming Papers, vol. 41, file: 1957 Election Policy: Manifestos, Memos, LAC.

70 Crepault to Diefenbaker, "NATO Stockpiling of Nuclear Weapons," 26 July 1957, Robinson Papers, vol. 8, file 8.1: Nuclear Weapons Policy, 1957–1958.

71 Ibid.

72 Ibid.

73 CDC minutes, 13 November 1957, Diefenbaker Papers, vol. 3, MG 01/XII/A/45 Defence – CDC, 1957–1959.

74 Ibid.

75 Permanent Representative of Canada to the North Atlantic Council and OEEC to Secretary of State for External Affairs, "The Present Position of NATO," 15 October 1957, ibid.

76 3 December 1957, Robinson Papers, vol. 1, file 1.7: December 1957.

77 Statement to External Affairs Committee, 5 December 1957, ibid.

78 Robinson, *Diefenbaker's World*, 31.

79 Cabinet Conclusions, 10 January 1958, paras. 17 and 18.

80 Cabinet Conclusions, 13 January 1958.

81 Pearkes to CDC, 10 February 1958, Diefenbaker Papers, vol. 3, MG 01/XII/A/45: Defence – CDC, 1957–1959.

82 J.W. Stambaugh to Kidd, 12 June 1957, Kidd Papers, vol. 5, file 19: Defeat of 1957, Correspondence, 1957–58.

83 Ibid., and H.J. MacDonald to Kidd, 17 June 1957, Kidd Papers, ibid.

84 Grant Deachman to Kidd, 21 June 1957, Kidd Papers, ibid.

85 See "Some Observations on How to Improve the Present Position of the Liberal Party," 21 September 1957, Kidd Papers, ibid.

86 Ibid.

87 Pickersgill, *The Road Back*, 17.

88 Canada, House of Commons, *Debates*, 20 January 1958, 3519–20.

89 Spencer, *Trumpets and Drums*, 49.

90 Cabinet Conclusions, 22 January 1958, paras. 6–8, and 24 January 1958, para. 1.

91 Pearkes to CDC, Top Secret, 10 February 1958, Diefenbaker Papers, vol. 3, MG 01/XII/A/45: Defence – CDC, 1957–1959.

92 "Advertising and Publicity Hints for Candidates," n.d., Fleming Papers, vol. 44, file: 1958 Campaign (3).

93 Spencer, *Trumpets and Drums*, 51.

94 See W.R. Brunt to all Candidates and Campaign Officials, "A Commentary on the Liberal Party's Policy Statement," 7 March 1958, Fleming Papers, vol. 44, file: 1958 Election – Campaign Material (1).

95 Diefenbaker was inspired by Eisenhower's presidential campaign of 1952, a very tangible example of the admiration with which he regarded the president; see Spencer, *Trumpets and Drums*, 50. See also "Advertising and Publicity Hints for Candidates," n.d., Fleming Papers, vol. 44, file: 1958 Campaign (3), and vol. 45, file: 1958 Election, Speeches.

96 "Talking Points for Progressive Conservative Speakers and Workers, General Election 1958, Confidential," n.d., Fleming Papers, vol. 44, file: 1958 Election – National Campaign Headquarters (4).

97 Grosart to Cabinet Ministers and Parliamentary Assistants, 24 February 1958, Fleming Papers, file: 1958 Election – National Campaign Headquarters (3).

98 "Campaign Circular No. 5," 14 March 1958, Fleming Papers, file: 1958 Election – National Campaign Headquarters (1).

99 Fleming Papers, *Globe and Mail* excerpt from 12 March 1958.

100 Godfrey Barrass to All Ontario Candidates, "Peace, Pearson and Missiles," 19 March 1958, Fleming Papers.

101 While campaigning in New Brunswick, Pearson promised to increase the numbers at Camp Gagetown and to reopen Camp Utopia in that province (ibid.).

102 "The Pearson Story, February 1958," Diefenbaker Papers, microfilm 7927, vol. 302, MG 01/VI/(335 Wpg s): The House of Commons – Members of the House – Winnipeg South Constituency, 1958–1962.

103 See various surveys and correspondences in the papers of T.W. Kent, vol. 2, 1988 accrual, Queen's University Archives.

104 Spencer, *Trumpets and Drums*, 54.

105 Ibid., 58.

106 Pickersgill, *The Road Back*, 24.

CHAPTER TWO

1 Quoted in Smith, *Rogue Tory*, 285.

2 Fleming, *So Very Near*, 1:475–8.

3 Newman, *Renegade in Power*, 86.

4 See the collected reference material at the Diefenbaker Canada Centre in Saskatoon.

5 Goose Bay was a product of the Destroyers for Bases Agreement between the United States and Great Britain in 1940. At the time, Newfoundland had not entered Confederation and, having declared bankruptcy during the Depression, was subject to a Commission of Government under the British.

6 CDC minutes, 28 April 1958, para. 13, John G. Diefenbaker Papers, vol. 3, MG 01/XII/A/45: Defence – CDC, 1957–1959, Diefenbaker Canada Centre.

7 Ibid.

8 Ibid.

9 Ibid.

10 Cabinet Conclusions, 29 April 1958, Privy Council RG 2, Library and Archives Canada (LAC).

11 Ibid.

12 See Diefenbaker Papers, microfilm 7811, MG 01/VI/154: Defence Research – Atomic Research, 1957–1963.

13 For the more technical aspects of the NORAD negotiations as well as the Canadian-American military discussions that preceded them, see Jockel, *No Boundaries Upstairs*, and McLin, *Canada's Changing Defense, 1957–1963*.

14 Cabinet Conclusions, 11 April 1958.

15 Cabinet Conclusions, 8 May 1958.

16 Ibid.

17 Robinson to Prime Minister (in Cabinet), 10 May 1958, H.B. Robinson Papers, vol. 1, file 1: 12 May 1958, LAC. (emphasis added).

18 Cabinet Conclusions, 10 May 1958.

19 Jockel, *No Boundaries Upstairs*, 117.

20 Cabinet Conclusions, 20 May 1958.

21 Cabinet Conclusions, 27 May 1958.

22 Jockel, *No Boundaries Upstairs*, 117. See also Canada, House of Commons, *Debates*, 10 June 1958, 1004.

23 Jockel, *No Boundaries Upstairs*. See also Canada, House of Commons, *Debates*, 19 June 1958, 1423.

24 Cabinet Conclusions, 8 May 1958.

25 CDC minutes, 28 April 1958, para. 18, Diefenbaker Papers, vol. 3, MG 01/XII/A/45: Defence – CDC, 1957–1959.

26 Cabinet Conclusions, 8 May 1958. Note that both Howard Green and Douglas Harkness were in attendance.

27 In 2007 dollars, the 1958 cost of the Arrow was $1.8 billion and the 1961 cost was $5.5 billion. The defence budget was $15.7 billion in 2006–2007. See www.dnd.ca/site/Reports/budget05/back05_e.asp and http://www.bankofcanada.ca/en/rates/inflation_calc.html.

28 Department of National Defence, "Aide Memoire for Discussions with the U.S. Secretary of State on Canada's Defence Problems," 10 July 1958, Robinson Papers, vol. 1, file 1.14.

29 Robinson, Notes on Meeting between Dulles and Smith, 10 July 1958, Robinson Papers, vol. 1, file 1.14.

30 On the Defence Production Sharing Agreement, see Kirton, "The Consequences of Integration." DPSA allowed Canadian defence products duty-free entry into the United States, notwithstanding the "Buy American" legislation of the United States.

31 Both Norman Robertson and Howard Green attended this meeting.

32 Bryce to the Prime Minister, "Air Defence Decisions," 31 July 1958, Diefenbaker Papers, vol. 3, MG 01/XII/A/45: Defence – CDC, 1957–1959.

33 Harkness, "The Nuclear Arms Question and the Political Crisis Which Arose from It in January and February 1963," August 1963, 2, Douglas S. Harkness Papers, vol. 57, file: The Nuclear Question, LAC.

34 Bryce to the Prime Minister, "Air Defence Decisions," 31 July 1958, Diefenbaker Papers, vol. 3, MG 01/XII/A/45: Defence – CDC, 1957–1959.

35 Cabinet Conclusions, 1 August 1958.

36 Department of External Affairs Memorandum to the CDC, "Continental Air Defence – Foreign Policy Implications," 14 August 1958, Diefenbaker Papers, vol. 10, MG 01/XIV/D/26.2.

37 Ibid.

38 Cabinet Conclusions, 8 September 1958.

39 Cabinet Conclusions, 22 September 1958.

40 Press release, Prime Minister's Office, 23 September 1958.

41 Cabinet Conclusions, 22 September 1958.

42 Cabinet Conclusions, 1 October 1958.

43 Pearkes had attended a NATO defence ministers' conference in mid-April. NATO's newly adopted strategy, MC–70, "Minimum Essential Force Requirements 1958–63," the focus of which was a "strong shield" using "modern weapons," formed the bulk of the discussion. Pearkes reported that talks were underway with interested members of the alliance, though no formal action would occur until the talks and reports were completed. See "Report on NATO Defence Ministers' Meeting, 15–17 April, 1958," 23 April 1958, Diefenbaker Papers, vol. 3, MG 01/XII/A/45 Defence – CDC, 1957–1959.

44 Jules Léger to Norman Robertson, c.c. Charles Ritchie, 17 April 1958, Robinson Papers, vol. 8, file 8.1: Nuclear Weapons Policy, 1957–1958. Granatstein cites Robertson's growing opposition to nuclear weapons from late 1958 to early 1959, which was definitely in full force by the time Howard Green became minister of external affairs in June 1959 (Granatstein, *A Man of Influence*, 336–8).

45 Léger to Charles Foulkes, 7 October 1958, Robinson Papers, vol. 8, file 8.2: Nuclear Weapons Policy, 1957–1958.

46 Cabinet Conclusions, 15 October 1958.

47 Fleming, *So Very Near*, 2:18.

48 Cabinet Conclusions, 15 October 1958.

49 Memorandum for File, "Acquisition and Storage of Defensive Nuclear Weapons and Warheads," 17 October 1958, Attachment: McCardle Memorandum for Minister, 15 October 1958, Diefenbaker Papers, vol. 10, MG 01/XIV/D/26.2.

50 Ibid. Diefenbaker highlighted this passage in the margin of the memo.

51 Ibid., Diefenbaker also highlighted this passage in the margin of the memorandum.

52 Robertson to Chairman, Chiefs of Staff and Secretary to the Cabinet, "Acquisition of Nuclear Weapons," 20 October 1958, Robinson Papers, vol. 8, file 8.2: Nuclear Weapons Policy, 1957–1958. Given Robertson's

opposition to nuclear weapons, it is ironic that cabinet approved his appointment as undersecretary of external affairs the very day it decided to undertake formal negotiations with the United States to acquire nuclear weapons. See Cabinet Conclusions, 15 October 1958.

53 DL (1) Division for File, "Control of Nuclear Weapons," 7 November 1958, Diefenbaker Papers, vol. 10, MG 01/XIV/D/26.2.

54 Ibid.

55 Cabinet Conclusions, 9 December 1958.

56 Ibid.

57 Robertson to Minister (in Cabinet), "Acquisition of Nuclear Weapons," 22 December 1958, Diefenbaker Papers, vol. 10, MG 01/XIV/D/26.2.

58 Cabinet Conclusions, 22 December 1958.

59 Bryce had urged Diefenbaker to announce the cancellation of the Arrow at the same time he announced that Canada had entered negotiations with the Americans for nuclear weapons. See Bryce to Diefenbaker, "The 105 Problem," 5 September 1958, Diefenbaker Papers, vol. 10, MG 01/XIV/D/26.2.

60 Cabinet Conclusions, 7 September 1958.

61 Bryce to Diefenbaker, "The 105 Problem," 5 September 1958, Diefenbaker Papers, vol. 10, MG 01/XIV/D/26.2.

62 By the end of 1958, every cabinet minister knew that the Arrow would be cancelled. See Cabinet Conclusions, 22 December 1958.

63 Canada, House of Commons, *Debates*, 20 February 1959, 1223.

64 *Globe and Mail*, 21 February 1959.

65 Jack Raymond, "US, Canada Near Atom Arms Pact – Ottawa Will Have an Equal Vote on Use of Weapons Based in Dominion," *New York Times*, 8 March 1959, Lester B. Pearson Papers, vol. 114, file: National Defence – Nuclear Weapons Storage in Canada, LAC.

66 Diefenbaker Papers, vol. 1, MG 01/XII/A/11: Avro Arrow – Letters, 1959. It should be noted that not all the mail received by Diefenbaker on this issue was negative; some Canadians applauded his decision, agreeing with the government that the CF–105 was simply too expensive to produce for the Canadian forces.

67 "History of the Ban the Bomb Movement by Douglas Campbell," n.d., CUCND-SUPA papers, vol. 1, file 10: CUCND Toronto Office 1960–61, Correspondence & Miscellaneous, McMaster University Library.

68 Ibid. See also Diefenbaker Papers, vol. 82, MG 01/XII/D/47: Defence Research – Atomic Research, Atomic Armament, 1959–61.

69 Canada, House of Commons, *Debates*, 10 March 1959, 1775; Douglas Le Pan (signed by Robertson) to the Minister, 10 March 1959, .

Diefenbaker Papers, vol. 104, MG 01/XII/F/100: Defence – Acquisition of Nuclear Weapons, n.d., 1959–1963.

70 Ibid.

CHAPTER THREE

1 Minister of National Defence to the Prime Minister, 6 January 1960, John G. Diefenbaker Papers, vol. 3, MG 01/VI/R/95, Diefenbaker Canada Centre.

2 Granatstein, *Canada, 1957–1967,* 102.

3 See Richard Bell's comment about Diefenbaker's use of King as a role model (Smith, *Rogue Tory,* 285).

4 Robertson to the Prime Minister, "Draft Bilateral Agreement with the United States on Cooperation on the Uses of Atomic Energy for Military Defence Purposes," 22 April 1959, H.B. Robinson Papers, vol. 8, file 8.8: Nuclear Policy, 1959, Library and Archives Canada (LAC). Noted in Bryce's handwriting across the top of this document is "Looks OK we better get ahead with it. B" and "approved by PM file: PCO RBB 29/4."

5 "Comparison of United States–United Kingdom Agreement with Proposed Canadian Agreement" (author unknown) n.d., Robinson Papers, vol. 8, file 8.8: Nuclear Policy, 1959.

6 CDC minutes, 22 April 1959, Diefenbaker Papers, vol. 3, MG 01/XII/A/45: Defence – CDC, 1957–59.

7 Cabinet Conclusions, 13 May 1959, Order in Council 1959–578, Privy Council Office, RG 2, LAC.

8 Robertson to the Prime Minister, "Instrument of Full Power to sign Canada–USA Agreement on the uses of atomic energy for mutual defence purposes," May 1959, Diefenbaker Papers, microfilm 7811, MG 01/VI/154: Defence Research – Atomic Research, 1957–1963.

9 Robinson, *Diefenbaker's World,* 107. Although Howard Green had not yet been appointed to his new portfolio, he attended the meeting in his capacity as minister of public works.

10 Robinson, *Diefenbaker's World,* 91. Thomas Delworth, interview with author, 18 May 1999.

11 Thomas Delworth, interview with author 18 May 1999.

12 Robinson, *Diefenbaker's World,* 37.

13 Diefenbaker, *The Years of Achievement, 1957 to 1962,* 123.

14 Robinson, *Diefenbaker's World,* 98.

15 His regular (and lengthy) letters to his mother illustrate the point; see Howard C. Green Papers, vol. 18, MSS 1060, Vancouver Municipal Archives.

16 Maxwell Yalden, interview with author, 13 April 1999.

17 Robinson, *Diefenbaker's World*, 108. The article was prepared by Christopher Hollis and appeared in the *Spectator*. See Robertson to Diefenbaker, Robinson Papers, vol. 8, file 8.8: Nuclear Policy, 1959.

18 Robertson did not have the prime minister's complete confidence. Robinson attributed this distrust to the fact that Robertson had denied Diefenbaker a diplomatic passport in 1945: before attending the U.N.'s founding conference in San Francisco, Diefenbaker had applied to the Department of External Affairs for a diplomatic passport, but Robertson, on instructions from Mackenzie King had refused Diefenbaker's request. Diefenbaker held quite a grudge (Robinson, *Diefenbaker's World*, 101).

19 Pearkes to the Prime Minister, 15 June 1959, Robinson Papers, vol. 8, file 8.8.

20 Ibid.

21 Léger to the Minister, 15 July 1959, Robinson Papers, vol. 8, file 8.8.

22 Pearkes to CDC, "Storage of Defensive Nuclear Weapons at Bases in Labrador and Newfoundland for the Use of United States Air Force Squadrons," 24 July 1959, Robinson Papers, vol. 8, file 8.8.

23 CDC minutes, 4 August 1959.

24 Cabinet Conclusions, 26 August 1959.

25 Granatstein, *Canada, 1957–1967*, 110.

26 Cabinet Conclusions, 26 August 1959.

27 Ibid.

28 Granatstein, *Canada, 1957–1967*, 110–11. Cabinet Conclusions, 26 August 1959.

29 Cabinet Conclusions, 27 August 1959.

30 Cabinet Conclusions, 26 August 1959.

31 Cabinet Conclusions, 11 September 1959.

32 Cabinet Conclusions, 22 September 1959.

33 See CDC minutes, 4 August 1959, and Cabinet Conclusions, 26 August and 11 September 1959.

34 Perhaps Green's continual emphasis on joint custody and control was interpreted as outright opposition. Given his naiveté on matters such as disarmament talks, it is entirely possible that he really believed that disarmament was an option and that if it proved to be impossible to secure some kind of agreement, nuclear weapons were acceptable. See Green Papers, vol. 18, Vancouver Municipal Archives.

35 Robinson, *Diefenbaker's World*, 111.

36 "Storage of Nuclear Weapons in Canada" (author unknown), 29 October 1959, Diefenbaker Papers, vol. 10, MG 01/XIV/D/26.2, and Robinson

Papers, vol. 8, file 8.10: Nuclear Policy, 1959. For example, if the Canadians demanded joint control in North America, would the Germans or the French demand the same arrangement for Canadian NATO forces stationed on their territory? This problem was developed in greater detail in Bryce, "Defence Questions for Discussions," Diefenbaker Papers, vol. 10, MG 01/XIV/D/26.2.

37 Department of External Affairs, "Canada–United States Defence Questions," 22 October 1959, Robinson Papers, vol. 8, file 8.10: Nuclear Policy, 1959.

38 "Storage of Nuclear Weapons in Canada" (author unknown) and Robinson Papers, vol. 8, file 8.10: Nuclear Policy, 1959.

39 Bryce, "Defence Questions for Discussions," Diefenbaker Papers, vol. 10, MG 01/XIV/D/26.2. See also Robinson Papers, vol. 8, file 8.10: Nuclear Policy, 1959.

40 Bryce, "Defence Questions for Discussions," and Robinson Papers, vol. 8, file 8.10: Nuclear Policy, 1959.

41 Bryce, "Defence Questions for Discussions."

42 Cabinet discussed preparations for the meeting at Camp David on 6 November 1959. The records of this discussion have been heavily excised under ss. 13(1)(a) and 15(1) of the Access to Information Act. However, there is little that cannot be determined from the briefing papers provided by the Department of External Affairs.

43 Cabinet Conclusions, 6 November 1959.

44 "Report on the Meeting of the Canada–United States Ministerial Committee on Joint Defence, 8–9 November 1959," Robinson Papers, vol. 8, file 8.10: Nuclear Policy, 1959.

45 Ibid.

46 Cabinet Conclusions, 10 November 1959.

47 Ibid.

48 "Storage of Nuclear Weapons in Canada" (author unknown) and Robinson Papers, vol. 8, file 8.10: Nuclear Policy, 1959.

49 Diefenbaker Papers, microfilm 7895, file 313.312: D-U – University Representatives – Control of Nuclear Weapons – Federal Government Executive – The Prime Minister of Canada – Requests and Appeals – Interviews – Delegations – University Representatives – Control of Nuclear Weapons, 1959–1960.

50 "History of the Ban the Bomb Movement by Douglas Campbell," n.d., CUCND-SUPA Papers, vol. 1, file 10: CUCND Toronto Office 1960–61, Correspondence and Miscellaneous, McMaster University Library.

51 Ibid.

52 Ibid.
53 Ibid. See also Moffatt, *History of the Canadian Peace Movement until 1969*, 147.
54 "Press Release – CCCRH Manifesto," February 1960, vol. 1, file 1; and Van Stolk to Walker, 10 August 1959, vol. 25, file 19: Maclean's Magazine; both in CCND papers, McMaster University Library.
55 David Lewis Stein, "Beginner's Guide to the Canadian Nuclear Disarmers," *Maclean's*, 7 October 1961, 10.
56 Wittner, *Resisting the Bomb, 1954–1970*, 32–3.
57 Christine Ball and Barbara Roberts suggest that Van Stolk's Edmonton Committee was a mothers' group. This is an overstatement. See Roberts, "Women's Peace Activism in Canada," and Ball, "The History of the Voice of Women/La Voix des Femmes: The Early Years."
58 Van Stolk to Walker, 10 August 1959, CCND papers, vol. 25, file 19: Maclean's Magazine. See also vol. 4, file 1: Correspondence – Mary Van Stolk, and several files in vol. 14 that contain a large quantity of material and correspondence between the CCCRH/CCND and SANE.
59 "Press Release – CCCRH Manifesto," February 1960, CCND papers, vol. 1, file 1. See also "History of the Edmonton Committee," September 1960, CCND papers, vol. 8, file 1; and David Lewis Stein, "A Beginner's Guide to Canada's Nuclear Disarmers," *Maclean's*, 7 October 1961.
60 CCND papers, vol. 4, file 1: Correspondence – Mary Van Stolk.
61 Van Stolk to H.L. Keenleyside, 19 September 1959, CCND papers, vol. 4, file 1: Correspondence – Mary Van Stolk.
62 "Report of the National Executive Secretary, Second Annual Meeting," March 1961, CCND papers, vol. 4, file 3: Mary Van Stolk – National Executive Secretary, CCCRH.
63 It was Keenleyside who suggested changing the name from "Canadian Committee for Sane Nuclear Policy" to the "Committee for the Control of Radiation Hazards" (Van Stolk to Walker, 10 August 1959, CCND papers, vol. 25, file 19: Maclean's Magazine). The existing Montreal Committee for the Control of Radiation Hazards made a similar suggestion.
64 "Report of the National Executive Secretary, Second Annual Meeting," March 1961, CCND papers, vol. 4, file 3: Mary Van Stolk – National Executive Secretary, CCCRH.
65 CCCRH by-laws, CCND papers, vol. 1, file 1.
66 Van Stolk to Walker, 10 August 1959, CCND papers, vol. 25, file 19: Maclean's Magazine.
67 Wittner, *Resisting the Bomb*, 52–4.

68 Ibid., 49–51.

69 Van Stolk to Walker, 10 August 1959, CCND papers, vol. 25, file 19: Maclean's Magazine.

70 CCND papers, vol. 1, file 1.

71 Ibid.

72 Ibid.

73 It is noteworthy that the early Canadian peace movement was predominantly Christian. See Socknat, *Witness against War*, 2–5.

74 Eugene Forsey wrote that Diefenbaker "had said that his door was always open to me, and it was (I was careful to appear at it as rarely as possible)." He considered Diefenbaker a "friend" and indicated that Diefenbaker had invited him to join the cabinet in 1957. Forsey seems to have kept his contact with Diefenbaker to matters involving the Canadian Labour Congress, not the CCCRH. In Forsey's case, nuclear weapons, the CCCRH, and nuclear disarmament did not warrant an index reference in his memoirs (Forsey, *A Life on the Fringe*, 86, 113–14).

75 CCND papers, vol. 1, file 1.

76 Selected correspondence from 1959 to 1963, CCND papers, vol. 25, file 19: Maclean's Magazine.

77 Blair Fraser to Van Stolk, 4 December 1960, CCND papers, vol. 25, file 19, Maclean's Magazine.

78 Banfield, *Political Influence*, 4–5.

79 Keenleyside to Diefenbaker, 20 January 1960, Diefenbaker Papers, vol. 3, file 154.5: Conf. Defence Research – Atomic Research – Radioactive Fallout – Confidential, 1960 VI/R/96.

80 Gowan Guest to Keenleyside, 9 February 1960, Diefenbaker Papers, vol. 3, file 154.5.

81 This is clear from the finding aid for Diefenbaker's personal papers. He kept correspondence files for everyone from "VIPS" (e.g., Eisenhower, Nixon, Macmillan, and Kennedy) to journalists (e.g., Blair Fraser) and political figures like (e.g., Eugene Forsey). Keenleyside is not in the list of separate files.

82 "Report of National Executive Secretary, Second Annual Meeting," March 1961, CCND papers, vol. 4, file 3.

83 See Levitt, *Pearson and Canada's Role in Nuclear Disarmament and Arms Control Negotiations*, for an overview of Canada's (with Pearson leading the way) involvement in U.N. disarmament conferences during the period preceding Pearson's leadership of the Liberal Party.

84 Pearson, "Statement on Control and Ownership of Tactical and Defensive Nuclear Weapons," 27 January 1960, Lester B. Pearson Papers, vol. 114, file: National Defence – Storage of Nuclear Weapons in Canada, LAC.

85 Robertson to the Minister, "Canadian Defence Policy – Position of the Leader of the Opposition," 2 December 1959, Diefenbaker Papers, vol. 10, MG 01/XIV/D/26.2.

86 Cabinet Conclusions, 30 December 1959; "Nuclear Weapons for Canadian Forces" (Draft; author unknown), 14 January 1960, Diefenbaker Papers, vol. 104, MG 01/XII/F/100.

87 Canada, House of Commons, *Debates*, 18 January 1960, 73.

88 "Nuclear Weapons for Canadian Forces" (Draft; author unknown), 14 January 1960, Diefenbaker Papers, vol. 104, MG 01/XII/F/100.

89 Canada, House of Commons, *Debates*, 20 January 1960, 133.

90 Minister of National Defence to the Prime Minister, "Acquisition and Control of Atomic Weapons," 11 January 1960, Diefenbaker Papers, vol. 10, MG 01/XIV/D/26.2. and vol. 3, MG 01/VI/R/94.

91 Minister of National Defence to the Prime Minister, 6 January 1960, Diefenbaker Papers, vol. 3, MG 01/VI/R/95.

92 Preston, *Canada in World Affairs*, 11:51–5, 57–9.

93 Bundy, *Danger and Survival*, 333.

94 Robinson, *Diefenbaker's World*, 131.

95 Note for file: Disarmament, 25 January 1960, Robinson Papers, vol. 2, file 2.16: January 1960.

96 Ibid.

97 For a detailed account of the U–2 incident, see Beschloss, *May-Day*.

98 Canada, House of Commons, *Debates*, 8 June 1959, 4413–14.

99 Eisenhower wrote: "Dear John, I thought that you would like to know that the conferees appointed by the House of Representatives and the Senate to consider appropriations for the Defense budget have recommended the appropriation of $244 million of the $294 million which had been requested by the Executive Branch for the Bomarc-B missile program. While this is, of course, not final since further legislative action must be taken, I hope that you will be as pleased as I was to know of this favorable development for the further improvement of continental defense. With warm regard, sincerely, Ike." This note does not indicate any concern on Diefenbaker's part about the coming of the Bomarc missile, something that the prime minister would likely have noted to the president. See Eisenhower to Diefenbaker, 29 June 1960, Diefenbaker Papers, vol. 7, MG 01/XII/A/232: Diefenbaker Correspondence (VIP) to Eisenhower, 1957–1961.

100 Despite their decision to work together, there were clear differences emerging between the Toronto and Montreal organizations. Toronto had the largest membership, which numbered between 100 and 120 members at its peak, and included a range of the political spectrum, from pacifists

to communists, with varying degrees of commitment to the cause. By
contrast, CUCND Montreal was smaller and dominated by ideologues,
particularly communists, Marxists, and Trotskyists, which did little to
enhance its credibility. Many Montreal members seemed to be more
interested in discussing the writings of revolutionaries than undertaking
action at the grassroots level to promote disarmament. In terms of policy,
both groups opposed nuclear weapons, but the Toronto branch supported Canada's involvement in NATO and NORAD (at least initially),
while students in Montreal wanted Canada to withdraw from both in
order to pursue a neutral foreign policy. Ultimately, while the Toronto
branch could be considered a group of pacifists and activists, the Montreal group was a collection of ideologues-of-the-moment, who seemed to
prefer to contemplate the ways of revolution without engaging in much
activity. See, for example, Ian Gentles's interview with author, 7 June
1999, and CUCND-SUPA papers, vol. 7, file: Early CUCND – Policy Statement, etc. See also "Members Universities of CUCND," Spring 1960,
CUCND-SUPA papers, vol. 1, file 10: CUCND Toronto Office 1960–61,
Correspondence and Miscellaneous.

101 Moffat, "North Bay Project," (n.d.), CCND papers, vol. 23, file 4: TCND
Miscellaneous Correspondence, 1962–1964.

102 See CUCND-SUPA Papers, vol. 8, files: Summer Projects; SUPA Summer
Projects in the Community 1965; and vol. 9, files: North Bay Project
Correspondence 1964–65 (Art Pape), North Bay Project Politics, Inter-
views, etc.; North Bay Project Preliminary Reports; North Bay Project:
Prospectus, Memo, Newsletter; SUPA papers: North Bay Project (Liora
Proctor); North Bay Project: Contacts & Interview List; North Bay Pro-
ject: Depth Interviews, Odds and Ends; North Bay Project: Economics
Committee.

103 Although Dempsey's columns inspired the creation of the Voice of
Women, it is difficult to determine the impact of the VOW on the noted
columnist. There is only the briefest reference to the VOW in her memoirs
– a single line devoted to the VOW – and it does not mention the role she
played in its creation. There is slightly more in the biography of Dempsey
written by her daughter-in-law. See Dempsey, *No Life for a Lady*, 100
and Davis Fisher, *Lotta Dempsey*, 50. Dempsey seems to have stayed
involved in the fight to ban nuclear weapons, even if not always offi-
cially, for she was a sponsor for the Benjamin Spock lecture in May 1964
in Toronto. See CCND papers, vol. 24, file 6: TCND – Dr. Benjamin Spock
Lecture. Dempsey, "Women's Section," Private Line, *Toronto Daily Star*,
17 May 1960.

104 Macpherson, *When in Doubt, Do Both*, 90. Also Dempsey, *Toronto Daily Star*.

105 Dempsey, *Toronto Daily Star*, 21 May 1960.

106 Dempsey, *Toronto Daily Star*, 30 May 1960.

107 Macpherson, *When in Doubt, Do Both*, 92–3.

108 Ball, "The History of the Voice of Women," 86, 96–7. For a treatment of women's traditional role within the peace movement, see Strong-Boag, "Peace-Making Women: Canada 1919–1939," 178.

109 VOW papers, vol. 1, file: Correspondence – MPs, Formation of VOW, LAC.

110 Ball, "The History of the Voice of Women," 100.

111 Josephine Davis to Maryon Pearson, 12 June 1960, VOW papers, vol. 1, file: Correspondence – MPs, Formation 1960–1963.

112 Ball, "The History of the Voice of Women," 105–7.

113 Roberts, "Women's Peace Activism in Canada," 307, fn 42. Roberts echoes sentiments expressed by Moffatt in *History of the Canadian Peace Movement*.

114 Ball, "The History of the Voice of Women," 118.

115 Olive Diefenbaker to Davis, 8 August 1960, VOW papers, vol. 1, file: Correspondence – MPs, Formation 1960–1963.

116 See Fairclough, *Saturday's Child*; also Fairclough to Davis, 26 July 1960, VOW papers, vol. 1, file: Correspondence – MPs, Formation 1960–1963.

117 Diefenbaker Papers, microfilm 7813, file 174: Defence Expenditure – Weapons, Ammunition, Explosives, Missiles, 1958–1963. See also microfilm 7811 for additional letters from this period.

118 Canada, House of Commons, *Debates*, 22 June 1960, 5239.

119 "Report of the National Executive Secretary, Second Annual Meeting," March 1961, CCND papers, vol. 4, file 3: Van Stolk as National Executive Secretary, CCCRH.

120 Pearson Papers, vol. 4, file 154.1: Nuclear Tests.

121 Davis to Maryon Pearson, 3 August 1960, Pearson Papers, vol. 91, file: External Affairs – Voice of Women, Part Two.

122 See Pearson Papers, vol. 4, file 154.1: Nuclear Tests from January 20, 1958.

123 A.E. Thompson to Mary Macdonald, 19 July 1960, Pearson papers, vol. 91, file: External Affairs – Voice of Women, Part Two.

124 Maryon Pearson to VOW, 30 July 1960, VOW papers, vol. 1, file: Correspondence – MPs, Formation 1960–1963.

125 Robinson to the Prime Minister, "Conversation with Eisenhower," 2 June 1960, Robinson papers, vol. 3, file 3.8: June 1960.

126 (As dictated by Bryce to Robinson) "Prime Minister's Visit to Washington: Matters Discussed, June 3, 1960," 7 June 1960 (Revised June 17, 1960), Robinson Papers, vol. 3, file 3.8: June 1960.

127 "Prime Minister's Conversation with President Eisenhower, June 3, 1960," 9 June 1960, Robinson Papers, vol. 3, file 3.8.

128 Canada, House of Commons, *Debates*, 22 June 1960, 5239; see also 4 July 1960, 5653.

129 Canada, House of Commons, *Debates*, 14 July 1960, 6271–2.

130 Robinson, *Diefenbaker's World*, 144.

131 Canada, House of Commons, *Debates*, 4 August 1960, 7557.

132 Robinson, *Diefenbaker's World*, 144.

133 Permanent Joint Board on Defence Canada–United States, "Journal of Discussions and Decisions for the Meeting Held at Camp Gagetown," 9 August 1960, Diefenbaker Papers, vol. 2, MG 01/VI/R/47 104: Secret Defence – Permanent Joint Board.

134 Kent pointed out that the electoral platform for the 1962 election was based on the 1958 leadership convention, not the Kingston Conference (Kent, *A Public Purpose*, 79).

135 Tom Kent's paper, "Towards a Philosophy of Social Security," generated the most commentary. Other papers included Maurice Lamontagne, "Growth, Price Stability, and the Problems of Unemployment"; Claude Morin, "Canadian Social Security: Problems and Perspectives"; William Mahoney, "The Aims of Organized Labour"; J. Wendell Macleod, "Basic Issues in Hospital and Medical Care Insurance"; W. Gibbings, "Prairie Grain Problems"; David L. MacFarlane, "Fair Shares for Agriculture"; A. Andras, "Some Comments on Unemployment Insurance"; Monteath Douglas, "Old Age Security"; Alan Jarvis, "The Environment"; Michael Barkway, "How Independent Can We Be?"; and André Laurendeau, "The Development of Canadian Values and Our Cultural Heritage." See Kent Papers, vol. 6, files: Study Conference on National Problems, Kingston, September 1960 (3) and (4).

136 James Eayrs, "Defending the Realm: A National Security Policy for Canada in the 1960s," and Harry Johnson, "External Economic Relations." Both papers encouraged the Canadian government to work toward greater cooperation with the Americans, which went against the grain of the prevailing tone of anti-Americanism. See R.M. MacIntosh, "The Kingston Conference September 1960," 4 October 1960, Kent Papers, vol. 6, file: Study Conference (1) Kingston 1960.

137 Eayrs, "Defending the Realm." Many of the ideas presented at this conference appeared in Eayrs's later work, *Northern Approaches: Canada and the Search for Peace* (Toronto, 1961).

138 Eayrs, "Defending the Realm."

139 Paul Hellyer, the Liberal Party's defence critic, spoke out against nuclear weapons in the House of Commons on 4 August 1960. Pearson did the same the following day (Canada, House of Commons, *Debates*, 4 August 1960, 7566–8, 7562, and 5 August 1960, 7606, 7610–11).

CHAPTER FOUR

1 John G. Diefenbaker Papers, vol. 9, MG 01/XII/A/306: Diefenbaker Correspondence (VIP) with Richard Nixon, 1958, 1961, Diefenbaker Canada Centre.
2 Heeney, *The Things That Are Caesar's*, 169.
3 See, for example, Preston, *Canada in World Affairs*, 68.
4 Harkness, "The Nuclear Arms Question," 3, Douglas S. Harkness Papers, vol. 57, file: The Nuclear Arms Question and the Political Crisis Which Arose from It in January and February 1963, Library and Archives Canada (LAC).
5 Ibid., 4.
6 Harkness to Diefenbaker, 17 November 1960, Diefenbaker Papers, vol. 104, MG 01/XII/F/100: Defence – Acquisition of Nuclear Weapons, n.d., 1959–1963.
7 Bryce to Robertson and Miller, "Recommendations on Nuclear Weapons," 30 November 1960, H.B. Robinson Papers, vol. 9, file 9.3, LAC.
8 Ibid.
9 Robertson to the Minister, 28 November 1960. Howard Green Papers (LAC), vol. 8, file 13: External Affairs Debate – memoranda, reports, notes, clippings, November 1960. Robertson cited in Canada, House of Commons, *Debates*, 19 January and 20 February 1959; and 18 January, 9 February, 4 and 14 July 1960. See Department of National Defence to CDC, "Memorandum on Nuclear Weapons," 5 December 1960, Robinson Papers, vol. 9, file 9.3. See also Green Papers (LAC), vol. 10, file 5.
10 Cabinet Conclusions, 1 December 1960, Privy Council, RG 2, LAC.
11 Cabinet Conclusions, 6 December 1960.
12 Ibid.
13 Ibid.
14 Ibid.
15 Diefenbaker, "Memorandum – Office of the Prime Minister," 27 December 1960, Diefenbaker Papers, vol. 70, MG 01/XII/C/342: Pound, M.R. – Political, 1957–1963.

16 Bryce to the Prime Minister, "Nuclear Weapons Policy Statement," 8
    January 1961, Diefenbaker Papers, vol. 104, MG 01/XII/F/100: Defence
    Acquisition of Nuclear Weapons 1959–1963.

17 For a contrasting point of view, see Simpson, "New Ways of Thinking
    about Nuclear Weapons and Canada's Defence Policy," in Story and
    Shepard, *The Diefenbaker Legacy*, 27–42. Simpson argued that Green
    and his supporters had control of cabinet nuclear policy by mid-1960.

18 Cabinet Conclusions, 14 February 1961.

19 Ibid. At a cabinet meeting on 17 February it was revealed that this opin-
    ion poll had been conducted by the CBC. At this particular meeting some
    members argued that a recent Gallup poll "produced diametrically oppo-
    site results" (paras. 1–2). This was not correct. The poll produced almost
    identical results. See note 60 below.

20 Cabinet Conclusions, 17 February 1961.

21 Ibid.

22 Ibid.

23 J.M. Shoemaker to Ross Campbell, "Correspondence from the Public on
    Nuclear Weapons," 17 February 1961, Green Papers (LAC), vol. 10, file
    12: Nuclear Weapons, Canadian Opposition to – correspondence, peti-
    tions, resolutions, 1961. The survey included only letters opposing
    nuclear weapons. Although few and far between, there are some letters in
    support of nuclear weapons found in the Diefenbaker Papers, microfilm
    7812, file 154.3: Defence Research – Atomic Research – Atomic
    Armament.

24 Canada, House of Commons, *Debates*, 2 February 1961, 1658.

25 Robinson, *Diefenbaker's World*, 169. Heeney's memoirs are silent on his
    role in arranging this first meeting between Kennedy and Diefenbaker,
    although Robinson makes up for this omission.

26 Robinson to Undersecretary, "Possible Visit to Washington by Prime
    Minister," 3 February 1961, Robinson Papers, vol. 4, file 4.3: Washing-
    ton – Eisenhower, January 1961, and Kennedy, February 1961.

27 Robertson, "President-elect Kennedy," 10 November 1960, Robinson
    Papers, vol. 3, file 3.13: November–December 1960.

28 Ibid.

29 Robinson, *Diefenbaker's World*, 168.

30 Heeney to Green, "Report of Meeting with Rusk," 9 January 1961,
    A.D.P. Heeney Papers, vol. 1, file: U.S., Ambassador to Washington,
    1961–1962, Correspondence, Memoranda, LAC. A solid and friendly
    relationship developed between Rusk and Heeney, not that it helped rela-

tions between the two leaders. See Heeney, *The Things That Are Caesar's*, 171–2.

31 Diefenbaker, "Conversation with Arnold Heeney," 17 January 1961, Diefenbaker Papers, vol. 86, MG 01/XII/D/149: Notes & Memos – Personal & Confidential – Typewritten, 1958–1963.

32 Robinson, "Memo for Diary File, Prime Minister's Visit to Washington," 19 January 1961, Robinson Papers, vol. 4, file 4.3: Eisenhower, January 1961, and Kennedy, February 1961.

33 Robertson, "President-elect Kennedy," 10 November 1960, Robinson Papers, vol. 3, file 3.13: November–December 1960.

34 "Diefenbaker, John (George)," December 1960, John F. Kennedy Papers, POF, vol. 113, file: Canada – Security 1961, John F. Kennedy Library, Boston.

35 "Memorandum for Meeting with Prime Minister Diefenbaker," n.d., Kennedy Papers, POF, vol. 113, file: Canada – Security 1961.

36 "Green, Howard (Charles)," December 1960, Kennedy Papers, POF, vol. 113, file: Canada – Security 1961.

37 "Memorandum for Meeting with Prime Minister Diefenbaker."

38 Ibid.

39 Ibid. As an illustration, Dean Rusk took time to make sure that the president knew how to pronounce Diefenbaker's name ("Deefen-BAKER," a memo indicated phonetically). See Rusk to Kennedy, "Diefenbaker Visit, February 17, 1961," Kennedy Papers, POF, vol. 113, file: Canada – Security 1961. It is surprising to see the thoroughness of the preparation for a visit universally considered an "informal" one, expected to last several hours at most. That Kennedy was advised how to pronounce Diefenbaker's name is significant in view of the prime minister's chagrin that Kennedy had, nonetheless, bungled his name, "Diefen-bawker." See Nash, *Kennedy and Diefenbaker*, 108.

40 "Memorandum for Meeting with Prime Minister Diefenbaker."

41 "Diefenbaker, John (George)," December 1960, Kennedy Papers, POF, vol. 113, file: Canada – Security 1961.

42 "Conversations between the President of the United States and the Prime Minister of Canada, February 20, 1961," Diefenbaker Papers, Interim vol. , MG 01/XIV/E/222 (Restricted) Defence (Haslam), Part 2. See also Robinson Papers, vol. 4, file 4.2: February 1961.

43 Ibid.

44 Ibid.

45 Ibid.

46 Ibid.

47 Heeney to Diefenbaker, 20 February 1961, Heeney Papers, vol. 1, file: US, Ambassador to Washington, 1961–1962, Correspondence, Memoranda.

48 Robinson to Rae, 21 February 1961, Robinson Papers, vol. 4, file 4.4: February 1961.

49 This assessment despite Diefenbaker's later words to the contrary about Kennedy's visit: "I became increasingly aware that President Kennedy had no knowledge of Canada whatsoever. More important, he was activated by the belief that Canada owed so great a debt to the United States that nothing but continuing subservience could repay it" Diefenbaker, *The Years of Achievement*, 171–2.

50 Robinson to Undersecretary, 21 February 1961, Robinson Papers, vol. 4, file 4.2: February 1961.

51 Ibid.

52 Diefenbaker, Notes of Kennedy Meeting, Robinson Papers, vol. 4, file 4.2: February 1961.

53 Diefenbaker, *The Years of Achievement*, 169 (emphasis in original).

54 "Memorandum of Conversation," 20 February 1961, 418. *Foreign Relations of the United States [FRUS]*, 1961–1963, 13:1147 (emphasis added).

55 Merchant to Kennedy, "Memorandum of Conversation," 8 March 1961, 419, *FRUS, 1961–1963*, 13:1150.

56 Robinson, *Diefenbaker's World*, 172.

57 Cabinet Conclusions, 21 February 1961.

58 Ibid.

59 Cabinet Conclusions, 17 February 1961. See above.

60 Harkness to Diefenbaker, 23 February 1961, Diefenbaker Papers, vol. 3, file 154, MG 01/VI/R/89: Conf. Defence Research – Atomic Research – Confidential. 1960–1961. The poll was conducted by Elliott-Haynes Ltd (Market Research and Analysis) and was based on 1,200 telephone calls to households in Halifax, Toronto, and Vancouver.

61 Harkness to Diefenbaker, 23 February 1961, Diefenbaker Papers, vol. 3, MG 01/VI/R/89.

62 On Merchant's sentiments, see Livingston Merchant Oral History Interview. Kennedy Library, Boston, Massachusetts. From the Canadian point of view, Heeney had learned from Dean Rusk in January 1961 that a highly regarded official was slated for Ottawa, not some "political hack."

63 Merchant to Kennedy, "Memorandum of Conversation," 8 March 1961, 419, *FRUS, 1961–1963*, 13:1150–1.

64 Ibid.

65 See Diefenbaker, *The Years of Achievement*, 169–70, for Diefenbaker's interpretation of the Bay of Pigs. Given the later hostility with which he regarded Kennedy, it is difficult to take seriously much of what he writes about their relationship, particularly the May 1961 visit to Ottawa.

66 Secretary of State to the Department of State, 14 May 1961, 420, *FRUS, 1961–1963*, 13:152–3.

67 State Department to American Consul in Geneva, cc American Embassy Ottawa, 12 May 1961, Kennedy Papers, POF, vol. 113, file: Canada – Kennedy Trip to Ottawa, 5/61 (D).

68 Secretary of State to the Department of State, 14 May 1961, 420, *FRUS, 1961–1963*, 13:152–3.

69 National Intelligence Estimate no. 99–61, "Trends in Canadian Foreign Policy," 2 May 1961, *FRUS, 1961–1963*, 13:152–3.

70 American Embassy (Ottawa), no. 908, 15 May 1961, and Rusk to White House, 15 May 1961, Kennedy Papers, NSF, vol. 18, file: Canada – General – 5/15/61–5/30/61.

71 Battle, "President Kennedy's Visit to Ottawa May 16–18, 1961," 14 April 1961, Kennedy Papers, NSF, vol. 18, file: Canada – General 4/61–5/14/61.

72 Ibid. The portion of this memorandum related to defence issues is highlighted in the margin by Kennedy.

73 American Embassy (Ottawa) to Secretary of State, no. 893, 11 May 1961, Robinson Papers, vol. 5, file 5.8: May 1961 (3). Merchant noted to Rusk: "Dept External Affairs was riddled with wishful thinkers who believed Soviets would be propitiated and disarmament prospects improved if only Canada did nothing to provoke Soviet Union such as accepting nuclear armaments. This he said was ridiculous but view strongly and widely held. Diefenbaker went on to say that cabinet must reach decision on this matter before much longer. *Intimation was clear his sympathies lie with us*" (emphasis added).

74 National Intelligence Estimate no. 99–61, "Trends in Canadian Foreign Policy," paras. 39–42, 2 May 1961, Kennedy Papers, POF, vol. 113, file: Canada – Kennedy Trip to Ottawa, 5/61 (D). It is difficult to determine what precisely Kennedy's briefing notes stated about nuclear weapons talks with the Canadians for the simple reason that this particular section of the briefing papers has been excised, in all copies, for reasons of national security. See, for example: "Talking Paper," 12 May 1961, Kennedy Papers, POF, vol. 113, file: Canada – Kennedy Trip to Ottawa, 5/61 (A), and file: Canada – Kennedy Trip to Ottawa, 5/61 (B).

75 See, Spencer, "External Affairs and Defence," *Canadian Annual Review for 1961*, 135–7.

76 American Embassy (Ottawa) to Secretary of State, "Preliminary and Tentative Assessment of JFK Visit to Ottawa 16–18 May," 19 May 1961, Kennedy Papers, NSF, vol. 18, file: Canada – General – 5/15/61–5/30/61.

77 Department of State, "Memoranda of Conversation, Trip to Ottawa, May 17, 1961 Subject: Disarmament," Kennedy Papers, NSF, vol. 18, file: Canada – General – Ottawa Trip 5/17/61. See also FRUS, *1961–1963*, vol. 13, Memo 421; OAS membership is also noted in memo 422, 1153–5. For the Canadian perspective, see "Visit of President Kennedy to Ottawa, 16–18 May 1961," Robinson Papers, vol. 5, file 5.7: May 1961 (2).

78 Department of State, "Memoranda of Conversation, Trip to Ottawa, May 17, 1961, Subject: NATO and Nuclear Weapons," file: Canada – General – Ottawa Trip 5/17/61. See also FRUS, *1961–1963*, vol. 13, memo 423, 1157–58.

79 Department of State, "Memoranda of Conversation, Trip to Ottawa, May 17, 1961. Subject: Disarmament," File: Canada – General – Ottawa Trip 5/17/61.

80 Ibid., "Subject: NATO and Nuclear Weapons." See also FRUS, *1961–1963*, vol. 13, memo 423, 1157–8.

81 Ibid.

82 "Visit of President Kennedy to Ottawa (Final)," May 1961, Robinson Papers, vol. 5, file 5.7: May 1961 (2).

83 "Visit of President Kennedy to Ottawa (Draft)," [proofread and corrected by Diefenbaker], May 1961, Robinson Papers, vol. 5, file 5.7.

84 "Visit of President Kennedy to Ottawa (Final Copy)," May 1961, Robinson Papers, vol. 5, file 5.7.

85 "Visit of President Kennedy to Ottawa (Draft)" and "Visit of President Kennedy to Ottawa (Final)," Robinson Papers, vol. 5, file 5.7."

86 "Visit of President Kennedy to Ottawa (Final)," May 1961, Robinson Papers, vol. 5, file 5.7.

87 Harkness to Jenny Coldman, 8 February 1961, Harkness Papers, vol. 27, file 42–66: Transportation and Testing of Atomic Weapons, 1961. This letter is typical of the response Harkness received following his comments at the end of January. See also VOW papers, vol. 1, file: Correspondence – MPs, Formation 1960–1963.

88 This was a particular problem for the Montreal CUCND, though even the more moderate Toronto organization allowed well-known communists such as Danny Goldstick, one of the founders of the student anti-nuclear campaign at the University of Toronto, to remain active in the group. See

Dimitri Roussopoulos to Mike Rowan, 13 February 1961, CUCND-SUPA papers, vol. 1, file 6: CUCND Correspondence, Toronto 1960–61.

89 See Marjorie Lamb, "The Promise and the Peril: A Question of Balance, Address to the Lions Club of Toronto (Central), King Edward Hotel," 25 June 1964, Walter Gordon Papers, vol. 6, file: Communism (3), LAC.

90 Ball, "The History of the Voice of Women," 453–5.

91 Robinson, *Diefenbaker's World*, 195–6.

92 "Visit of President Kennedy to Ottawa (Final Copy)," May 1961, Robinson Papers, vol. 5, file 5.7.

93 Ibid.

94 "Visit of President Kennedy to Ottawa (Draft)," Robinson Papers, vol. 5, file 5.7."

95 Ibid.

96 "Foreign Policy," January 1961, Kent Papers, vol. 6, file: National Rally Text and Follow-Up, January 1961.

97 "Defence Policy," Kent Papers, vol. 6, ibid.

98 "Visit of President Kennedy to Ottawa (Draft)," Robinson Papers, vol. 5, file 5.7.

99 "Trends in Canadian Foreign Policy," Kennedy Papers, POF, vol. 113, file: Canada – Kennedy Trip to Ottawa 5/61 (D).

100 Ibid.

101 "Pearson, Lester Bowles ("Mike")," May 1961, Kennedy Papers, POF, vol. 113, file: Canada – Kennedy Trip to Ottawa, 5/61 (C).

102 Memorandum for Messrs. Rostow and Sorenson, Kennedy Papers, vol. 18, NSF, file: Canada – General – 4/61–5/14/61.

103 Secretary of State to the President, 13 May 1961, Kennedy Papers, vol. 18, NSF, file: Canada – General – 4/61–5/14/61.

104 Diefenbaker, *The Years of Achievement*, 171.

105 American Embassy (Ottawa) to Secretary of State, no. 923, "Preliminary and Tentative Assessment of JFK Visit to Ottawa 16–18 May," 19 May 1961. Kennedy Papers, NSF, vol. 18, file: Canada – General – 5/15/61–5/30/61.

106 Diefenbaker, *The Years of Achievement*, 171.

107 Secretary of State to the President, 13 May 1961, Kennedy Papers, vol. 18, NSF, file: Canada – General – 4/61–5/14/61.

108 Diefenbaker, *The Years of Achievement*, 183.

109 Robinson, *Diefenbaker's World*, 206.

110 Robinson, "Memorandum for File," 31 May 1983, Robinson Papers, vol. 5, file 5.7: May 1961 (2).

111 Robinson, *Diefenbaker's World*, 208.

112 When he learned of the injury, Diefenbaker wrote a letter to Kennedy expressing his concern as well as his regret that it had been sustained in Ottawa. See Diefenbaker to Kennedy, 8 June 1961, Robinson Papers, vol. 5, file 5.7: May 1961 (2).

CHAPTER FIVE

1 Rostow to Kennedy, "Follow-Up from Canada," 22 May 1961, John F. Kennedy Papers, NSF, vol. 18, file: Canada – General – 5/15/61–5/30/61, Kennedy Library.

2 Merchant (Ottawa) to Secretary of State, no. 930, 23 May 1961, Kennedy Papers, ibid.

3 Merchant (Ottawa) to Secretary of State, no. 1016, 12 June 1961, Kennedy Papers, NSF, vol. 18, file: Canada – General – 6/61–9/61.

4 Merchant (Ottawa) to Secretary of State, no. 934, 24 May 1961 and Merchant to Secretary of State, no. 950, 28 May 1961, Kennedy Papers, NSF, vol. 18, file: Canada – General – 5/15/61–5/30/61.

5 Merchant (Ottawa) to Secretary of State, 31 May 1961, ibid.

6 Ibid.

7 The only nuclear issue discussed in cabinet at this time was the SWAP agreement, approved by cabinet on 8 June 1961. See also Cabinet Conclusions, 23 May 1961, Privy Council Office, RG 2, Library and Archives Canada (LAC).

8 Cabinet Conclusions, 24 July 1961.

9 Notes re RBB letter, 8 July 1961, John G. Diefenbaker Papers, vol. 86, MG 01/XII/D/152: Nuclear Weapons – Kennedy Memo 1961, Diefenbaker Canada Centre.

10 Cabinet Conclusions, 24 July 1961.

11 Ibid.

12 Ibid.

13 Bryce to Diefenbaker, 4 August 1961, Diefenbaker Papers, vol. 86, MG 01/XII/D/152: Nuclear Weapons – Kennedy Memo 1961. The letter was highly confidential, with a request that the original be burned. The original could not be found in the Diefenbaker Papers.

14 These systems included the Bomarc at North Bay and La Macaza, the Honest John rocket used by the army in Europe, and the F–104G and F–101B interceptor aircraft, both used by the RCAF in NORAD. The F–101B was approved only the day before the CBC broadcast.

15 Former chairman of the Chiefs of Staff Committee General Foulkes supported the acquisition of nuclear weapons, as did the president of King's College in Halifax. See Ottawa Embassy to Secretary of State, no. G–329,

27 June 1961, Kennedy Papers, NSF, vol. 18, file: Canada – General – 6/61–9/61.

16 Each of the chosen anti-nuclear activists had been the subject of a previous report to Washington: Feinberg, in Toronto Consul Dispatch no. 76, 19 May 1961; Macklin, in Vancouver Dispatch, no. 241, 5 June 1961; and Keenleyside, in Toronto Dispatch no. 76, 30 March 1961. See Kennedy Papers, NSF, vol. 18, file: Canada – General.

17 Embassy (Ottawa) to Secretary of State, no. G–329, 27 June 1961, Kennedy Papers, NSF, vol. 18, file: Canada – General – 6/61–9/61.

18 Merchant (Ottawa) to Secretary of State, no. 138, 15 August 1961, Kennedy Papers, NSF, vol. 20, file: Canada – Subjects: Diefenbaker Correspondence, 8/11/61–10/10/62. Includes text draft letter from Diefenbaker to Kennedy of 11 August 1961.

19 See "Chronology of Government Statements regarding Negotiations on Acquisition and Storage of Nuclear Weapons," n.d., Progressive Conservative Party (PCP) papers, vol. 421, file: Government Statements on Nuclear Weapons, LAC. See also Diefenbaker Papers, vol. 176, MG 01/VII/A/1646.2: Nuclear Weapons 1961–1962 Statements.

20 Robinson, *Diefenbaker's World*, 229–30.

21 Notes re RBB letter, 8 July 1961, Diefenbaker Papers, vol. 86, MG 01/XII/D/152: Nuclear Weapons – Kennedy Memo 1961.

22 Harkness, "The Nuclear Arms Question," 5–6, Douglas S. Harkness Papers, vol. 57, LAC. See also the string of correspondence between Green and Harkness in H.B. Robinson Papers, vol. 9, LAC, and Harkness Papers, vols. 10 and 57.

23 Cabinet Conclusions, 22 August 1961.

24 Ibid.

25 Ibid. (emphasis added).

26 Ibid.

27 Cabinet Conclusions, 23 August 1961.

28 Ibid.

29 Cabinet Conclusions, 22, 23, and 25 August 1961.

30 Cabinet Conclusions, 31 August 1961.

31 See Diefenbaker Papers, vol. 17, MG 01/XIV/E/222: Defence (Haslam), part 2 (1961–1963).

32 Spencer, "External Affairs and Defence," *Canadian Annual Review for 1961*, 155.

33 Cabinet Conclusions, 14 September 1961.

34 W. Armstrong (Ottawa) to Secretary of State, no. 291, 15 September 1961, Kennedy Papers, NSF, vol. 18, file: Canada – General – 6/61–9/61. Armstrong noted rumours that Green might be removed from his

portfolio, though he could not confirm that they were true, arguing that Green seemed more "realistic about the world situation" with "no signs of insecurity in office."

35 D.B.D. to Bryce, "Draft of Proposed Agreement on Nuclear Warheads," 19 September 1961, Robinson Papers, vol. 9, file 9.1: Nuclear Weapons Policy, 1961.

36 Armstrong (Ottawa) to Secretary of State, no. 316, 20 September 1961, Kennedy Papers, NSF, vol. 20, file: Canada – Subjects: Diefenbaker Correspondence, 01/20/61–8/10/61.

37 Canada, House of Commons, *Debates*, 20 September 1961, 8596.

38 Notes for Diefenbaker Speech, "The Nation's Business," 20 September 1961, Diefenbaker Papers, vol. 17, MG 01/XIV/E/222: Defence (Haslam), Part 2 (1961–1963).

39 Armstrong (Ottawa) to Secretary of State, no. 327, 22 September 1961, Kennedy Papers, NSF, vol. 18, file: Canada – General – 6/61–9/61.

40 Beschloss, *The Crisis Years*, 315. Although Diefenbaker had mentioned upcoming American disarmament proposals in his statement before the House of Commons on 20 September, there is no indication that Kennedy had discussed the proposals with him in advance of his U.N. address, aside from references to a new policy during the May visit.

41 Canada, House of Commons, *Debates*, 26 September 1961, 8903.

42 Beschloss, *The Crisis Years*, 316–26. See also Cabinet Conclusions, 27 September 1961. One minister noted the government's earlier concern that negotiations, which would inevitably leak out, would make it seem that the government was willing to take nuclear weapons. With Kennedy's statement in the United Nations about American opposition to proliferation, this was no longer a concern. It is difficult to determine who made this statement, since Green was absent from cabinet that day.

43 "Special News Bulletin, a Letter from the President, September 1961," VOW papers, vol. 5, file: Radiation Hazards and Fall-Out [5–1], LAC.

44 VOW to Diefenbaker, 17 September 1961, Diefenbaker Papers, microfilm 7895, file 313.312 D-V: Voice of Women Federal Government Executive – The Prime Minister of Canada – Requests and Appeals – Interviews – Delegations – Voice of Women, 1960–1962.

45 This came from a comment made in the House of Commons on 23 September. See Robinson to Undersecretary, "Meeting with VOW" (based on notes by John Diefenbaker), 5 October 1961, Robinson Papers, vol. 9, file 9.1: Nuclear Weapons Policy, 1961. See also Diefenbaker Papers, microfilm 7895, file 313.312 D-V: Voice of Women Federal Government

Executive – The Prime Minister of Canada – Requests and Appeals – Interviews – Delegations – Voice of Women, 1960–1962.

46 Robinson to Undersecretary, "Meeting with vow" (based on notes by John Diefenbaker), 5 October 1961, Robinson Papers, vol. 9, file 9.1: Nuclear Weapons Policy, 1961. See also Diefenbaker Papers, microfilm 7895, file 313.312 d-v: Voice of Women Federal Government Executive – The Prime Minister of Canada – Requests and Appeals – Interviews – Delegations – Voice of Women. 1960–1962.

47 cccrh records indicate 160,000 signatures, while *The Canadian Annual Review of 1961*, 156, reports 142,000 names. Later ccnd documents put the figure at 180,000. ccnd papers, vol. 18, file 12: ccnd Ottawa Delegation, 16 April 1962: News Release, McMaster University Library. See also Nash, *Kennedy and Diefenbaker*, 141.

48 David Lewis Stein, "Beginner's Guide to the Canadian Nuclear Disarmers." *Maclean's*, 7 October 1961.

49 Thomson had been moderator of the United Church of Canada, dean of divinity and professor of philosophy of religion at McGill, a former president of the University of Saskatchewan, and president of the board of directors for the cbc and the United Nations Club of Canada.

50 ccnd papers, vol. 2, file 13: Correspondence, H.L. Keenleyside.

51 Thomson was not overly enthusiastic about his new position in the organization. His reluctance stemmed from a variety of sources: his teaching and church commitments, a recent illness, and his age. Because of these things, he refused to get involved in the day-to-day business of the cccrh, acting more as a figurehead than a leader. See Thomson to Hunnius, 2 August 1961, ccnd papers, vol. 3, file 9.

52 ccnd papers, vol. 2, file 13: Correspondence, H.L. Keenleyside

53 ccnd papers, vol. 19, file 11: National Petition 1961, Subject Matter.

54 Ibid., "Suggestions for Petitioners."

55 ccnd papers, vol. 19, file 8: National Petition 1961, Branch Memos.

56 Ibid.

57 Ibid.

58 ccnd papers, vol. 19, file 11: "Suggestions for Petitioners," and file 10: Original Signers of the 1961 National Petition.

59 David Lewis Stein, "Beginner's Guide to the Canadian Nuclear Disarmers," *Maclean's*, 7 October 1961, 10.

60 Cabinet Conclusions, 6 October 1961.

61 Robinson to Undersecretary, "Nuclear Weapons Policy," 6 October 1961, Robinson Papers, vol. 9, file 9.1: Nuclear Weapons Policy, 1961.

62 Ibid.

63 Ibid.

64 Ibid.

65 Robinson to Undersecretary, "Nuclear Weapons Policy," 7 October 1961, Robinson Papers, vol. 9, file 9.1: Nuclear Weapons Policy, 1961.

66 As one member of the American Embassy in Ottawa noted in a telegram dated 7 October 1961, "Prime Minister's closest official assistants thought until yesterday that he was of the same wave length as Defense Minister, but their confidence is now badly shaken by his statement of yesterday." See Linville (Ottawa) to Secretary of State, no. 386, 7 October 1961, Kennedy Papers, NSF, vol. 18, file: Canada – General – 10/61–01/62.

67 Spencer, "External Affairs and Defence," *Canadian Annual Review for 1961*, 156–7. See also Cabinet Conclusions, 21 November 1961.

68 Cabinet Conclusions, 30 November 1961.

69 Ibid.

70 Diefenbaker received a copy of a speech by James Thorson of the CCCRH, given in Manitoba on 5 November. Diefenbaker's copy of the speech includes underlined portions, particularly reports of pressure from Washington to accept nuclear weapons. See Diefenbaker Papers, vol. 176, MG 01/VII/A/1646.2: Nuclear Weapons, 1961–1962.

71 Harkness to Green, 19 December 1961, Robinson Papers, vol. 9, file 9.1: Nuclear Weapons Policy, 1961. See also Harkness Papers, vol. 57.

72 Harkness, "Address to the Air Industries and Transport Association," 1 November 1961, Diefenbaker Papers, vol. 17, MG 01/XIV/E/222: Defence (Haslam), Part 2, 1961–1963.

73 *Ottawa Citizen*, 3 November 1961.

74 Linville (Ottawa) to Secretary of State, no. 386, 7 October 1961, Kennedy Papers, NSF, vol. 18, file: Canada – General – 10/61–01/62.

75 Armstrong (Ottawa) to Secretary of State, no. 406, 12 October 1961, Kennedy Papers, NSF, vol. 18, file: Canada – General – 10/61–01/62.

76 Merchant to Kennedy, 10 November 1961, Kennedy Papers, NSF, vol. 18, file: Canada – General – 10/61–01/62. When Merchant later talked to Diefenbaker about the status of nuclear negotiations, the prime minister promised to bring the issue to cabinet. Nothing was done. As a result, Merchant continued to warn the White House to expect no progress in this area because of Diefenbaker's preoccupation with public opinion and the division within his cabinet. See Embassy (Ottawa) to State Department, no. 19, *FRUS, 1961–1963*, 13:1163–4.

77 Merchant (Ottawa) to Secretary of State, no. A–196, 22 November 1961, *FRUS, 1961–1963*, 13:1163–4.

78 Heeney (Washington) to Diefenbaker, 3 November 1961, Diefenbaker
   Papers, vol. 17, MG 01/XIV/E/222: Defence (Haslam), part 2, 1961–1963.

79 Cabinet Conclusions, 18 December 1961.

80 Canadian Institute of Public Opinion, "Ranking of Issues Facing Canada
   Today, February 1962." National Liberal Federation (NLF) Papers, vol.
   757, file: Political Surveys and Presentations (1), LAC.

81 Robinson to Undersecretary, "Prime Minister's Request for Information
   on Defence Matters," 10 January 1962, Robinson Papers, vol. 9, file 9.4:
   Nuclear Weapons Policy, 1962.

82 Robinson to the Prime Minister, 16 January 1962, Robinson Papers, vol.
   9, file 9.4.

83 Canada, House of Commons, *Debates*, 22 January 1962, 65.

84 Embassy (Ottawa) to State Department, no. 873, 8 March 1962, *FRUS,
   1961–1963*, 13:1168–9; Le Pan to Pearson, 21 February 1962, and
   Pearson to Le Pan, 28 February 1962, Lester B. Pearson Papers, vol. 49,
   file 802.2: Nuclear Policy, part 1, LAC.

85 Le Pan to Pearson, 21 February 1962, and Pearson to Le Pan, 28 February 1962, Pearson Papers, vol. 49, file 802.2: Nuclear Policy, part 1.

86 See, for instance, Edmonton news conference, 24 February 1962, PCP
   papers, vol. 421, file: Government Statements on Nuclear Weapons,
   March 1962. As well, see Canada, House of Commons, *Debates*, 26 February 1962, 1250–1; Robinson Papers, "Nuclear Weapons Policy," 27
   February 1962, vol. 9, file 9.4: Nuclear Weapons Policy, 1962.

87 Robinson, "Nuclear Weapons Policy," 27 February 1962, Robinson
   Papers, vol. 9, file 9.4: Nuclear Weapons Policy, 1962.

88 "Liberal Victory Planning Bulletin, no. 25," 8 June 1962, NLF papers,
   vol. 689, file: National Office – General Correspondence, Elections
   1962–1963.

89 Robinson to Diefenbaker, 4 April 1962, Robinson Papers, vol. 6, file 6.1:
   April 1962.

90 "Trends in Canadian Foreign Policy," Kennedy Papers, POF, vol. 113,
   file: Canada – Kennedy Trip to Ottawa 5/61 (D).

91 Robinson, *Diefenbaker's World*, 268–9.

92 Merchant to George Ball, 5 May 1962, Kennedy Papers, NSF, vol. 18,
   file: Canada – General – Rostow Memorandum 5/16/61 and Related
   Material 5/61–5/63.

93 Ibid.

94 Ibid.

95 Ibid.

96 Ibid.

97 Bundy to Ball, 8 May 1962, and Acting Secretary of State to Embassy (Ottawa), no. 1081, 8 May 1962, NSF, vol. 18, file: Canada – General – Rostow Memorandum 5/16/61 and Related Material 5/61–5/63.

98 Ibid.

99 Merchant (Ottawa) to Secretary and Undersecretary of State, 13 May 1962, Kennedy Papers, NSF, vol. 18, Canada – General – Rostow Memorandum 5/16/61 and Related Material 5/61–5/63.

100 Ibid.

101 "Memorandum of Conversation, Canadian Ambassador's Farewell Call," 17 April 1962, 432, *FRUS, 1961–1963*, 13:1170–1.

102 During the campaign, Canadian and American representatives of the Permanent Joint Board on Defence met at Fort Benning, Georgia, where the Americans expressed their continued concern about the non-nuclear status of the Bomarc missile. See "Permanent Joint Board on Defence, April 30–May 3, 1962," 3–4, Robinson Papers. See also D.L. Wilgress to Bryce, 11 May 1962, and Bryce to Wilgress, 14 May 1962, Robinson Papers, vol. 9, file 9.4: Nuclear Weapons Policy, 1962.

103 "Possible Points for Discussion with the new Ambassador of Canada," Kennedy Papers, POF, vol. 113, file: Canada – Security 1962.

104 Robinson, "Conversations with Ambassador Merchant and Mr. Armstrong of American Embassy, May 9, 1962," Robinson Papers, vol. 6, file 6.2: May–August 1962.

105 White, *The Making of the President, 1960*. See also Walter Gray, "The Men behind the Political Machines," *Globe Magazine*, 10 March 1962, Allister Grosart Papers, vol. 8, file 13: Conservative Campaign Manager, Clippings, 1936–1974, LAC.

106 NLF papers, vols. 686, 687, and 688, Files: Correspondence and Memoranda (1) (2) (3); vol. 689, files: National Office – General Correspondence, Elections 1962–1963, Election Campaign – General Correspondence, 1962, National Office – General Correspondence, Elections 1962–1963 (2); vol. 692, file: Election: Pre-campaign Strategy, 1961–1962; vol. 704, file: Campaign Bulletin, 1961–1962. See also Thomas W. Kent Papers, vols. 1, 2, and 7 (1988 accrual), Queen's University Archives.

107 "Meeting of the National Campaign Committee, 15–16 April 1962," PCP papers, vol. 384, file: Election 1962 – National Campaign Committee.

108 "The Campaign Themes," n.d., PCP papers, vol. 387, file: Campaign Strategy – Memorandum – Election 1962.

109 Walter Gray, "The Men behind the Political Machines," *Globe Magazine*, 10 March 1962, Grosart Papers, vol. 8, file 13: Conservative Campaign Manager, Clippings, 1936–1974.

110 "Campaign College for Candidates," n.d., Kent Papers (1994 accrual), vol. 4, file: Government Briefs, Drafts, Reports, etc., 1957–1962.

111 Goodman, *Life of the Party*, 94. This was actually a reference to the 1963 Annual General Meeting, but when asked about it, he indicated that this was how party policy was made generally (E.A. Goodman, interview with author, 8 April 1999).

112 See PCP papers, vol. 384, file: Election 1962, Issues Survey.

113 "Report on the Presentation of the National Petition to the Prime Minister," n.d., CCND papers, vol. 18, file 1: Third Annual Conference, February 26–27, 1962.

114 Mary Macdonald to James Thomson, 26 September 1961, CCND papers, vol. 3, file 9. This letter acknowledges receipt of request for assistance to finance the CCCRH; also letters from early October 1961 from Thomson to Beland Honderich and B.K. Thall at the *Toronto Daily Star* requesting financial assistance for the CCCRH.

115 As part of a desire to become more broadly based, members debated whether to change the name of the CCCRH to more accurately reflect its opposition to nuclear weapons. They also began to consider joining forces with the university campaign as a means of expanding general membership more quickly. The debate began in the autumn of 1961, just as the petition efforts were winding down, and culminated in February 1962 at the organization's annual meeting. Though it was not completely without controversy, most members supported both measures. While some favoured the inclusion of "survival" or "peace" in the new name, more typical was the response from Margaret Hanley of the Calgary Committee for the Control of Radiation Hazards. She wrote: "We favour uniting with CUCND. We would like to see our name changed to 'Canadian Campaign for Nuclear Disarmament.' This expresses what we see as our main purpose, and unites us with the campaign in Great Britain." This statement captured what many regarded as the main purpose of the merger and name change. See William J. Smith to CCCRH Executive, 19 December 1961, and Margaret Hanley to CCCRH Executive, 20 February 1962, CCND papers, vol. 1, file 2: Correspondence Regarding Name of Organization.

116 Hunnius to Hugh Brock, 2 April 1962, CCND papers, vol. 18, file 3: Easter Demonstration 1962.

117 This was modelled on the Danish Campaign for Nuclear Disarmament, which had met with some success (F.C. Hunnius, interview with author, 15 April 1999). These members included Justice Thorson, J.R. Kidd, Eugene Forsey, Claude Jodoin, Yousuf Karsh, Major General W.H.S. Macklin, and Josie Quart.

118 Hunnius to Stig Harvor, 29 March 1962, CCND papers, vol. 18. file 3: Easter Demonstration 1962; Thomson to various MPs and Senators, n.d.; CCND papers, vol. 18, file 13: Letters to MPs, Senators, Ottawa Delegation, April 1962.

119 "Questions Lobbyists Should Ask MPs." CCND papers, vol. 18, file 13.

120 "CCND Ottawa Delegation Schedule April 16," n.d., CCND papers, vol. 18, file 14: Ottawa Delegation April 1962, Presentation of Policy to Prime Minister.

121 General Message from T.C. Douglas, 3 April 1962, CCND papers, vol. 18, file 14.

122 "CCND Ottawa Delegation Schedule April 16," CCND papers, vol. 18, file 14.

123 "Questionnaire for 1962 Election Campaign," CCND papers, vol. 18, file 15: Questionnaire to all candidates, election 1962, drafts and correspondence.

124 To better illustrate the consequences of the shortage of volunteers, one need only look at how the CCND dealt with Ontario ridings. Essentially, four branches – Toronto, Ottawa, London, and Welland – ran the province's anti-nuclear lobby. The Toronto CCND, the largest in the province (and in the country, for that matter), was responsible for 40 ridings, including all the ridings in Toronto and York, as well as all ridings north of Toronto, spanning the province from Grey County to Algoma; Toronto members had to deal not only with a large number of ridings but with the vast territory they covered. The Ottawa CCND had helped to organize the April parliamentary lobby, as well as its own region of 19 ridings. The London CCND, with a small but solid core, was responsible for 15 ridings, from Windsor to Kitchener-Waterloo. The Welland branch was responsible for a more manageable 11 ridings in and around the city, from Brantford to Niagara Falls, including Hamilton. Eighty-five ridings, with three to four candidates in each, meant that volunteers had to contact between 255 and 340 people. See "Ridings Divided among Branches," 10 May 1962, CCND papers, vol. 18, file 18: Election 1962 – Ontario Ridings Branch Assignments.

125 Hunnius to David Gauthier, 1 May 1962, CCND papers, vol. 18, file 16: Guide, Statement, Questionnaire – MP candidates, 1962.

126 Fleming, *So Very Near*, 2:502–3.

127 Sharp, *Which Reminds Me*, 94–5.

128 Some speculated that the party decided to nominate a candidate, even if the riding was a lost cause, when Sharp refused to "make a deal" with them. This fact is noted in Smith's article on the campaign, but there is no mention of the NDP offer to Sharp in his own recollections. To be fair, although there are no references to Social Credit or the NDP in Sharp's account of the campaign, this does not mean that the suggestion the NDP was willing to sit out the race if concessions were won from Sharp is groundless (Smith, "The Campaign in Eglinton," 73).

129 Smith, "The Campaign in Eglinton," 73.

130 Gauthier to Hunnius, 24 April 1962, and Hunnius to Gauthier, 1 May 1962, CCND papers, vol. 18, file 16: Guide, Statement, Questionnaire – MP candidates, 1962.

131 Smith, "The Campaign in Eglinton," 83.

132 Fleming, *So Very Near*, 2:504.

133 Land, *Eglinton*, 135.

134 Smith, "The Campaign in Eglinton," 85.

135 Ibid., 83.

136 Organizers estimated that 2,000 attended the rally following the march; see CCND papers, vol. 18, file 3: Easter Demonstration 1962.

137 The CPRI was created by Norman Alcock in November 1961 to act as a research institute for nuclear issues; see Paul and Laulicht, *In Your Opinion*, vol. 1. One prime example of this phenomenon is the VOW's Josephine Davis. She wrote letters and worked on behalf of the CPRI during the campaign, rather than for the CCND or VOW. Other members of the VOW also worked for the CPRI to raise money during the spring of 1962, rather than for the CCND election campaign designed by Hunnius. See Diefenbaker Papers, microfilm 7969, vol. 418, MG 01/VI/601.68: Social Welfare – Associations, Clubs and Societies – Women's Organizations – Voice of Women, 1961–1963.

138 Ian Gentles, interview with author, 7 June 1999; F.C. Hunnius, interview with author, 15 April 1999.

139 At the Pearson Centennial Conference in April 1997, many former Liberal MPs asserted that the Liberals had won the 1962 election by reducing Diefenbaker's majority to a minority government. However, Paul Hellyer contradicted this point of view (Paul Hellyer, interview with author, 14 May 1999.

140 John Lamont to Kent and Davey, 25 June 1962, Kent Papers, vol. 2, file: July 1962.

141 "Liberal Victory Planning Bulletin, No. 25," 8 June 1962, NLF Papers, vol. 689, file: National Office – General Correspondence, Elections 1962–1963.

142 The program included surcharges on imports, reductions in government expenditures totalling $250 million, and loans from the United States and Great Britain (as well as from the IMF) to help bolster the dollar and Canada's foreign exchange reserves.

143 Smith, *Rogue Tory*, 430.

144 Spencer, *Trumpets and Drums*, 66.

CHAPTER SIX

1 Note that this was two days after Kennedy learned of the missile build-up in Cuba, but several days before Diefenbaker learned about it. See State Department to Embassy (Ottawa), 18 October 1962, John F. Kennedy Papers, NSF, vol. 20, file: Canada – Subjects: Diefenbaker Correspondence, 10/11/62–10/21/62, Kennedy Library.

2 Robinson, "Nuclear Weapons Policy," 16 October 1962, H.B. Robinson Papers, vol. 9, file 9.4: Nuclear Weapons Policy, 1962, Library and Archives Canada (LAC).

3 Canada, House of Commons, *Debates*, 18 October 1962, 656–7.

4 Bundy, *Danger and Survival*, 392–3.

5 Robinson, *Diefenbaker's World*, 284.

6 Kennedy approached Erwin Griswold, the dean of Harvard Law School, about the post in Ottawa, but Griswold refused it; see Griswold to Kennedy, 1 August 1962, Kennedy Papers, POF, vol. 113, file: Canada – General, 1962. The new American ambassador, Walton Butterworth, did not arrive in Ottawa until the middle of December. Butterworth had served in Ottawa in 1932. His position prior to Ottawa in 1962 was American representative to the European Communities, a post he had held since late 1959. Butterworth presented his credentials on 11 December 1962. His final note in the report of his initial conversation with Diefenbaker was simply that the prime minister did not raise the subject of nuclear weapons negotiations. See no. 442, Embassy Ottawa to Department of State, 17 December 1962, no. 797, *FRUS, 1961–1963*, 13:1191–2.

7 Robinson, *Diefenbaker's World*, 285–6; Nash, *Kennedy and Diefenbaker*, 184.

8 Harkness, "The Nuclear Arms Question," 8, Douglas S. Harkness Papers, vol. 57, LAC.

9 Ibid., 9.

10 Notes for Parliament – Cuban Missile Crisis Debate, 22 October 1962, Diefenbaker Papers, vol. 56, MG 01/XII/C/120: Cuba 1960–1962.

11 Canada, House of Commons, *Debates*, 22 October 1962, 805–8.

12 Granatstein, *Canada, 1957–1967*, 115.

13 Robertson to the Minister, "Cuba," 24 October 1962, Diefenbaker Papers, vol. 56, MG 01/XII/C/120: Cuba 1960–1962.

14 Robinson, *Diefenbaker's World*, 289.

15 There are five defence readiness conditions (i.e., "DEFCON") used between the Joint Chiefs of Staff and commanders of unified commands. The levels decrease numerically as the military severity increases in a given situation. The peacetime level is DEFCON–5, while maximum readiness is DEFCON–1.

16 Cabinet Conclusions, 23 October 1962, Privy Council Office, RG 2, LAC.

17 Harkness, "The Nuclear Arms Question," 9, Harkness Papers, vol. 57.

18 Cabinet Conclusions, 23 October 1962.

19 Harkness, "The Nuclear Arms Question," 11, Harkness Papers, vol. 57.

20 Ibid., 13. Did Diefenbaker know what his minister of defence was doing? Some of his closest advisers believed that he did; Bryce, for instance, was convinced that Diefenbaker had turned a blind eye and preferred to allow an informal alert over a formal one. As Robinson wrote, "Not much escaped the Diefenbaker antennae" (*Diefenbaker's World*, 288). However, in cabinet on 25 October, Diefenbaker made a point of insisting during discussions of the War Book that "no action was to be taken to put Canadian forces on an Alert footing without his approval."

21 Kennedy had every reason to expect that this would be Diefenbaker's reaction. See briefing notes from Diefenbaker visit to Washington as well as Kennedy visit to Ottawa in which the prime minister's sensitivities are oft-noted (chap. 4).

22 Cabinet Conclusions, 30 October 1962.

23 Secretary of State for External Affairs to the Prime Minister, "Provision of Nuclear Warheads," 26 October 1962, Diefenbaker Papers, vol. 17, MG 01/XIV/E/222: Defence (Haslam), part 2.

24 Cabinet Conclusions, 30 October 1962.

25 Harkness, "The Nuclear Arms Question," 15–16, Harkness Papers, vol. 57.

26 Ibid.

27 Robert McNamara suggested that he and Harkness discuss nuclear weapons at the NATO ministers' meeting in mid-December in Paris. See McNamara to Harkness, 8 November 1962, Harkness Papers, vol. 57, file: The Nuclear Arms Crisis, Reference 1961–1963.

28 Harkness, "The Nuclear Arms Question," 16–17.

29 Bryce, "Lessons of the Cuban Crisis," 20 November 1962, Robinson Papers, vol. 9, file 9.4: Nuclear Weapons Policy, 1962.

30 Harkness, "The Nuclear Arms Question," 17.

31 M.J. Deacey to Thérèse Casgrain, 12 October 1962; Claude Gauthier to Diefenbaker regarding Casgrain and VOW, 11 October 1962. In what was described to Diefenbaker as an "annual event," Gauthier relayed Casgrain's request for a meeting with Diefenbaker on 1 November, promising to bring with her between 250 and 300 members of the VOW. See Diefenbaker Papers, microfilm 7895, vol. 234, file 313.312 D-V: Voice of Women Federal Government Executive – The Prime Minister of Canada – Requests and Appeals – Interviews – Delegations – Voice of Women, 1960–1962.

32 The Diefenbaker and Pearson Papers are filled with letters from the anti-nuclear movement as well as from ordinary Canadians regarding the Cuban Missile Crisis.

33 Embassy (Ottawa) to Department of State A–572, 28 December 1962, Kennedy Papers, NSF, vol. 18, file: Canada – General – 10/62–1/63. See also Spencer, "External Affairs and Defence," *Canadian Annual Review for 1962*, 149.

34 Diefenbaker Papers, microfilm 7895, vol. 234, file 313.312 D-V: Voice of Women Federal Government Executive – The Prime Minister of Canada – Requests and Appeals – Interviews – Delegations – Voice of Women, 1960–1962.

35 Ibid. See also Brief to Prime Minister Diefenbaker, 1 November 1962, VOW papers, vol. 7, file VOW Briefs and Statements, 1962 [7–9], LAC.

36 Casgrain to Diefenbaker, 29 October 1962, Diefenbaker Papers, microfilm 7895, vol. 234, file 313.312 D-V: Voice of Women Federal Government Executive – The Prime Minister of Canada – Requests and Appeals – Interviews – Delegations – Voice of Women, 1960–1962.

37 Thomson to CCND and CUCND Membership, 26 November 1962, CCND papers, vol. 19, file 1: Replies and Donations for Ottawa Lobby 1962, LAC.

38 The Liberal caucus, for instance, agreed to meet with lobbyists even though most members opposed their position; see Paul Martin to CCND, 23 October 1962, CCND papers, vol. 19, file 3: MPS' replies to lobby; Hellyer, *Damn the Torpedoes*, 25.

39 Ibid.

40 CCND papers, vol. 19, files 1 and 3.

41 CCND papers, vol. 19, file 1: Replies.

42 Merchant to Rusk and Ball, no. 441, n.d., *FRUS, 1961–1963,* 13:1190–1.

43 Ibid.

44 Hellyer, *Damn the Torpedoes,* 20.

45 Ibid., 24.

46 Paul Hellyer, interview with author, 14 May 1999. See also Ignatieff, *The Making of a Peacemonger,* 206–07.

47 Hellyer, "Following the NATO Parliamentary Conference held in Paris, November 1962," 29 November 1962, Lester B. Pearson Papers, vol. 55, file: NATO Parliamentary Conference, LAC.

48 Hellyer, *Damn the Torpedoes,* 25–6; Spencer, "External Affairs and Defence," *Canadian Annual Review for 1962,* 144.

49 Hellyer, *Damn the Torpedoes,* 25; Pickersgill, *The Road Back,* 181–4.

50 John Gellner to Hellyer, 21 December 1962, Pearson Papers, vol. 49, file 806.2: Nuclear Policy, part 1.

51 Pearson Papers, vol. 49, file 806.2: Nuclear Policy, part 1.

52 Pickersgill, "Defence Policy," 3 January 1963, Pearson Papers, vol. 49, file 806.2: Nuclear Policy, part 1.

53 Pickersgill, *The Road Back,* 183.

54 Ibid.

55 See Spencer, "External Affairs and Defence," *Canadian Annual Review for 1963,* 284–5.

56 English, *The Worldly Years,* 249.

57 Kent, *A Public Purpose,* 189.

58 Ibid., 187.

59 For examples of Kent's involvement in the transformation of proposals into policy, see Thomas W. Kent Papers, vols. 1, 2, 6 and 7, Queen's University Archives.

60 Kent, *A Public Purpose,* 188–9.

61 Ibid., 189.

62 This suggestion was something that Pearson had recommended in the days following the missile crisis.

63 Kent, "Defence Note," 7 January 1963, Kent Papers, vol. 2, series 1, file: T.W. Kent, Correspondence, January–February 1963 (1).

64 Pearson, *Words and Occasions,* 203–4.

65 Pearson, *Mike: Memoirs,* 3:70–1.

66 Saywell, "Parliament and Politics," *Canadian Annual Review for 1963,* 34.

67 Embassy (Ottawa) to Department of State A–572, 28 December 1962, Kennedy Papers, NSF, vol. 18, file: Canada – General – 10/62–1/63. See also Spencer, "External Affairs and Defence," *Canadian Annual Review for 1962,* 149.

68 Camp, "Telex Poll," 2 March 1962, Diefenbaker Papers, vol. 176, MG 01/VII/A/1646.2: Nuclear Weapons, 1961–1962.

69 "Penetration Survey," 15–16, Kent Papers, vol. 2, file: T.W. Kent, Correspondence, January – February 1963 (1). See also Walter Gordon Papers, vol. 19, file 12, LAC. Note that both Kent and Gordon saw the results and recommendations contained in the survey.

70 "Penetration Survey," 47.

71 Ibid., 48.

72 Ibid.

73 Kent noted that there were rumblings in December 1962 that Robert Winters should replace Pearson as leader (*A Public Purpose*, 184). Hellyer echoed these sentiments in an interview with the author on 14 May 1999.

74 Kent, *A Public Purpose*, 186.

75 Ibid., 192.

76 Kent letter to author, 27 March 1999.

77 English, *The Worldly Years*, 262.

78 Butterworth (Ottawa), "Pearson's Nuclear Statement," no. 897, 14 January 1963, Kennedy Papers, POF, vol. 18, file: Canada – General – 10/62–1/63.

79 English, *The Worldly Years*, 251.

80 Spencer, "External Affairs and Defence," *Canadian Annual Review for 1963*, 287–8; Pearson Papers, vol. 50, file 806.2: Nuclear Policy, part 4.

81 Ian Gentles, interview with author, 7 June 1999.

82 Pearson Papers, vol. 51, file 806.2: Nuclear Policy.

83 Pearson, *Mike: Memoirs*, 3:71. See also Pearson Papers, vol. 50, files 806.2, parts 2–5.

84 Diefenbaker Papers, microfilm 7969, vol. 418, MG 01/VI/601.68: Social Welfare – Associations, Clubs and Societies – Women's Organizations – Voice of Women. 1961–1963.

85 See Harkness, "The Nuclear Arms Question," 20–2, Harkness Papers, vol. 57. Also E.A. Goodman, interview with author, 8 April 1999.

86 Goodman, *Life of the Party*, 95–9. Goodman interview.

87 Goodman, *Life of the Party*, 94–5. See PCP papers, vol. 292, Files PCSF Annual Meeting – 1963; Annual Meeting, 1963 Resolutions (1); Annual Meeting, 1963 Resolutions (2); Annual Meeting, 1963 Resolutions (3).

88 Goodman, *Life of the Party*, 99–101.

89 Goodman interview. Goodman was true to his word and resigned from the party on 5 February 1963 when Defence Minister Harkness also resigned his position.

90 Harkness, "The Nuclear Arms Question," 23–4, Harkness Papers, vol. 57.
91 Ibid., 32.
92 Canada, House of Commons, *Debates*, 25 January 1963, 3125–39.
93 Harkness, "Statement in House of Commons," 28 January 1963, Harkness Papers, vol. 57, file: The Nuclear Arms Question – Background Correspondence, 1963.
94 Tyler to Ball, 29 January 1963, no. 443, *FRUS, 1961–1963*, 13:1193.
95 Robinson to Campbell, 23 January 1963, Robinson Papers, vol. 9, file 9.6: Nuclear Weapons – Policy and Negotiations, January 1 – April 30, 1963.
96 Department of State, "Press Release no. 59 – United States and Canadian Negotiations Regarding Nuclear Weapons," 30 January 1963, no. 444, *FRUS, 1961–1963*, 13:1195–6.
97 Collection of typed and handwritten notes, Howard C. Green Papers, vol. 18, file 10: Canadian–U.S. Relations Re: Nuclear Weapons, 1959–1963, Vancouver Municipal Archives.
98 Harkness, "The Nuclear Arms Question," 46, Harkness Papers, vol. 57.
99 Spencer, "External Affairs and Defence," *Canadian Annual Review for 1963*, 295–7.
100 Robertson to Diefenbaker, 30 January 1963, Green Papers (Vancouver), vol. 18, file 10: Canadian-US Relations Re: Nuclear Weapons, 1959–1963.
101 Harkness, "The Nuclear Arms Question," 56, Harkness Papers, vol. 57.
102 Spencer, *Trumpets and Drums*, 81.
103 Ibid., 80.
104 Mary Macdonald to Pearson, "Nuclear Defence Policy," 18 January 1963, Pearson papers, vol. 50, file 806.2, part 3. See also Davey to Pearson, Gordon, and Kent, 31 January 1963, NLF papers, vol. 689, file: National Office – General Correspondence, Elections 1962–1963.
105 "Lester Pearson and Nuclear Warheads – A Riot of Indecision," Diefenbaker Papers, vol. 17, MG 01/XIV/E/222: (Haslam) Defence, part 2.
106 English, *The Worldly Years*, 292.
107 Alex Mogelon to NLF, 16 August 1960, NLF papers, vol. 702, file: Comics, 1960; *Marketing*, 2 October 1959.
108 English, *The Worldly Years*, 292.
109 "The Election Colouring Book 1963," NLF papers, vol. 704, file: Colouring Book, Election 1963.
110 Davey, "Press Release," 12 March 1963, NLF papers, vol. 694, file: Memos from Keith Davey to Provincial Campaign Chairmen & Communications Chairmen, 1963.

111 Davey, "Third Report," 15 March 1963, NLF papers, vol. 698, file: Reports to Hon. L.B. Pearson from Keith Davey, 1963 Election. See also vol. 696, file: Truth Squad 1963.

112 English, *The Worldly Years*, 264. Interestingly, the photo of Diefenbaker is less flattering on the cover of Smith's, *Rogue Tory* than on the 1963 edition of *Newsweek* (which likely says more about standards and expectations at the end of the 1990s than the same concerns in the 1960s).

113 *Newsweek*, 18 February 1963, PCP papers, vol. 389, file: Election 1963 – Candidates, Memorandum.

114 Camp to Constituency Presidents, 13 February 1963, PCP papers, vol. 389, Camp to Don Watson, 14 February 1963, PCP papers, vol. 388, file: Election, 1963 – Camp, Dalton. See also "Relationship of Grahams to Kennedy," 13 February 1963, and Bradley Gundy to Camp, 13 February, 1963, PCP papers, vol. 388. Gundy wrote: "Newsweek's treatment of the PM is so grossly disrespectful that I am horrified. It seems incredible that a self-respecting journal would release anything so indecent and utterly lacking in moral fibre. For sheer insolence the piece exceeds anything I have read in a long while."

115 English, *The Worldly Years*, 264. The White House and the Pentagon obliged. See note in Kennedy Papers, POF, vol. 113, file: Canada – General, 1963.

116 Butterworth to State Department, 27 March 1963, Kennedy Papers, NSF, vol. 18, file: Canada – General – Rostow Memorandum. See also Newman, *Renegade in Power*, 266.

117 Embassy (Ottawa) to Secretary of State, 7 April 1963, and Butterworth to Secretary of State, 8 April 1963, Kennedy Papers, POF, vol. 18, file: Canada – General – 4/1/63–4/10/63. See also Smith, *Rogue Tory*, 507–9.

118 Spencer, "External Affairs and Defence," *Canadian Annual Review for 1963*, 23. Kennedy was upset that his secretary of defense would make such an impolitic statement, commenting to *Newsweek*'s editor Bradlee, "Everyone ought to run for office. That's all there is to it" (Bradlee, *Conversations with Kennedy*, 162).

119 William Brubeck to Bundy, "Outlook for New Canadian Government and Possible US Tactics," 11 April 1963, Kennedy Papers, NSF, vol. 18, file: Canada – General – 4/11/63–5/3/63.

120 Kent, *A Public Purpose*, 192. Paul Hellyer, interview with author, 14 May 1999.

121 English, *Worldly Years*, 267; Butterworth to Secretary of State, 22 April 1963, Kennedy Papers, NSF, vol. 18, file: Canada – General – 4/11/63–5/3/63.

CONCLUSION

1 The Trade Expansion Act and Columbia River Treaty were the other two outstanding issues. Brubeck to Bundy, "Outlook for New Canadian Government and Possible US Tactics," 11 April 1963, John F. Kennedy Papers, NSF, vol. 18, file: Canada – General – 4/11/63–5/3/63, Kennedy Library.

2 "Visit of Prime Minister Pearson, May 10–11, 1963," 6 May 1963, Kennedy Papers, NSF, vol. 19, file: Canada – Subjects – Pearson Visit, Briefing Book, 5/63.

3 DLW to State Department, 11 May 1963, Kennedy Papers, NSF, file: Canada – Subject: Pearson Visit, 5/63 – 5/11/63–5/30/63.

4 English, *Worldly Years*, 269–70.

5 "Visit of Prime Minister Pearson, May 10–11, 1963," 6 May 1963, Kennedy Papers, NSF, vol. 19, file: Canada – Subjects – Pearson Visit, Briefing Book, 5/63.

6 Legere to Bundy, 7 May 1963, Kennedy Papers, NSF, vol. 19, file: Canada – Subjects – Pearson Visit, 5/6/63–5/10/63.

7 "Joint Communiqué Following Meeting Between President J.F. Kennedy and Prime Minister Lester B. Pearson, Hyannis Port, Mass., May 10 and 11, 1963," ibid.

8 DLW to State Department, 11 May 1963, Kennedy Papers, NSF, vol. 19, file: Canada – Subject: Pearson Visit, 5/63 – 5/11/63–5/30/63. "U.S.-Canadian Nuclear Relations," 16 May 1963, ibid., file: Canada – Subjects: Pearson Visit, 5/63 – Memorandum of Conversation.

9 Butterworth, 6 April 1963, and Bundy to Butterworth, 11 April 1963, Kennedy Papers, NSF, vol. 18, file: Canada – General – Rostow Memorandum 5/16/61 and Related Material 5/61–5/63. See also Memorandum for the Record, 9 May 1963, Kennedy Papers, NSF, vol. 19, file: Canada – Subjects: Pearson Visit, 5/63 – Memorandum of Conversation.

10 Bradlee, *Conversations with Kennedy*, 167, 182–4.

11 See Diefenbaker Papers, vol. 88, MG 01/XII/D/204: United States – Kennedy, 1957–68; Robinson, "Memorandum for File," 31 May 1983, Robinson Papers, vol. 5, file 5.7: May 1961 (2).

12 Clearwater, *Canadian Nuclear Weapons*, 33–43, for a detailed account of the political discussions in cabinet, the Cabinet Defence Committee, and Parliament surrounding the final negotiations. See Clearwater's appendix for the full agreement.

13 The Voice of Women remained intact but became more radical as it turned its attentions to the war in Vietnam. The CCND, however, disappeared, and CUCND was reborn as the more radical Students United for Peace Action (SUPA).

Bibliography

PRIMARY SOURCES

Manuscript Collections

Canadian Committee for the Control of Radiation Hazards
(CCCRH)/Canadian Committee for Nuclear Disarmament (CCND). The
William Ready Division of Archives and Research Collections,
McMaster University Library, Hamilton, Ontario
Combined Universities Campaign for Nuclear Disarmament – Students
United for Peace Action. (CUCND-SUPA). The William Ready Division
of Archives and Research Collections, McMaster University Library,
Hamilton, Canada
Rt. Hon. John G. Diefenbaker Papers. Diefenbaker Canada Centre,
Saskatoon
Donald M. Fleming Papers. Library and Archives Canada, Ottawa
Walter Gordon Papers. Library and Archives Canada, Ottawa
Howard Green Papers. Library and Archives Canada, Ottawa
Howard C. Green Papers. Vancouver Municipal Archives, Vancouver
Allister Grosart Papers. Library and Archives Canada, Ottawa
Douglas S. Harkness Papers. Library and Archives Canada, Ottawa
A.D.P. Heeney Papers. Library and Archives Canada, Ottawa
John F. Kennedy Papers. John F. Kennedy Presidential Library, Boston
Thomas W. Kent Papers. Queen's University Archives, Kingston. 1988 &
1994 accruals
H.E. Kidd Papers. Library and Archives Canada, Ottawa
National Liberal Federation Papers. Library and Archives Canada,
Ottawa

Rt. Hon. Lester B. Pearson Papers. Library and Archives Canada, Ottawa
Progressive Conservative Party Papers. Library and Archives Canada, Ottawa
Norman A. Robertson Papers. Library and Archives Canada, Ottawa
H.B. Robinson Papers. Library and Archives Canada, Ottawa
Sidney Smith Papers. University of Toronto Archives, Toronto
Voice of Women. Library and Archives Canada, Ottawa

Record Groups (Library and Archives Canada, Ottawa)

Department of External Affairs, RG 25
Department of National Defence, RG 24
Royal Canadian Mounted Police/Canadian Security Intelligence Service, RG 146
Privy Council Office, RG 2

Interviews

Thomas Delworth
Ian Gentles
E.A. Goodman
Paul Hellyer
F.C. and Valerie Hunnius
Maxwell Yalden

SECONDARY SOURCES

Ball, Christine. "The History of the Voice of Women/La Voix des Femmes: The Early Years." PHD dissertation. Toronto: University of Toronto, OISE, 1994
Banfield, Edward C. *Political Influence: A New Theory of Urban Politics*. New York: Free Press; and London: Collier Macmillan, 1961
Bashevkin, Sylvia. *Toeing the Lines: Women and Party Politics in English Canada*. Toronto: University of Toronto Press, 1985
Beattie, Margaret Eileen. *A Brief History of the Student Christian Movement in Canada, 1921–1974*. Toronto: SCM, 1975
Beschloss, Michael. *Mayday: Eisenhower, Khrushchev, and the U-2 Affair*. New York: Harper & Row, 1986
– *The Crisis Years: Kennedy and Khrushchev, 1960–1963*. New York: HarperCollins, 1991

Bothwell, Robert. *Eldorado: Canada's National Uranium Company.*
Toronto: University of Toronto Press, 1984
– *Nucleus: The History of Atomic Energy of Canada, Limited.* Toronto:
University of Toronto Press, 1988
Bothwell, Robert, and William Kilbourn. *C.D. Howe: A Biography.*
Toronto: McClelland & Stewart, 1979
Bothwell, Robert, Ian Drummond, and John English. *Canada since 1945:
Power, Politics, and Provincialism.* Revised edition. Toronto:
University of Toronto Press, 1989
Bradlee, Benjamin C. *Conversations with Kennedy.* New York: W.W.
Norton, 1975
Bundy, McGeorge. *Danger and Survival.* New York: Random House,
1988
Burt, Sandra, "Organized Women's Groups and the State." In *Policy
Communities and Public Policy in Canada,* ed. William Coleman and
Grace Skogstad. Toronto: Copp Clark Pitman, 1990
Casgrain, Thérèse F. *A Woman in a Man's World.* Trans. Joyce Marshall.
Toronto: McClelland & Stewart, 1972
Cigler, Allan J., and Burdett A. Loomis. *Interest Group Politics.* 5th
edition. Washington: CQ Press, 1998
Clearwater, John. *Canadian Nuclear Weapons: The Untold Story of
Canada's Cold War Arsenal.* Toronto: Dundurn Press, 1998
Clemens, Elisabeth Stephanie. *The People's Lobby: Organizational
Innovation and the Rise of Interest Group Politics in the United States.*
Chicago: University of Chicago Press, 1997
Conant, Melvin. *The Long Polar Watch: Canada and the Defense of
North America.* New York: Harper, 1962
Crozier, Michel. *The Bureaucratic Phenomenon.* Chicago: University of
Chicago Press, 1963
Davey, Keith. *The Rainmaker: A Passion for Politics.* Toronto: Stoddart,
1986
Davis Fisher, Carolyn. *Lotta Dempsey: The Lady Was a Star.* Toronto:
Belsten, 1995
Dempsey, Lotta. *No Life for a Lady.* Don Mills: Musson, 1976
Diefenbaker, John G. *The Crusading Years. 1895–1956.* Vol. 1 of *One
Canada: Memoirs of the Right Honourable John G. Diefenbaker.*
Toronto: Macmillan of Canada, 1975
– *The Years of Achievement.* Vol. 2 of *One Canada: Memoirs of the
Right Honourable John G. Diefenbaker.* Toronto: Macmillan of
Canada, 1976

– *The Tumultuous Years.* Vol. 3 of *One Canada: Memoirs of the Right Honourable John G. Diefenbaker.* Toronto: Macmillan of Canada, 1977

Dyck, Perry Rand. *Provincial Politics in Canada.* Scarborough: Prentice-Hall Canada, 1986

Eayrs, James. "Canadian Policy and Opinion during the Suez Crisis." *International Journal* 12 (Spring 1957): 97–108

Endicott, Stephen. *Endicott: Rebel Out of China.* Toronto: University of Toronto Press, 1980

English, John. *The Decline of Politics: The Conservatives and the Party System, 1901–1920.* Toronto: University of Toronto Press, 1977

– *Shadow of Heaven.* Vol. 1 of *The Life of Lester Pearson, 1897–1948.* Toronto: Lester & Orpen Dennys, 1989

– *The Worldly Years.* Vol. 2 of *The Life of Lester Pearson 1949–1972.* Toronto: Alfred A. Knopf, 1992

Fairclough, Ellen Louks. *Saturday's Child: Memoirs of Canada's First Female Cabinet Minister.* Toronto: University of Toronto Press, 1995

Fleming, Donald M. *So Very Near: The Political Memoirs of the Honourable Donald M. Fleming.* 2 vols. Toronto: McClelland & Stewart, 1985

Foreign Relations of the United States, 1961–1963. Vol. 13: *Western Europe and Canada.* Washington: State Department, Bureau of Public Affairs, 1994

Forsey, Eugene. A Life on the Fringe: The Memoirs of Eugene Forsey. Toronto: Oxford University Press, 1990

Fursenko, A.V. *One Hell of a Gamble: Khrushchev, Castro, and Kennedy, 1958–1964.* New York: W.W. Norton, 1997

Garson, G. David. *Group Theories of Politics.* Beverly Hills: Sage Publications, 1978

Ghent, Jocelyn Maynard. "Canada, the United States, and the Cuban Missile Crisis." *Pacific Historical Review*, May 1979, 159–84

– "Did He Fall or Was He Pushed? The Kennedy Administration and the Collapse of the Diefenbaker Government." *International History Review*, 1979

Ghent-Mallet, Jocelyn. "Deploying Nuclear Weapons, 1962–63." In *Canadian Foreign Policy: Selected Cases*, ed. Don Munton and John Kirton. Scarborough: Prentice-Hall Canada, 1992

Ghent-Mallet, Jocelyn, and Don Munton. "Confronting Kennedy and the Missiles in Cuba, 1962." In *Canadian Foreign Policy: Selected Cases*, ed. Don Munton and John Kirton. Scarborough: Prentice-Hall Canada, 1992

Giangrande, Carole. *The Nuclear North: The People, the Regions, and the Arms Race*. Toronto: Anansi, 1983

Goldfarb, Martin, and Thomas Axworthy. *Marching to a Different Drummer: An Essay on the Liberals and Conservatives in Convention*. Toronto: Stoddart Publishing Co. Limited, 1988

Goodman, E.A. *Life of the Party: The Memoirs of Eddie Goodman*. Toronto: Key Porter, 1988

Goodwin, Doris Kearns. *The Fitzgeralds and the Kennedys: An American Saga*. New York: Simon & Schuster, 1987

Gordon, Walter. *Walter L. Gordon: A Political Memoir*. Toronto: McClelland & Stewart, 1977

Granatstein, J.L. *A Man of Influence: Norman A. Robertson and Canadian Statecraft, 1929–68*. Toronto: Deneau, 1981

– *The Ottawa Men: The Civil Service Mandarins, 1935–1957*. Toronto: Oxford University Press, 1982

– *Canada, 1957–1967: The Years of Uncertainty and Innovation*. Toronto: McClelland & Stewart, 1986

– "When Push Comes to Shove: Canada and the United States." In *Kennedy's Quest for Victory: American Foreign Policy, 1961–1963*, ed. Thomas G. Paterson. New York: Oxford University Press, 1989

– *Yankee Go Home: Canadians and Anti-Americanism*. Toronto: HarperCollins, 1996

Grant, George. *Lament for a Nation: The Defeat of Canadian Nationalism*. Toronto: McClelland & Stewart, 1965

Hamilton, Nigel. *JFK, Reckless Youth*. New York: Random House, 1992

Haydon, Peter T. *The 1962 Cuban Missile Crisis: Canadian Involvement Reconsidered*. Toronto: Canadian Institute of Strategic Studies, 1993

Heeney, A.D.P. *The Things That Are Caesar's: Memoirs of a Canadian Civil Servant*, ed. Brian Heeney. Toronto: University of Toronto Press, 1972

Hellyer, Paul. *Damn the Torpedoes: My Fight to Unify Canada's Armed Forces*. Toronto: McClelland & Stewart, 1990

Hertzman, Lewis, John Warnock, and Thomas Hockin. *Alliances and Illusions: Canada and the NATO-NORAD Question*. Edmonton: Hurtig, 1969

Hilliker, John. "The Politicians and the 'Pearsonalities': The Diefenbaker Government and the Conduct of Canadian External Relations." In *Canadian Foreign Policy: Historical Readings*, ed. J.L. Granatstein. Revised edition. Toronto: Copp Clark Pitman, 1993

Hilliker, John and Donald Barry. *Canada's Department of External
    Affairs*. Vol. 2. *Coming of Age, 1946–1968*. Institute of Public
    Administration of Canada. Montreal & Kingston: McGill-Queen's
    University Press, 1995

Hrebenar, Ronald J. *Interest Group Politics in America*. 3rd edition.
    Armnk: M.E. Sharpe, 1997

Immerman, Richard H., ed. *John Foster Dulles and The Diplomacy of
    the Cold War*. Princeton: Princeton University Press, 1990

Ignatieff, George. *The Making of a Peacemonger*. Toronto: University of
    Toronto Press, 1985

Ippolito, Dennis S. *Political Parties, Interest Groups, and Public Policy:
    Group Influence in American Politics*. Englewood Cliffs, NJ:
    Prentice-Hall, 1980

Jockel, Joseph T. *No Boundaries Upstairs: Canada, the United States,
    and the Origins of North American Air Defence, 1945–1958*.
    Vancouver: University of British Columbia Press, 1987

Kealey, Linda, and Joan Sangster, eds. *Beyond the Vote: Canadian
    Women and Politics*. Toronto: University of Toronto Press, 1989

Keating, Tom, and Larry Pratt. *Canada, NATO, and the Bomb: The
    Western Alliance in Crisis*. Edmonton: Hurtig, 1988

Keenleyside, H.L. *Memoirs of Hugh L. Keenleyside*. Vol. 2. Toronto:
    McClelland & Stewart, 1982

Kennedy, Robert F. *Thirteen Days: A Memoir of the Cuban Missile
    Crisis*. New York: Norton, 1971

Kent, Tom. *A Public Purpose: An Experience of Liberal Opposition and
    Canadian Government*. Montreal & Kingston: McGill-Queen's
    University Press, 1988

Kirton, John. "The Consequences of Integration: The Case of the Defence
    Production Sharing Agreements." In *Continental Community?
    Independence and Integration in North America*, ed. W. Andrew
    Axline et. al., Toronto: McClelland & Stewart, 1974

Kostash, Myrna. *Long Way from Home: The Story of the Sixties Generation
    in Canada*. Toronto: James Lorimer, 1980

Land, Brian. *Eglinton*. Toronto: Peter Martin, 1965

Laycock, David H. *Populism and Democratic Thought in the Canadian
    Prairies, 1910 to 1945*. Toronto: University of Toronto Press,
    1990

Legault, Albert, and Michel Fortmann. *A Diplomacy of Hope: Canada
    and Disarmament, 1945–1988*. Trans. Derek Ellington. Montreal &
    Kingston: McGill-Queen's University Press, 1992

Levitt, Joseph. *Pearson and Canada's Role in Nuclear Disarmament and Arms Control Negotiations, 1945–1957*. Montreal & Kingston: McGill-Queen's University Press, 1993

Loewen, Candace. "Mike Hears Voices: Voice of Women and Lester Pearson, 1960–1963." *Atlantis* 12 (Spring 1987):24–30

Lyon, Peyton V. *Canada in World Affairs*. Vol. 12: *1961–1963*. Toronto: Oxford University Press, 1968

McCall, Christina. *Grits: An Intimate Portrait of the Liberal Party*. Toronto: Macmillan of Canada, 1982

McLin, Jon B. *Canada's Changing Defense Policy, 1957–1963: The Problems of a Middle Power in Alliance*. Baltimore: Johns Hopkins Press, 1967

Macpherson, Kay. *When in Doubt Do Both: The Times of My Life*. Toronto: University of Toronto Press, 1994

Macpherson, Kay, and Meg Sears. "The Voice of Women: A History." In *Women in the Canadian Mosaic*, ed. Gwen Matheson. Toronto: Peter Martin, 1976

Malecki, Edward S., and H.R. Mahood. *Group Politics: A New Emphasis*. New York: Scribner, 1972

Maloney, Sean M. *War without Battles: Canada's NATO Brigade in Germany, 1958–1993*. Toronto: McGraw-Hill Ryerson, 1997

– "Canadian Shield: Canada's National Security Strategy and Nuclear Weapons, 1951–1971 *(NATO, NORAD)*." PHD dissertation, Philadelphia: Temple University, 1998

Martin, Paul. *A Very Public Life*. 2 vols. Ottawa: Deneau, 1983–1985

Meisel, John. *The Canadian General Election of 1957*. Toronto: University of Toronto Press, 1962

– *Papers on the 1962 Election: Fifteen Papers on the Canadian General Election of 1962*. Toronto: University of Toronto Press, 1964

Michels, Robert. *Political Parties: A Sociological Study of the Oligarchical Tendencies of Modern Democracy*. New York: Hearst's International Library, 1915

Minifie, James M. *Peacemaker or Powder-Monkey: Canada's Role in a Revolutionary World*. Toronto: McClelland & Stewart, 1961

Moffatt, Gary. *History of the Canadian Peace Movement until 1969*. St. Catharines: Grape Vine Press, 1969

Munton, Don, and John Kirton, eds. *Canadian Foreign Policy: Selected Cases*. Scarborough: Prentice-Hall Canada, 1992

Nash, Knowlton. *Kennedy and Diefenbaker: Fear and Loathing across the Undefended Border*. Toronto: McClelland & Stewart, 1990

Newman, Peter C. *Renegade in Power: The Diefenbaker Years.* Toronto: McClelland & Stewart, 1963

Nicholson, Patrick. *Vision and Indecision.* Don Mills: Longmans Canada, 1968

Owram, Douglas. *The Government Generation: Canadian Intellectuals and the State, 1900–1945.* Toronto: University of Toronto Press, 1986

– *Born at the Right Time: A History of the Baby Boom Generation.* University of Toronto Press, 1996

Page, Benjamin, and Robert Shapiro. *The Rational Public.* Chicago: University of Chicago Press, 1992

Paul, John, and Jerome Laulicht. *In Your Opinion.* Vol. 1. *Leaders' and Voters' Attitudes on Defence and Disarmament.* Toronto: Canadian Peace Research Institute and Oakville: Esperanto Press. 1963

Pearson, Geoffrey. *Seize the Day.* Ottawa: Carleton University Press, 1993

Pearson, Lester B. *Words and Occasions.* Toronto: University of Toronto Press, 1970

– *Mike: The Memoirs of the Right Honourable Lester B. Pearson.* 3 vols. Toronto: University of Toronto Press, 1972–75

Perlin, George C. *The Tory Syndrome: Leadership Politics in the Progressive Conservative Party.* Montreal: McGill-Queen's University Press, 1980

Pickersgill, J.W. *The Road Back: By a Liberal in Opposition.* Toronto: University of Toronto Press, 1986

– *Seeing Canada Whole: A Memoir.* Toronto: Fitzhenry & Whiteside, 1994

Pierson, Ruth Roach, ed. *Women and Peace: Theoretical, Historical, and Practical Perspectives.* London: Croom Helm, 1987

Preston, Richard A. *Canada in World Affairs.* Vol. 11: *1959–1961.* Toronto: Oxford University Press, 1965

Pross, Paul A., ed. *Pressure Group Behaviour in Canadian Politics.* Scarborough: McGraw-Hill Ryerson, 1975

– *Group Politics and Public Policy.* Toronto: Oxford University Press, 1986

Reeves, Richard. *President Kennedy: Profile of Power.* New York: Simon & Schuster, 1993

Reeves, Thomas C. *A Question of Character: A Life of John F. Kennedy.* Toronto: Collier Macmillan Canada, 1991

Regenstreif, Peter. *The Diefenbaker Interlude: Parties and Voting in Canada, an Interpretation.* Toronto: Longmans, 1965

Richter, Andrew. "'Strategic Theoretical Parasitism' Reconsidered: Canadian Thinking on Nuclear Weapons and Strategy, 1950–1963." *International Journal* (Canadian Institute of International Affairs), 55 (Summer 2000):401–26

– *Avoiding Armageddon: Canadian Military Strategy and Nuclear Weapons, 1950–1963*. Vancouver: University of British Columbia Press, 2002

Ritchie, Charles. *Diplomatic Passport: More Undiplomatic Diaries, 1946–1962*. Toronto: Macmillan of Canada, 1983

Roberts, Barbara. "Women's Peace Activism in Canada." In *Beyond the Vote: Canadian Women and Politics*, ed. Linda Kealey and Joan Sangster. Toronto: University of Toronto Press, 1989

Robin, Martin. *Canadian Provincial Politics: The Party Systems of the Ten Provinces*. 2nd edition. Scarborough: Prentice-Hall of Canada, 1978

Robinson, H.B. *Diefenbaker's World: A Populist in Foreign Affairs*. Toronto: University of Toronto Press, 1989

Rothenberg, Lawrence S. *Linking Citizens to Government: Interest Group Politics at Common Cause*. Cambridge: Cambridge University Press, 1992

Roy, Reginald H. *For Most Conspicuous Bravery: A Biography of Major-General George R. Pearkes*. Vancouver: University of British Columbia Press, 1977

Rush, Michael, ed. *Parliament and Pressure Politics*. New York: Oxford University Press, 1990

Salisbury, Robert Holt. *Interest Group Politics in America*. New York: Harper & Row, 1970

Saywell, John T. "Parliament and Politics." In *Canadian Annual Review for 1963, ed. Saywell*. Toronto: University of Toronto Press, 1964

Sévigny, Pierre. *This Game of Politics*. Toronto & Montreal: McClelland & Stewart, 1965

Sharp, Mitchell. *Which Reminds Me ...* Toronto: University of Toronto Press, 1994

Simpson, Erika. "New Ways of Thinking about Nuclear Weapons and Canada's Defence Policy," In *The Diefenbaker Legacy: Canadian Politics, Law, and Society since 1957*, ed. Donald C. Story and R. Bruce Shepard. Regina: Canadian Plains Research Center, 1998

– *NATO and the Bomb: Canadian Defenders Confront Critics*, Montreal & Kingston: McGill-Queen's Press, 2001

Smith, David E., *The Regional Decline of a National Party: Liberals on the Prairies*. Toronto: University of Toronto Press, 1981

Smith, Denis. "The Campaign in Eglinton." In *Papers on the 1962 Election*, ed. John Meisel. Toronto: University of Toronto Press, 1964
– *Gentle Patriot: A Political Biography of Walter Gordon*. Edmonton: Hurtig, 1973
– *Rogue Tory: The Life and Legend of John G. Diefenbaker*. Toronto: Macfarlane Walter & Ross, 1995
Socknat, Thomas. *Witness against War: Pacifism in Canada, 1900–1945*. Toronto: University of Toronto Press, 1987
Spencer, Dick. *Trumpets and Drums: John Diefenbaker on the Campaign Trail*. Vancouver & Toronto: Greystone Books, 1994
Spencer, Robert. "External Affairs and Defence." In *Canadian Annual Review for 1960*, ed. John T. Saywell. Toronto: University of Toronto Press, 1961
– "External Affairs and Defence." In *Canadian Annual Review for 1961*, ed. John T. Saywell. Toronto: University of Toronto Press, 1962
– "External Affairs and Defence." In *Canadian Annual Review for 1962*, ed. John T. Saywell. Toronto: University of Toronto Press, 1963
– "External Affairs and Defence." In *Canadian Annual Review for 1963*, ed. John T. Saywell. Toronto: University of Toronto Press, 1964
Story, D.C., and R. Bruce Shepard. *The Diefenbaker Legacy: Canadian Politics, Law, and Society since 1957*. Regina: Canadian Plains Research Center, 1998
Strong-Boag, Veronica. "Peace-Making Women: Canada 1919–1939." In *Women and Peace*, ed. Ruth Roach Pierson. London: Croom Helm, 1987
Stursberg, Peter. *Leadership Gained: Diefenbaker, 1956–1962*. Toronto: University of Toronto Press, 1975
– *Diefenbaker: Leadership Lost, 1962–1967*. Toronto: University of Toronto Press, 1976
Thomson, Dale C. *Louis St. Laurent Canadian*. Toronto: Macmillan of Canada, 1967
Thorburn, Hugh G. "Parliament and Policy-Making." *Canadian Journal of Economics and Political Science* 23 (November 1957):516–31
The True North Strong and Free? Proceedings of a Public Inquiry into Canadian Defence Policy and Nuclear Arms. Vancouver: Gordon Soules, 1987
Warnock, John W. *Partner to Behemoth: The Military Policy of a Satellite Canada*. Toronto: New Press, 1970
Wearing, Joseph. *The L-Shaped Party: The Liberal Party of Canada, 1958–1980*. Toronto: McGraw-Hill Ryerson, 1981

Whitaker, Reginald. *The Government Party: Organizing and Financing the Liberal Party of Canada, 1930–58.* Toronto: University of Toronto Press, 1977

White, Theodore H. *The Making of the President, 1960.* Toronto: McClelland & Stewart, 1961

Williamson, Janice, and Deborah Gorham, eds. *Up and Doing: Canadian Women and Peace.* Toronto: Women's Press, 1989

Wittner, Lawrence S. *Resisting the Bomb, 1954–1970.* Vol. 2 of *A History of the World Nuclear Disarmament Movement.* Stanford: Stanford University Press, 1997

Index

36–7, 41, 43–6, 56–7, 60, 63,
74, 82, 90, 119, 151; American
consultation with Canada, 14,
15; anti-nuclear activists, 140;
background, 12; and consultation with CDC, 12–14; Cuban
Missile Crisis, 148, 151–2;
Diefenbaker's political concerns
about, 14, 34; and Green, 54,
56; and Hellyer, 157; Liberal
Party reversal on nuclear role,
157–61 negotiations, 14–15, 29,
33–4; North Bay, 77; nuclear
negotiations with Kennedy, 94,
103–4, 106, 151–2; parliamentary approval, 35–6; Pearson's
criticisms of Canadian role in,
110–11; relationship to NATO,
14–15, 34–6, 60, 116; Sky
Hawk, 57–8; SWAP agreement,
114–15

North Atlantic Treaty Organization (NATO): anti-nuclear activists, 140; and Canada's nuclear
policy, 56, 90, 118–19, 126,
128–9, 151–2, 156–7, 158–9;
and Canadian sovereignty, 40,
48–9; consistency of Canada's
nuclear policy within it and
NORAD, 60; and Cuban Missile
Crisis, 148, 151; and External
Affairs' views on nuclear policy,
72–3; Diefenbaker's distinction
between it and NORAD, 116;
Diefenbaker's discussions with
Kennedy about, 105–6, 111; and
Green, 54, 56, 62, 104; Kennedy
administration and nuclear
negotiations, 103–4, 111; and
NORAD, 14–15, 34–6, 48–9; conferences, 18, 20, 154–5, 156;
nuclear policy of, 18–20, 42–6,
53, 82, 118–19, 126, 133;

Pearson's opposition to nuclear
weapons in, 72–3, 110, 157–8;
political considerations, 7; separate nuclear agreement for, 74;
Suez Crisis effect on, 5; SWAP
agreement, 108–9

North Bay. *See* Bomarc bases

Nowlan, George, 8

nuclear weapons: agreement
(final), 171–3; Anglo-American
model, 19, 32, 41, 52–3, 97,
99–100, 102, 109, 159–60;
anti-nuclear movement, 31, 50,
64–8, 70–1, 75, 78–82, 108,
124–7, 130, 140, 153–5;
Argentia, 30, 60, 76; Bomarc
bases, 39, 41, 75–7, 120, 126,
128, 130, 131, 174; Bomarc
missile, 30, 37–9, 41, 42, 48–50,
55, 61, 72–7, 106, 116, 128,
130, 157, 169; Bryce on, 17–18,
129–30, 153; cabinet discussions
on, 17, 20–1, 32, 36–7, 41, 42,
46–8, 52, 58, 59, 63–4, 73–4,
90–2, 102–3, 116–17, 118–19,
120–1, 151–2, 164, 165–6; CDC
discussions on, 16–17, 24 ,
29–31, 36, 53, 58–9; Cuban
Missile Crisis, 147–51; custody
and control of, 39–41, 44, 46,
59, 60, 63, 72, 90–1, 115; Dept
of External Affairs and, 42–6,
50, 62, 64, 72–3, 83, 86, 93,
107, 122, 147–9; Dept of
National Defence and, 43–6, 86,
146–7; Diefenbaker and, xv,
16–18, 20–1, 24, 29–31, 32,
36–7, 41, 42, 46–9, 51, 52–3,
55–9, 62–4, 71, 73–4, 80–6,
90–2, 94–104, 106–10, 112–24,
128–34, 146–7, 150–3, 162–6,
175–7; double perimeter,
118–19; economic consider-